The Sporting News

TAKE ME OUT TO THE BALL PARK

The Sporting News
TAKE ME OUT TO THE BALL PARK

Written by **LOWELL REIDENBAUGH**

Illustrations by **AMADEE**

Editor
CRAIG CARTER

Design
BILL PERRY

Associate Editors
JOE HOPPEL and DAVE SLOAN

President and Chief Executive Officer
RICHARD WATERS

Editor/The Sporting News
DICK KAEGEL

Director of Books and Periodicals
RON SMITH

Published in the United States by The Sporting News Publishing Co., 1212 North Lindbergh Boulevard, St. Louis, Missouri 63132.

ISBN: 0-89204-101-3
10 9 8 7 6 5 4 3 2 1

First Edition

Nine of the ball park illustrations in this book were drawn originally by Gene Mack and updated by Amadee. They originally were published in *The Boston Globe* and later in a Gene Mack book published by *The Sporting News*. The nine parks are: Braves Field in Boston; Crosley Field in Cincinnati; Municipal Stadium-League Park in Cleveland; Ebbets Field in Brooklyn; the Polo Grounds in New York; Shibe Park in Philadelphia; Forbes Field in Pittsburgh; Sportsman's Park in St. Louis, and Griffith Stadium in Washington.

Color Photography Credits

Janis Rettaliata: Page 33, 183 (inset). **Richard Pilling:** Page 34 (2), 36 (below), 108 (2), 109, 182, 183, 250 (above). **Sports Photo File, Mitchell Reibel:** Page 35, 177, 181, 252-253. **California Angels:** 36. **Earnie Glazener:** 36-37, 105. **Atlanta Braves:** 38. **Bill Smith:** 38-39. **Joe Hoppel:** 106. **Kansas City Royals:** 106-107. **Detroit Tigers:** 107. **Carl Skalak Jr.:** 110 (left). **Focus on Sports:** 110 (right), 177 (above left). **Jayne Kamin:** 111. **Howard Zyrb:** 177 (above right), 178-179. **Bruce Bisping:** 180 (above). **Montreal Expos:** 180 (below). **Jack Zehrt:** 249, 250 (below). **Dennis Desprois:** 250-251. **Robert B. Shaver:** 254. **Seattle Mariners:** 255.

Black and White Photography Credits

Library of Congress: Page 7, 60, 66, 170-171, 208. **Paul Tepley:** 96. **Minneapolis Star and Tribune:** 157. **Bruce Bisping:** 159. **George Gojkovich:** 229. **Jack Zehrt:** 236, 241. **Dennis Desprois:** 259. **Russ Reed:** 260-261.

The remainder of the photographs are from THE SPORTING NEWS archives and courtesy of major league baseball teams.

TABLE OF CONTENTS

Introduction

Construction on the new Brooklyn baseball park was rapidly nearing completion when a sharp-eyed subaltern made a startling discovery. The architects had neglected to include a press box.

That oversight was remedied by assigning the Fourth Estate to the first several rows of the grandstand until more satisfactory arrangements could be made.

When the gala opening day arrived, every self-respecting citizen of Flatbush was jammed against the gates, clamoring for admittance. But another horrifying discovery was made. The park superintendent had forgotten the key to the park.

Ultimately, the gates swung open and the noisy multitudes poured into Ebbets Field, ogling and admiring every feature that Charles Ebbets had provided for their enjoyment.

Finally, the band struck up patriotic airs, the players concluded the pregame drills, the groundkeepers completed their chores and the dignitaries and the players started their march to center field for flag-raising ceremonies, striding awkwardly all the way in an effort to stay in step.

The procession arrived at its destination and Ebbets, bursting with pardonable pride, turned to an aide.

"The flag, please," he said.

"Sorry Charley," came the mournful tone. "We forgot the flag."

Such is the romance of major league ball parks. No two are alike. No two speak the same language. Each has a character of its own. Each revives torrents of memories, whether they are the multi-purpose arenas of the present or the haphazard structures of days long gone.

Every ball park reminds someone—a schoolboy playing hookey, an industrial giant on an extended lunch hour or a housewife on an escape from domestic drudgery—of a memorable event when a man and a moment met in unforgettable achievement; a game-winning home run, a glittering no-hitter, a spectacular catch or a positively ludicrous episode like that which amused a handful of spectators on a steamy afternoon in Philadelphia about a half century ago.

The incident occurred at Baker Bowl, where a 40-foot wall loomed less than 300 feet away in right field. For most of the game, Phillies' hits had caromed off the wall, keeping Hack Wilson in a constant chase. He was near exhaustion, not only from his daylight exercises, but also from the previous night's exercises in Philadelphia's speakeasies.

When the action was halted to permit a change of Brooklyn pitchers, Wilson sought out a soft spot to gather his thoughts and catch his breath. He had scarcely found repose, when another baseball ricocheted off the wall.

Leaping to his feet, he retrieved the ball and fired a perfect throw to second base that would have nailed any adventurous baserunner.

To his chargin, Wilson discovered that he had made a textbook play on a ball heaved by Walter Beck, furious at being removed from the mound and known thereafter as Boom-Boom.

Before the era when civic arenas were erected on spacious plots that permitted parking areas as well as a stadium, the configuration of a ball park was determined by the dimensions of the acreage on which it was built.

As a consequence, one park would favor a lefthanded hitter while discriminating against a righthander. Other parks presented a reverse situation.

One would present an inviting target for the batter who hit high, majestic flies, another would prove a delight to line-drive hitters. A popular subject for speculation in the 1940s was: "What would Joe DiMaggio hit if he played half his games in Fenway Park, with its Green Monster in left field, and what would Ted Williams hit if he were a Yankee and played half his games in the Stadium, with its beckoning right-field seats?"

The Polo Grounds, with a 483-foot deep center field and chummy foul lines, was a singular pleasure for a batter who could drop a pop fly over the nearby fences, like Dusty Rhodes in the 1954 World Series, but sheer horror for one who drilled a ball into a long putout in center field, a la Vic Wertz in the same Series.

For years Forbes Field, with its wide open outfield expanses, was a paradise for three-base hits. The major league record for a season still belongs to an old Pirate, Chief Wilson, who set the mark in 1912.

Before Branch Rickey, or one of his contemporaries, devised a running track to serve as a warning to outfielders in hot pursuit of fly balls, it

was not unusual for clubs to build banks as a caution for flychasers. At Fenway Park such an incline was known as "Duffy's Cliff," in tribute to Red Sox outfielder Duffy Lewis, who mastered ascent and descent with equal facility.

The same could not be said of Smead Jolley, a Boston outfielder of questionable talent. Smead spent long hours trying to master the cliff, but invariably fell on his face. In total frustration after such an experience, he muttered to whomever would listen that, "They taught me how to climb up the damn hill, but not how to come down."

Time and techniques have eliminated many of the storied parks with peculiarities that gave them character. The trend toward stereotyped stadiums has produced handsome enclosures with a sameness extending from Philadelphia to Pittsburgh to Cincinnati to St. Louis to Atlanta.

But similarity does not necessarily preclude happy memories, whether it's a far distant spot where Greg Luzinski poled a home run in Veterans Stadium, a point where Willie Stargell deposited one in Three Rivers Stadium, the spot where Pete Rose crashed into Ray Fosse to win the 1970 All-Star Game at Riverfront, where Lou Brock stole his record base at Busch Memorial or where Hank Aaron socked his 715th homer at Atlanta-Fulton County.

Reminiscences, like beauty, remain in the mind of the beholder. They know no age and are always available for instant recall whether they are recent, like a Bruce Sutter strikeout of Gorman Thomas to clinch a world championship, or a flagless dedication at a long-since demolished Ebbets Field in 1913.

All might not have gone according to plan when Ebbets Field opened officially on April 9, 1913, but things went smoothly when Owner Charles Ebbets (above) threw out the first ball for the 1914 opener.

ANAHEIM STADIUM

Anaheim

When William Wrigley Jr. purchased the Los Angeles Angels from Johnny Powers in 1921, the Pacific Coast League team played its home games at Washington Park at the intersection of Washington and Hill streets.

Two years later, when the city refused to build underground parking facilities, Wrigley drew up plans to build a new park at 42nd and Avalon—22,000-seat Wrigley Field.

The new park was dedicated in September 1925, prior to a game with the San Francisco Seals, and served as a PCL base until 1958, when the franchise was transferred to Spokane to make way for the newly arrived Dodgers from Brooklyn.

Following three years of idleness, the old structure was reactivated in 1961 as the home of a new major league club, an American League expansion franchise named, not surprisingly, the Los Angeles Angels.

When a curious public wondered why the Angels did not move into the Los Angeles Coliseum as co-tenants with the Dodgers, Commissioner Ford Frick explained that a major league rule, enacted only a few months earlier, prohibited a second major league club from playing within five miles of the first.

"The Angels accepted the rule," said Frick, "and also agreed to play at least two years in Chavez Ravine (the Dodgers' new park about to be constructed)."

The Angels made their A.L. debut on the road in 1961, winning one of eight games. In their inaugural at Wrigley Field, they were defeated by Minnesota, 4-2, before almost 12,000. Tom Morgan accounted for the Angels' first home victory the next day with a 12-inning, 6-5 decision over the Twins.

Wrigley Field, with its 345-foot power alleys, was a slugger's delight. The Angels, led by Leon Wagner, Steve Bilko and Ted Kluszewski, made capital of the chummy confines, but so did the opposition. When the curtain fell on the 1961 season, with Ryne Duren losing the finale to Cleveland, 8-5, before 9,868, Wrigley Field owned the distinction of being the most productive home run park in the American League. The Angels occupied eighth place in the 10-club circuit.

Curiously, Roger Maris of the Yankees clouted only two of his record 61 home runs in Los Angeles that season.

At the gate the Angels topped the 600,000 mark. Their largest crowd, 19,930, turned out for a game with New York.

At the close of the '61 season, Wrigley Field was abandoned again. The Angels moved into Dodger Stadium as tenants of the N.L. club. Their old park at 42nd and Avalon was dismantled to make room for Gilbert Lindsay Park, a public playground.

Respectability crowned the Angels' efforts in 1962 when, in the spacious new park, they drew 1.1 million customers and leaped into third place, earning for Bill Rigney recognition as Major League Manager of the Year.

The campaign was less than a month old when Bo Belinsky, a 25-year-old lefthander with playboy tendencies, created headlines by pitching the Angels' first no-hitter, a 2-0 victory over Baltimore before 15,886. The May 5 win was the fourth in a row for the unbeaten Belinsky, who won only six more games the remainder of the season and was back in the minors before the close of the 1963 season.

As Belinsky faded so did the Angels. They plunged to ninth in 1963 and even though they climbed to fifth in '64, their attendance dropped to 700,000.

Off the field the Angels were faring just about as badly. On one occasion an Angel accountant discovered that the Dodgers were drawing 76 percent of the customers in Chavez Ravine but the Angels were paying for 50 percent of the toilet paper. An adjustment was made.

At another time it was determined that the Angels, whose offices were in the windowless basement at Dodger Stadium, were paying half of the cost for keeping the park's windows clean. Once more the Angels sought redress and gained satisfaction.

On still another day, Angels Owner Gene Autry learned that he was paying for the care and watering of the stadium grass when his club was at home. At the time tenant Autry also was in the hotel business. He confided to a reporter, "I'd have a hell of a time getting people who rent my rooms to water the posies. That's the responsibili-

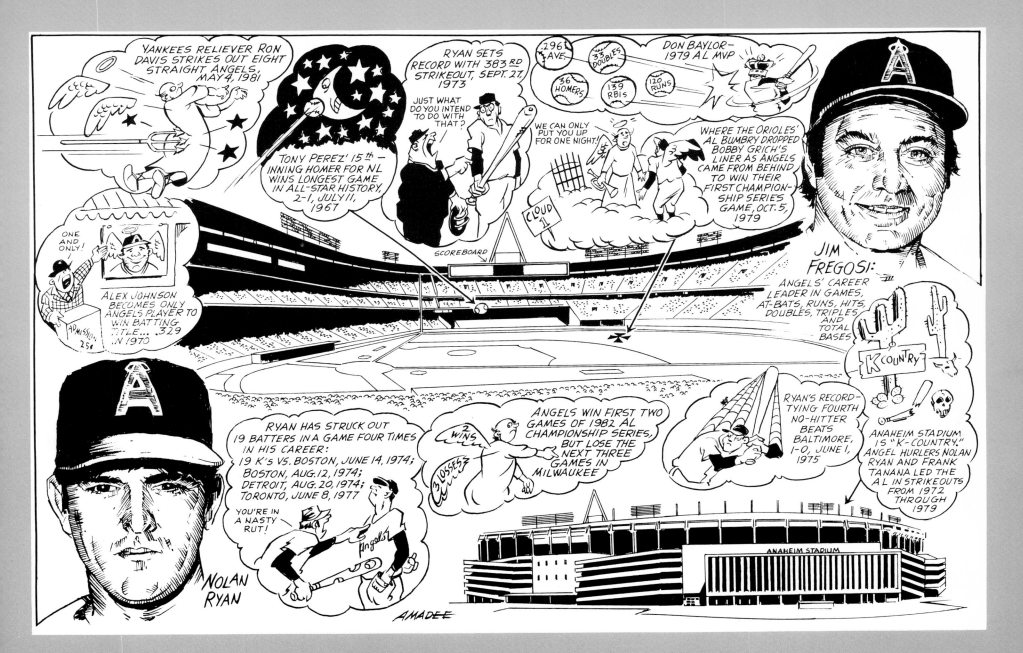

ty of the landlord."

"Not so," replied landlord Walter O'Malley. "The Angels play as many games in our 'hotel' as we do. Are we supposed to let everything die when they're at home?"

On that point the Angels struck out.

By September 2, 1965, the Angels, in keeping with their forthcoming move to Anaheim, were prepared to announce a change in their name. Henceforth they would be the California Angels. Club executive Bob Reynolds explained: "In the last five years we have been the only American League club in the state of California. We have had people from all over the state become Angels fans.

"You might say we are the team of the Golden West and therefore we want to remain a part of the entire state."

The Angels bade farewell to Chavez Ravine in impressive fashion on September 22, 1965, sweeping the Boston Red Sox, 10-1 and 2-0, before only 3,353. Two days earlier they had attracted only 945 for an afternoon game with Baltimore.

On the last day the Angels rapped 19 hits, their season high, in the opener. George Brunet yielded only two hits in the nightcap. The two victories gave the Angels a four-year log in the Dodgers' park of 170-153.

Their 1965 attendance was 566,727, giving the A.L. club a four-year gate of 3,292,244, which left little profit after paying the rent.

Under terms of their lease agreement, the Angels paid $200,000 in annual rent, or 7½ percent of net receipts, whichever was larger. They kept half of the concessions receipts and none of the parking. At Anaheim, they were to retain two-thirds of parking income, while the other terms remained the same.

At the time it aspired to major league status, Anaheim had a population of only 150,000, but there were 600,000 people within a five-mile radius, one million within 10 miles, three million within 20 miles and six million within 30 miles. The area was described as one of the youngest, richest and fastest growing regions in the country.

The contract between the city and the Angels

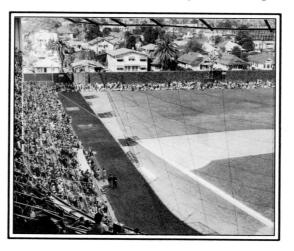

was signed on August 8, 1964. By terms of the agreement, the Angels were to occupy the park for 35 years—or until the year 2001—after which they could exercise three 10-year options.

Ground-breaking ceremonies for the stadium on State College Boulevard were held on August 31, 1964. The first spades were turned by Anaheim Mayor C.L. (Chuck) Chandler, Autry and Del Webb, whose company was awarded the construction contract.

Among the other celebrities on hand was Sam Yorty, the Los Angeles mayor, who arrived by helicopter. He told the crowd, "I want to congrat-ulate you on your progressive and forward-looking step. Had we the same foresight and been able to build a ball park like you are doing, we would still have the Angels."

From world-famous Disneyland, two miles away, came a fire engine carrying cartoon characters Mickey Mouse, Goofy and Pluto, who presented a "pennant" to Bill Rigney.

Webb, a co-owner of the New York Yankees, assured the audience, "This will be my dream stadium. I've tried to observe the right and wrong of every stadium in the country. We want to get all the right things in this one and leave out all the wrong things."

Earlier, Webb had declared, "The move of the Angels from Los Angeles is important to the success of the American League. All you have to do is look at what happened in cities like St. Louis and Philadelphia, where two teams once played in the same park, to realize it is not good."

True to Webb's promise, the stadium was completed on schedule, but there were frustrating delays. A month-long strike retarded the construction schedule. Later, picketing by a non-construction union caused a four-day stoppage. But 200 laborers, working until 2:30 a.m. in the final week, applied the finishing touches so that the $24 million structure could be finished on time.

Initially, the three-tier stadium had a seating capacity of 43,250, but additions through the years enlarged it to 65,158.

The Angels' desire "to bring the fans back to the game and the game back to the fans" developed the park theme of "Convenience, Comfort and Courtesy."

Known as the "Big-A," the stadium is the centerpiece of a 140-acre plot that contains ground level parking facilities for 12,000 cars and more

During their first American League season, 1961, the Angels played at Los Angeles' Wrigley Field, a longtime minor league park noted for its vine-covered outfield wall (above) and office tower (right).

than 200 buses.

Two escalators, one at first base and the other at third, 16 ramps and four elevators help move customers quickly to the vari-colored levels. The distance from the playing field to the last row of seats on the top level is only 109 feet.

Playing field dimensions were determined by air density and wind tests at the normal game times, 1:30 and 8:00 p.m. As a result, the foul lines are 333 feet, power alleys 370 feet and the center-field wall 404 feet. The outfield wall is eight feet high.

The stadium got its nickname, the Big-A, from the A-frame scoreboard which rose 230 feet and was visible from the five freeways that serve the stadium. A giant halo topped the $1 million scoreboard, which was erected by Standard Oil of California in exchange for advertising considerations.

When the stadium underwent construction to be completely enclosed in 1979, a new video scoreboard was installed on the facade of the left-center field roof. The Big-A board, meanwhile, was preserved and moved to the edge of the stadium parking lot.

The construction increased the seating capacity to over 65,000 and among those things added to the stadium were new executive boxes, media boxes and a new sound system.

The first American League game in the Big-A,

on April 19, 1966, was a 3-1 victory for the Chicago White Sox. Tommy John and Eddie Fisher combined to hold the Angels to four hits, one of which was a second-inning home run by Rick Reichardt. Tommy Agee's homer tied the score in the sixth inning before singles by Don Buford and Floyd Robinson plated the deciding runs in the

eighth inning.

The start of the inaugural was delayed 20 minutes as the result of a broken water main that flooded one of the city's main thoroughfares and created a gigantic traffic jam.

The Angels did not distinguish themselves in their first season at Anaheim, finishing in sixth place, but they did surprisingly well at the turnstiles. The season gate topped 1.4 million.

More than 46,000 watched the longest All-Star Game at Anaheim on July 11, 1967, when Tony Perez's 15th-inning homer off Jim (Catfish) Hunter gave the National League a 2-1 triumph.

Although the Angels lost in their first Cham-

pionship Series appearance in 1979 in four games, they won their only game in Anaheim. They beat the Baltimore Orioles when Baltimore center fielder Al Bumbry dropped Bobby Grich's line drive, allowing the tying run to score in the ninth inning. The game ended a few minutes later when teammate Larry Harlow doubled home the deciding run.

The Angels went on to lose the Championship Series in four games.

The Angels had to wait three years to get another crack at a postseason appearance. After acquiring slugging outfielder Reggie Jackson as a free agent, the ex-Yankee tied for the league lead in homers with 39 and drove in 101 runs in 1982. Teamed with Don Baylor, Fred Lynn and Rod Carew, Jackson not only gave the Angels another former MVP award winner, but made the Angels a devastating offensive team. California set numerous club batting records during the '82 season.

But even with a powerful lineup and a pitching staff that ranked second in the American League, the Angels lost to the Milwaukee Brewers in the Championship Series. They won the first two contests, both played at the Big-A, 8-3 and 4-2 behind Tommy John and Bruce Kison. They lost the next three games in Milwaukee, however, becoming the first team ever to squander a 2-0 series lead.

After calling the Dodgers' park in Chavez Ravine home from 1962 through 1965, the Angels moved into Anaheim Stadium (above). Now fully enclosed, the "Big-A" had a different look in 1966 (right).

ARLINGTON STADIUM

Arlington

When Richard W. Burnett purchased the Dallas club of the Texas League in 1948, he almost immediately began to promote the city as a major league site.

Major league baseball did not arrive, however, until 1972, long after Burnett's death. When that magical day eventually came, the team did not carry the Dallas name, but was known as the Texas Rangers, headquartered in Arlington, Tex., midway between Dallas and Fort Worth.

The two North Texas cities entered Organized Baseball in 1886 as members of the Texas League. The loop suspended operations several times before commencing a long and impressive reign in 1907. Dallas and Fort Worth served as two of its most influential members.

Dallas' original playing site, known as Gaston Park, was located at Second and Parry streets, a spot now occupied by the Music Hall of the Texas State Fairgrounds.

In 1919, the club moved to a new stadium at West Jefferson and Comal in the Oak Cliff section on the west side of the Trinity River. The park was known as Gardner Park for the club owner, Joe Gardner.

Following a fire in 1924, a new park was built on the opposite side of the street. Initially, the capacity was 7,000 and subsequently was increased to 8,000.

Another fire destroyed that park on September 10, 1940, shortly after the close of the season. A partial stadium was available for the start of the 1941 season, but the $137,000, roofless stadium was not ready for dedication until July 29, when the home team defeated Shreveport, 6-3. Park capacity was 10,571.

As the name of the team changed through the years, so did the name of the park. In the early years of the 20th century, the team was known as the Giants, a tribute to the New York National League club and its manager, John McGraw, who had a strong affinity for the city.

When the team was known as the Steers, the park bore a similar name. When George Schepps bought the club in October of 1938, he changed the name to Rebels and the name of the park accordingly. When oilman Dick Burnett bought the club on April 6, 1948, he rechristened the team the Eagles and renamed the stadium Burnett Field.

Perhaps the most spectacular event during Burnett's ownership occurred on opening day in 1950, but it was not at Burnett Field.

Rather, it took place in the Cotton Bowl, where the Eagles had transferred their inaugural so they could attract 53,578 fans, a minor league record at the time, for their April 11 opener against Tulsa.

The Oilers clobbered the home forces, 10-3, but the customers streamed from the stadium feeling rewarded for having seen such Hall of Famers as Ty Cobb, Tris Speaker, Dizzy Dean, Mickey Cochrane, Home Run Baker, Charley Gehringer, plus some lesser lights, all attired in Dallas uniforms, who performed in pregame ceremonies.

The original Fort Worth park in the 1880s was located in the "Prairie" area near downtown and was known simply as "the ball park."

When a city fireman named Hayne lost his life while fighting a huge conflagration in 1890, the ball field was named Hayne's Park.

The park remained in use until 1900, when a new facility was built on North Main Street. In recognition of the team's name, the park was known as Panther Park. This facility endured into the 1920s, and was the home of the Fort Worth team, now known as the Cats, when it captured six consecutive Texas League championships.

In 1926, a new stadium was constructed on the east side of Main Street, a few blocks from the former park, and was named LaGrave Field in honor of Paul LaGrave, the club's business manager who died in 1929.

During their years as a power in the Texas League, the Cats captured eight Dixie Series titles in competition with the Southern Association champions. In the same period, from 1920 to '56, Dallas teams won three titles.

Fire destroyed LaGrave Field on May 17, 1949. On July 5, 1950, LaGrave Field was ready for rededication, after having been rebuilt by the parent Brooklyn Dodgers as one of the most modern parks in Organized Baseball.

In 1965 the Texas League franchise, known as the Dallas-Fort Worth Spurs, performed at Turn-

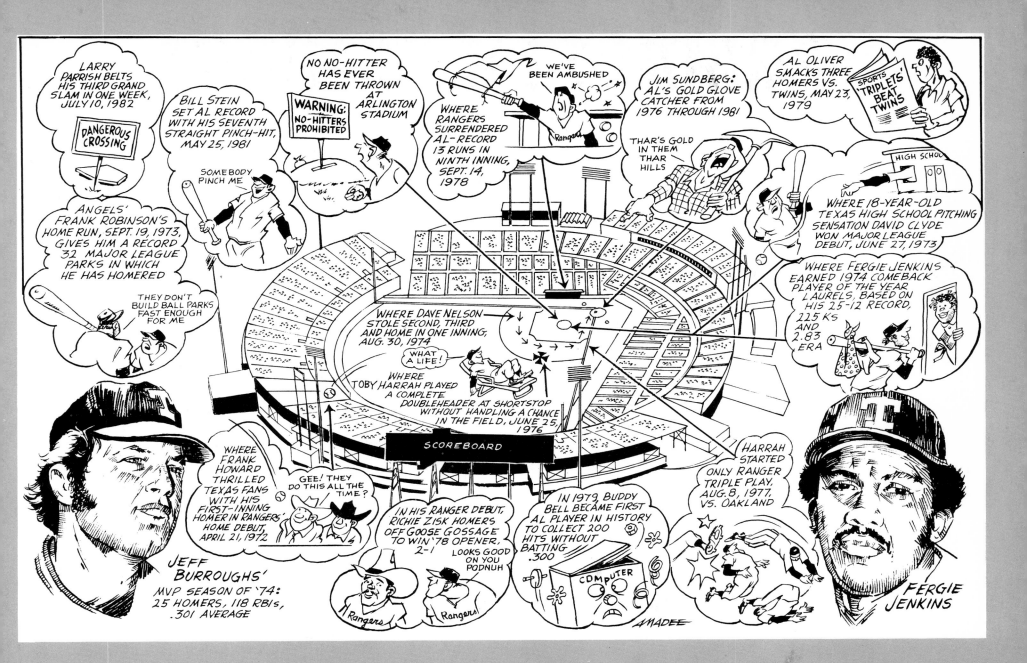

pike Stadium, in Arlington, Tex. This stadium was located on a 137-acre tract just north of the former Arlington Downs race track and near the Six Flags Over Texas amusement park.

The $1.5 million facility had 325-foot foul lines and a center-field fence 400 feet away. The parking lot could accommodate 2,500 cars but that area could be expanded to 10,000 vehicles when required.

Plans for a park to serve both cities were first advanced in 1959 when the owners of the Dallas-Fort Worth franchise in the American Association, J. W. Bateson and Amon Carter Jr., envisioned a franchise in the projected Continental League.

But American League expansion dealt a death blow to the Continental League and to North Texas hopes for an early entry into the major leagues.

In the fall of 1959 the Texas Legislature authorized the formation of a Bi-County Sports Committee, empowered to issue $9.5 million in revenue bonds for the construction of a major league stadium if the voters approved. They did.

Because the stadium was built in a natural bowl, with a playing surface 40 feet below the surrounding territory, it was estimated that an identical park built elsewhere could have cost as much as $15 million.

"No excavation—except to connect dugouts directly with dressing rooms—would be necessary if the stadium were enlarged to seat more than 50,000," announced Mayor Tommy Vandergriff of Arlington.

The Turnpike Stadium opener, delayed as long as possible to permit workmen to apply the finishing touches, was held on April 23, 1965, and 7,231 watched the Spurs defeat Albuquerque. As it was, laborers needed every possible moment to complete the 10,000-seat project.

The final piece of sod was layed 36 hours before the first pitch. The foul lines were drawn during pregame practice on opening night and the lights atop 150-foot towers were not completely adjusted until the previous night.

The stadium was expanded for the first time in 1970, when the capacity was doubled to 20,000.

A second enlargement took place after the 1971 season, following the announcement that Bob Short would transfer the Washington Senators to Texas. When this move was completed, there were seats for 35,694 customers. In 1978 the park was expanded to its present capacity, 41,284.

When all enlargement projects were completed, fence measurements in the stadium were 330 feet on the foul lines, 380 feet in the power alleys and 400 feet to center field.

With the advent of major league baseball, the name of the club was changed from Senators to Rangers, a name that George Schepps had favored in 1958 when he served as general manager of the Dallas club owned by J.W. Bateson.

In moving to Arlington, Bob Short paid the six surviving Texas League clubs—Shreveport, San Antonio, Memphis, Little Rock, Amarillo and El Paso—$40,000 apiece for territorial invasion. He also agreed that the Rangers would meet a Texas League all-star team annually with no cost to the minor league teams.

By this time, the park also had a new name. Turnpike Stadium was considered inappropriate for the home of a major league club, and leading newspapers in the area urged that it be named Vandergriff Stadium in honor of the Arlington mayor who had labored long and diligently in making the stadium a reality.

Vandergriff, however, rejected the suggestion and the stadium was named for the city.

The moment that Dick Burnett had dreamed of nearly a quarter of a century earlier arrived on April 21, 1972. The honor of throwing out the first ball was accorded to Vandergriff, who delivered the righthanded pitch from a spot between American League President Joe Cronin and Bob Short.

A crowd of 20,105—or at least those who were not snared in a mammoth traffic jam that developed at two toll plazas on the Dallas-Fort Worth Turnpike—received its first big league thrill in the first inning when Frank Howard clouted a 400-foot line drive home run over the center-field fence. Dave Nelson also homered for the Rangers, but the biggest bat was wielded by Lenny Randle, who slammed a double and two singles good for four runs batted in. At game's end the left-field scoreboard, shaped like the state of Texas, showed a 7-6 victory for Ted Williams' Rangers over the California Angels.

Arlington Stadium reverberated to its first capacity crowd on June 27, 1973 when David Clyde, an 18-year-old lefthander who signed for a $125,000 bonus after graduating from Westchester High School in Houston, pitched five innings in his professional debut, struck out eight and allowed one hit, a two-run homer by Mike Adams of the Minnesota Twins.

Clyde called it a night with a 4-2 lead and was credited with a 4-3 victory with relief help from Bill Gogolewski.

In his second appearance on July 2, 1973, Clyde attracted more than 33,000 customers to Arlington Stadium. He hurled six innings and departed the game because of a finger blister, leading 4-3. Ineffective relief pitching deprived the

Turnpike Stadium (above) held only 10,000 fans in 1969, but a year later the first expansion of the minor league park doubled its seating capacity.

youngster of another victory.

Hall of Famer Frank Robinson, then a member of the California Angels, established a major league record at Arlington Stadium on September 19, 1973 when he homered in his 32nd major league park. The one-time star of the Cincinnati Reds and Baltimore Orioles had connected previously in such unused or extinct parks as Ebbets Field, the Polo Grounds, Connie Mack Stadium, RFK Stadium, Kansas City Municipal Stadium, Forbes Field, Crosley Field, the Los Angeles Coliseum, Colt Stadium in Houston, Sportsman's Park in St. Louis and Roosevelt Stadium in Jersey City, where the Brooklyn Dodgers played occasionally in the 1950s.

Three sluggers have rapped three home runs in a single game at Arlington Stadium: John Mayberry of Kansas City in 1975; Al Oliver of the Rangers in 1979, and George Brett, also of K.C., in 1979.

Larry Parrish of the Rangers also hit three home runs, not in the same game, but in the same week in 1982. What made Parrish's feat unique is that each of the clouts was a grand slam—and tied the major league record. After connecting at Oakland on July 4, Parrish hit the last two at home: on July 7 against Boston and July 10 against Detroit.

On two occasions dramatic home runs won opening day games for the Rangers. Toby Harrah's round-tripper in the 10th inning clinched a victory in 1977 and Richie Zisk's homer did the same in 1978.

Harrah also earned headlines for his performance on June 25, 1976. The shortstop played an entire doubleheader without a single fielding chance.

Dave Nelson gained a spot in the record book on August 30, 1974 by stealing second, third and home in the first inning. His achievement could not avert a defeat, however, as the Rangers bowed to Cleveland, 7-3.

Bill Stein of the Rangers set an American League record at Arlington on May 25, 1981 by rapping his seventh consecutive pinch-hit.

Three years earlier, on September 14, 1978, the California Angels, victims of the Rangers on inaugural night in 1972, scored an A.L. record 13 runs in the ninth inning, en route to a 16-1 shellacking of the Rangers.

Turnpike Stadium grew from a 20,000-seat facility (above left) in 1971 to a 35,694-seat structure (above right) in 1972 and, with the arrival of the Texas Rangers, was renamed Arlington Stadium.

18

Arlington Stadium hadn't undergone its 1978 expansion—more than 5,500 seats were added, bringing capacity to 41,284—when this full house (above) attended a Rangers game.

ATLANTA STADIUM

Atlanta

Professional baseball was introduced to Atlanta in 1885 and quickly developed into a recreational staple through the promotional energies of Henry W. Grady, the brilliant managing editor of the Atlanta Constitution.

When the Southern League was organized, Grady was elected president. He conducted league business from his newspaper office, from where he also supervised the editorial page of the Constitution as well as the news columns, a responsibility that enabled him to publish baseball news on page one.

When the editor-in-chief threatened to bill Grady for the wire tolls resulting from the transmission of baseball news, Henry replied, "That's okay, but I'm going to have baseball news just the same."

Grady also was the Constitution's baseball writer, regularly dictating game accounts to his personal secretary from Peters Park, the city's first professional field at North Avenue and Peachtree Street.

Grady did more than report on ball games. He wrote articles encouraging the community's society folks to attend games and warned the players against the evils of associating with questionable characters during off-duty hours.

Atlanta's bluebloods reacted kindly to Grady's pleadings. Accounts of early games noted the presence of burly Bob Toombs, an ex-senator and Civil War general, and Ben Hill, a longtime power in Georgia politics.

Prior to the advent of professional ball, citi-

zens watched spirited matches by amateurs on a playing field on Hunter Street just west of Oakland Cemetery. In 1866, two years after the city succumbed to the Yankee torch, a contest was waged between the "Atlantas" and the "Gate City Nine." Although the "Atlantas" had been proclaimed "the finest team in the world," they fell a bit short of that exalted distinction on this particular day. They lost the four-hour and 30-minute game, 127-29.

The home run hitting of Tom Johnson, the Gate

City third baseman, produced wide-eyed amazement among the spectators, many of whom had arrived four hours before the first pitch. Johnson's home run ball was not found for two weeks, at which time the distance was measured and found to be a quarter of a mile. Whether the latter portion of the distance was downhill was not disclosed.

The captain of the winning team, it was noted, was struck in the abdomen by a line drive and fell to the ground. As small children wept, the gallant leader struggled to his feet and, thankfully, recovered sufficiently to continue in the game.

Justly proud of their accomplishment, the Gate City team had the game ball gilded and placed on display in the window of Dr. Taylor's drugstore at Peachtree and Decatur streets.

Huge throngs gazed on it "as though it were some great man lying in state."

As a result of its humiliation, the Atlanta club disbanded, but the Gate City Nine went on to record 36 wins, losing only to a team of college students from Athens, Ga.

The popularity of the Gate City team throughout the Southeast was credited with the birth and quick acceptance of the Southern League club.

Peters Park, named for Richard Peters, an early baseball enthusiast, consisted of a grandstand and bleachers and was enclosed by a high wire fence. It also was the home of a pennant-winning team in 1885, the first year of the Southern League.

In 1892, the team, known by this time as the

Chief Noc-a-homa (above) lives quietly in his left-field tepee until a Braves' home run necessitates his celebrated war dance.

Crackers, moved to Brisbane Park at Cumley, Ira and Glenn streets. Later in the same decade the team transferred to the old Show Grounds at Boulevard, Jackson and Irvin streets.

The Southern League functioned during this period with the exception of 1890, '91 and '97 before reorganizing as the Southern Association in 1901. The Crackers were not in the S.A. in 1901, but entered the circuit in 1902 as a replacement for the Selma, Ala. team.

In their first season in the Southern Association, the Crackers were owned by Abner Powell who, as operator of the New Orleans franchise in the 1880s, introduced the raincheck and ladies day to baseball.

In this era, games were played at Piedmont Park, 10th Street and Piedmont Avenue, but after Powell sold the club to local interests following the 1903 campaign, games were shifted to Ponce de Leon Park, so named because of an amusement park that gave its name to Ponce de Leon Avenue.

The 11,000-seat all-wood structure was destroyed by a spectacular fire in the early morning of Saturday, September 9, 1923. The blaze, of undetermined origin, was discovered by a night watchman at a nearby health spa that was owned by Rell J. Spiller, who also owned the ball club and park.

According to one account, "within 15 minutes the tinder-dry grandstand and bleachers collapsed, sending flames 100 feet in the air. The park, situated in a sort of amphitheater, offered the spectacle of a burning, crackling inferno.

"Telephone poles on Ponce de Leon Avenue, caught by the leaping flames, became pillars of fire. While the whole scene was lit up with noonday brilliance, the snapping of the high power

wires from time to time suddenly changed the lighting to a bluish hue.

"Billboards on the side of the park, fence posts, trees and even the leaves of trees were burning and sending myriads of sparks into the air, showering the neighborhood with a rain of fire. Thousands of citizens crowded nearby streets to watch the spectacular fire, the glow of which could be seen for miles around."

The fire consumed all the Crackers' trophies, equipment, uniforms and records. And it nearly cost them a secretary, Silver Bill Stickney, who was asleep in his quarters under the grandstand. Silver Bill was rescued with great difficulty but suffered burns on his legs and body.

The Crackers played the remaining games of

the 1923 season at Grant Field, home of the Georgia Tech athletic teams.

Before the embers of the Ponce de Leon Park fire had cooled, R.J. Spiller announced he would rebuild the structure. Spiller was as good as his promise and on opening day 1924, spectators were welcomed to a $250,000 palace with concrete stands and a 15,000-seat capacity. Named Spiller Park, it was called "the most magnificent park in the minor leagues."

The stadium retained Spiller's name until 1932, when it was rechristened Ponce de Leon Park. At that time the foul lines measured 365 feet to left field and 321 feet to right. The scoreboard in center field was 462 feet from home plate. In front of the scoreboard there was a

Ponce de Leon Park (above), home of the Atlanta Crackers, was modified in 1949 when Earl Mann reduced home run distances by planting a hedge from the left-field foul pole to center field.

magnolia tree that resisted the long-distance efforts of all sluggers except one. Only Eddie Mathews, a Cracker in 1950-51 before embarking on a Hall of Fame career with the Braves, was able to drive a ball into the magnolia tree.

When the club encountered rough financial waters in 1932, the Coca-Cola Company came to its rescue and operated the team. Former Brooklyn manager Wilbert Robinson served as president and pilot.

When Robinson died suddenly in 1934, Earl Mann, who had been a ball park vendor as early as 1916, was installed as president.

The Earl Mann era in Atlanta represented independent baseball operation at its most lucrative level. Mann built winning teams, drew capacity crowds and sold players to major league organizations at handsome profits.

In 1947 the Crackers played to 404,000 fans at home and opened the 1948 season on the same impressive note. The inaugural against Birmingham attracted a Ponce de Leon record throng of 21,812. Spectators spilled onto the field and many were perched atop the four-deck series of signs in right field. Mann estimated that 5,000 fans had been turned away.

Mann purchased the club and park from Coca-Cola for $700,000 in 1949 and shortly thereafter made the home run distances more equitable for all batters.

A hedge was planted from the left-field foul line to center field, reducing the distance for home runs from 365 feet to 330. The center field distance was cut to 410 feet. But almost immediately problems developed.

Under new ground rules, an outfielder making a catch was required to remain within the hedge for the catch to be legal. If the momentum of the drive carried him through the shrubbery, it was a home run. Protests and confusion brought quick results. A four-foot high cyclone fence was erected in front of the hedge after the first home series.

Mann operated the Crackers until after the 1959 season, when he returned the franchise to the Southern Association while retaining Ponce de Leon Park. The Los Angeles Dodgers operated a farm club in 1960-61. In 1962-63, the St. Louis Cardinals placed an International League farm club at Ponce de Leon Park. In 1964 the club was a link in the Minnesota Twins' chain. The 1965 Crackers were a farm of the Milwaukee Braves and played in new Atlanta-Fulton County Stadium, which became the home of the Braves in 1966.

In November 1965 Ponce de Leon Park, once a showplace of minor league baseball, was sold to a real estate developer for $1.25 million. Commercial properties now occupy the 23-acre plot.

Action on Atlanta's modern sports stadium commenced on March 5, 1964 when Mayor Ivan Allen Jr. announced: "I have the verbal commitment of a major league baseball club to move its franchise to Atlanta if we have a stadium available by 1966." Speculation focused on the Braves and Phillies.

The next afternoon the proposition was submitted to the board of aldermen, which unanimously approved plans for an $18 million stadium complex. The selected location was an urban renewal area a quarter mile from the state capitol

The Braves and Pirates, shown (above) during opening-day ceremonies in 1966, kicked off the first major league season in Atlanta's new three-tiered, circular stadium.

and six miles from the Atlanta airport.

Within 12 months after the first spade was turned the stadium was completed. Prior to the 1977 season, more seats were added, bringing the seating capacity of the three-tier circular structure to 52,785 for baseball and 60,748 for football. The stadium is 750.5 feet in diameter and occupies 19.4 acres. The playing field is 33 feet below the level of the 10,000-car parking area.

Initially, the playing field dimensions were 325 feet on the foul lines, 402 feet to the center field fence and 375 feet in the power alleys. From the beginning the stadium was a home run hitters' paradise. To provide some relief for harried pitchers, the power alleys were lengthened to 385 feet in the 1970s.

The Braves arrived in Atlanta in 1966 and with the Pittsburgh Pirates as their opponents, treated more than 50,000 customers to a first-game bombardment that included two home runs by Joe Torre and one each by Jim Pagliaroni and Willie Stargell. The 13th-inning blow by Stargell was hit with a runner on base and produced a 3-2 Pittsburgh victory.

Despite a fifth-place finish, the Braves attracted 1.5 million customers in their first season in Atlanta. They followed with five more million-plus gates before slipping below the mark.

The Braves captured the National League West Division championship in 1969 but were eliminated in three games by the New York Mets, losing at home 9-5 and 11-6 before crowds of more than 50,000.

The Braves had to wait another 13 seasons before they won their second N.L. West title. Powered by 36 home runs and 109 RBIs from National League MVP Dale Murphy, the Braves

edged out defending champ Los Angeles by one game on the final day of the 1982 regular season.

But Atlanta's big bats went silent in the playoffs (a .169 team batting average) as they lost to eventual World Series champion St. Louis in three straight in the League Championship Series.

The '82 season was a memorable one for Braves' fans for another reason: The team established a modern major league record for most victories at the start of a season (13), from April 6 to April 21.

Pitching accomplishments in Atlanta Stadium have been relatively few, although Phil Niekro hurled a no-hitter there against the San Diego Padres on August 5, 1973.

The emphasis in Atlanta Stadium, however, has been on hitting—long-range blasting. Even Houston's knuckleballer Joe Niekro got into the act on May 29, 1976 when he not only socked a home run, but also defeated brother Phil, 4-3.

Willie McCovey of San Francisco clouted his 500th career home run on June 30, 1978, but the

greatest swell of national excitement was created by Henry Aaron. The slugging outfielder, who had powered 398 major league home runs before the Braves abandoned Milwaukee, smacked his 500th career round-tripper before the home folks on July 14, 1968, his 600th on April 27, 1971, and his 700th on July 21, 1973.

The most dramatic moment in Aaron's illustrious career and in the history of the Atlanta-Fulton County Stadium occurred on April 8, 1974, a few days after Aaron had equalled Babe Ruth's record of 714 lifetime home runs with a drive against Jack Billingham in Cincinnati.

In the Braves' first home appearance of the season, and with network TV cameras grinding from every conceivable position, Henry slammed a fourth-inning pitch from Los Angeles' Al Downing over the left-field fence. The time was 9:07 p.m.

As Aaron circled the bases and as Chief Noc-a-homa, the pseudo redskin, put a few extra frills on his war dance outside his left-field tepee, reliever Tom House retrieved the historic baseball and 53,775 rose in unison for a lengthy, lung-clearing salute.

The Hammer was greeted at home plate by his teammates and carried briefly on their shoulders. He trotted to a special box where he embraced his wife and parents.

The arduous climb and the long-anticipated moment were over. But Henry's career endured for 40 more home runs. He was traded to the Milwaukee Brewers at the end of the season and served two years as a designated hitter-outfielder and finished his career with 755 home runs.

But the magic moment in his 23-year major league career belonged to Atlanta Stadium on April 8, 1974.

Seat 107 in Atlanta Stadium's upper-deck stands (above) bears the mark of Hank Aaron's 557th career home run, a mammoth shot recorded for posterity by artist Wayland Moore.

The overview (above) of Atlanta Stadium shows its close proximity to downtown Atlanta and Georgia's state Capitol.

MEMORIAL STADIUM

Baltimore

Frank Robinson was a 31-year-old outfielder for the Baltimore Orioles when he stepped to the plate in the fourth inning of the fourth game of the World Series at Memorial Stadium, on October 9, 1966.

A week earlier, Robinson had clinched the Triple Crown of the American League. Within a few weeks, he would be named the league's Most Valuable Player, matching his achievement in the National League five years earlier, when he was a member of the Cincinnati Reds.

On this October afternoon, the Orioles were in a scoreless deadlock with the Los Angeles Dodgers, heavily favored to capture the world championship because of their superlative pitching staff, built around Sandy Koufax and Don Drysdale.

But Koufax had lost the second game of the Series to Jim Palmer, 6-0, and now Drysdale was matching zeroes with Dave McNally. One more victory and the Orioles would be kings of baseball.

And one pitch was all that Robinson needed, crashing a 410-foot home run into the left-field bleachers to settle a battle of twin four-hitters, 1-0.

There was no finer hour for the 54,458 fans at Memorial Stadium, or perhaps in Baltimore baseball history. In 13 years, the club that had been the ragtag remnants of the St. Louis Browns had crested as ruler of baseball.

Fame and respect were a long time arriving at that section of 33rd Street known as Babe Ruth Plaza. By one calculation, Memorial Stadium is the eighth park to serve Baltimore baseball teams since the sport took root in the City of Monuments more than a century ago.

From the Madison Avenue Grounds, where inter-city games were played in earliest times, the city's baseball activity shifted to Newington Park, on a plot bordered by Baker, Gold and Calhoun streets and Pennsylvania Avenue. This facility was home to the Lord Baltimores of the National Association and the Orioles of the American Association until 1883, when action shifted to a site on Greenmount Avenue.

In the 1890s, local sports fans got their baseball kicks at Union Park, where they screamed themselves hoarse for John McGraw, Wilbert Robinson and Hugh Jennings, the nucleus of a hard-bitten troupe that won three consecutive National League pennants.

When the city was awarded a franchise in Ban Johnson's infant American League in 1901, games were played in a park at 10th Street and York Road. After two unprofitable seasons, the A.L. franchise was shifted to New York, where it later became the Yankees. Baltimore was left with only an International League baseball team.

But even the minor leagues were not without rewards. For one thing, there was Jack Dunn, who became Mr. Baseball to the Chesapeake area in the decades ahead. In 1914 he discovered a teen-age lefthander from St. Mary's Industrial School who won 22 games as a rookie. Before long the youngster was sold to the Boston Red Sox. And within another short period of time he was a household name: Babe Ruth.

When the Federal League, a new self-proclaimed major circuit, set up shop just one block away from Dunn's park in 1914, death appeared imminent for the International League franchise. But somehow—perhaps by selling Ruth and others before they had fully matured as players—Dunn survived. And when the Feds later tossed in the towel, Dunn bought their Terrapin Park, rechristened it Oriole Park and embarked upon a new era of prosperity.

It was here that Dunn scaled his highest peaks, winning seven consecutive International League championships from 1919 to 1925. He developed such stars as Lefty Grove, George Earnshaw, Max Bishop and Joe Boley, mainstays of pennant-winning Philadelphia A's clubs in 1929-31.

Oriole Park suffered a sudden and inglorious demise on July 4, 1944. Dunn had passed from the scene and the club was managed by Tommy Thomas, who was awakened at his home on St. Paul Street that night by a bright glare. Checking it out, he found the ball park a mass of flames. The efforts of firefighters proved futile as flames raced throughout the antiquated structure. "It was," reported one witness, "like a huge ball of fire swept through the stands."

After the disaster, the Orioles departed on a two-week trip, during which Municipal Stadium,

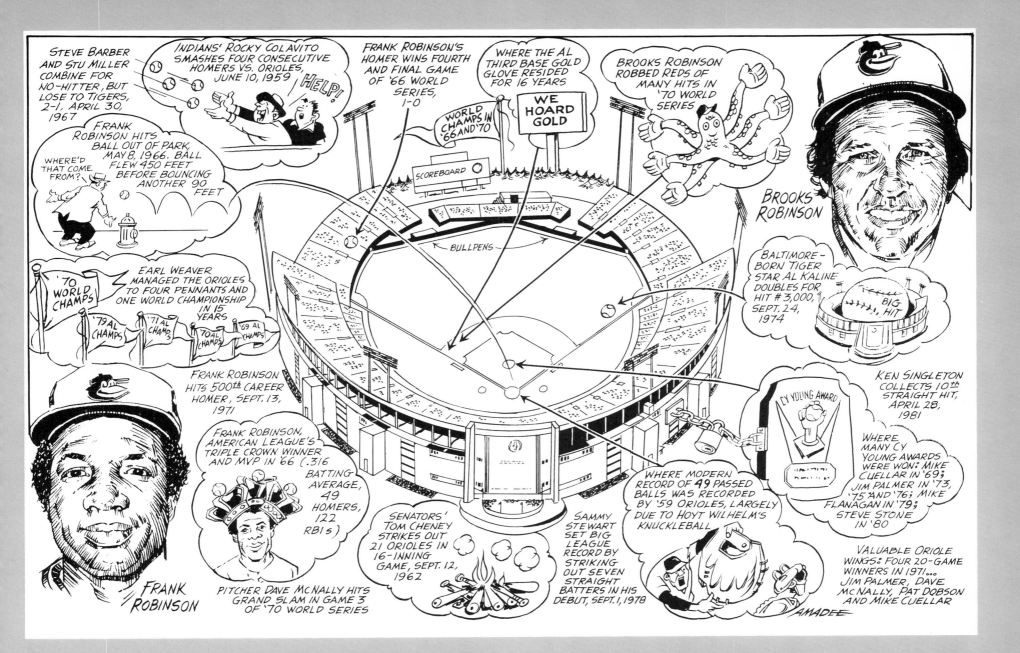

designed for football, was prepared for baseball.

The Orioles did not win the pennant that season, but before the year was out they attracted 52,000 spectators to a Junior World Series game with Louisville. That attendance figure focused attention on Baltimore's potential as a major league city because at the same time, the St. Louis Cardinals and Browns were playing to a World Series crowd of 31,000 at Sportsman's Park.

In 1950, the Orioles moved into a new facility, 31,000-seat Memorial Stadium.

In anticipation of a major league franchise, the city fathers rebuilt Memorial Stadium in 1953 as a multi-purpose facility with an unroofed second deck. And, after more than a 50-year absence— or since Boston defeated the Orioles, 9-5, in 1902 —the city celebrated its return to the American League on April 15, 1954.

The game, preceded by a gigantic parade, attracted more than 46,000, including Vice President Richard Nixon. Also there was Mrs. John McGraw, a native of Baltimore and widow of the Little Napoleon who had done so much to popularize the game in Baltimore 60 years earlier.

To assist the crowd in following the progress of the contest, there was a newly installed scoreboard in right field. It featured more than 40 miles of electrical wiring and no moving parts— only lights against a black enamel background— all at a cost of $152,000.

Completing the momentous inaugural, Bob Turley scattered seven hits and struck out nine, while Vern Stephens and Clint Courtney hit home runs to give the Orioles a 3-1 victory over Chicago.

Initially, the stadium lacked a center-field fence, with only a hedge serving as a barrier in that sector. Eventually, a wire fence replaced the hedge, providing the props for one of the more humorous incidents in the stadium's history.

It occurred the day that Jackie Brandt, whose delightful eccentricities flavored the Baltimore scene for years, back-pedaled on a long fly ball and banged into the fence, where he remained for several moments as he struggled to free his feet, which were caught on the bottom portion of the fence.

Progress was slow and painful in the Orioles' first season, but there were memorable events such as Bob Kennedy's grand-slam homer, the club's first, on July 30. In the same game Don Larsen blanked the New York Yankees, 10-0, thus ruining Casey Stengel's 65th birthday.

Terrapin Park (above left) was jammed for Baltimore's Federal League opener. Renamed Oriole Park, it hosted International League games (above right) before being destroyed by fire (right).

More than one million fans clicked Memorial Stadium turnstiles in 1954, but they had little to applaud in the power department. The Orioles socked only 19 home runs in the spacious arena, their opponents 23.

Through the years the stadium has undergone numerous minor alterations. In 1961, there were new dugouts, new bullpens and new box seats for the customers, raising the park's capacity to over 49,000.

Field dimensions have remained relatively unchanged, measuring 309 feet down each foul line and 410 feet to center field.

From its unimpressive start, home run production has escalated remarkably. In 1980, the stadium ranked third in the American League in the number of round-trippers.

Today, Baltimore fans relish the memory of such power feats as Rocky Colavito's four consecutive home runs for the Cleveland Indians on June 10, 1959; Frank Robinson's gargantuan home run of May 8, 1966—the 450-foot wallop representing the only drive ever to sail out of the park—and pitcher Dave McNally's grand-slam homer in the third game of the 1970 World Series against the Cincinnati Reds.

Other memorable blows were struck by Robinson on September 13, 1971 (his 500th major league homer); by hometown product Al Kaline on September 24, 1974 (his 3,000th major league hit for the Detroit Tigers); by John Lowenstein on October 3, 1979 (his 10th-inning homer enabled the Orioles to defeat the California Angels, 6-3, in the first game of the Championship

Series), and by Ken Singleton on April 26-27-28, 1981 (10 consecutive hits).

There are two spots on the Memorial Stadium diamond that stick out because of the great baseball feats performed there.

First, there is the pitching mound that has served as a launching pad for four no-hit games. The first was thrown by a young Hoyt Wilhelm against the New York Yankees, 1-0, on September 20, 1958. Wilhelm, of course, went on to become one of the greatest relief pitchers in the history of the game.

Also on this miniature Olympus, four Cy Young Award winners have labored with distinction for the Orioles, including Mike Cuellar in 1969, Jim Palmer in 1973, 1975 and 1976, Mike Flanagan

in 1979 and Steve Stone in 1980.

This pitching mound was also the working area for four 20-game winners in 1971: Palmer, McNally, Cuellar and Pat Dobson.

In addition, Tom Cheney of the Washington Senators fanned 21 Orioles in a 16-inning game on September 12, 1962. And Sammy Stewart established a major league record by striking out seven consecutive batters in his debut, September 1, 1978.

The other playing area venerated by longtime Bird watchers extends in all directions from third base. It represents the acreage once patrolled so dramatically and efficiently by Brooks Robinson, winner of 16 Gold Glove Awards between 1960 and 1975. Brooks was so lustrous during the 1970 World Series that the Cincinnati Reds, victims of his spectacular thievery, respectfully christened him "Hoover," as in the vacuum sweeper.

And then there are those areas that will be associated forever with the name of Gus Triandos, a catcher of above-average talents whose efforts in the early years of the franchise stimulated teammates and fans to both pity and praise him.

In 1958, Triandos smacked 13 home runs at Memorial Stadium, contributing to his total of 30 round-trippers that tied the league record for catchers.

The following season, Big Gus played a scrambling game behind the plate, committing 28 passed balls as Oriole backstops set a modern major league record of 49, most of them attribut-

Opened in 1950, Memorial Stadium (above) was rebuilt after only three years in anticipation of major league baseball. A second deck was added to the ball park.

Baltimore's minor league team moved into Municipal Stadium (above) after the 1944 fire at Oriole Park. Municipal, also called Baltimore Stadium and Babe Ruth Stadium, was designed for football.

able to Hoyt Wilhelm's erratic knuckleball.

The Orioles were victimized in a strange game at Memorial Stadium on April 30, 1967. Steve Barber of the home club had a no-hitter with two outs in the ninth inning, but control problems plagued him—he walked 10 batters in the game—and he was replaced by Stu Miller with the game tied, 1-1. Miller came in and made Don Wert hit the ball to shortstop Luis Aparicio. But second baseman Mark Belanger dropped Aparicio's throw on the attempted forceout, as the leading run scored. Miller retired the next batter to preserve the no-hitter, but the Orioles lost, 2-1.

Baltimore fans are not likely to forget Earl Weaver's last day as manager. The Orioles and Milwaukee Brewers were tied for first place in the American League East Division and met in the 1982 season finale on October 3 at Memorial Stadium.

The Brewers won the game, 10-2, to clinch the division, but Baltimore fans gave Weaver an emotional farewell even in defeat. They gave the man who had produced six division titles, four A.L. pennants and one world championship (1970) in 15 seasons a long, thunderous standing ovation.

The most depressing event in the history of Memorial Stadium, however, was neither record numbers of passed balls, Weaver's retirement nor the seventh game of the 1971 and 1979 World Series, both of which ended in an Oriole defeat. It was, instead, a tragedy in the left-field stands.

On May 2, 1964, children riding an escalator were crushed against a portable barricade for nearly 30 seconds before the power could be shut off.

One 14-year-old girl was killed and 46 others injured on what had been designated as Safety Patrol Day.

Baltimore's Memorial Stadium as it appeared in 1962 (top), eight years after the city landed the American League's St. Louis Browns, and as it looked in 1982 (bottom and right).

32

Boston's Fenway Park (left) played host to its first game in 1912 and is tied with Tiger Stadium as the second-oldest existing park in baseball. Among its many charms are the "Green Monster" (right) staring menacingly at the batter and the left-field scoreboard (above), one of the few still operated by hand.

When Anaheim Stadium was enclosed in 1979 (below), the A-frame scoreboard in left field (above left) was moved to the edge of the stadium parking lot.

36

The view (above) from the right-field foul pole at Arlington Stadium shows a spacious outfield with a left-field scoreboard that constantly reminds fans that the stadium is home of the Texas Rangers.

Comiskey Park (above and right) is the oldest stadium still in use by a major league team. The Stadium's exploding scoreboard (shown before being remodeled prior to the 1982 season), has entertained White Sox fans for many years. The three-tiered, circular Atlanta Stadium (above) long has been a paradise for National League home run hitters.

BRAVES FIELD

Boston

During a Detroit Tigers visit to Boston in 1915, Ty Cobb made a personal inspection of the new baseball park on Commonwealth Avenue.

From home plate, the famed Georgia Peach squinted down the 402-foot foul lines, then checked the center-field fence 550 feet away and announced:

"Nobody will ever hit a baseball out of this park."

Generally, Cobb was accurate in matters pertaining to baseball. But he misfired on this prediction, although for 10 years he appeared to have called the turn correctly.

On May 28, 1925, five years after the advent of the lively ball, Frank (Pancho) Snyder, a New York catcher with undistinguished hitting credentials, smacked a pitch from Larry Benton over the left-field wall. The drive cleared the barrier by about 20 feet and was 15 feet fair.

The impact of Snyder's achievement was still fresh when Bernie Neis did even better. A 160-pound outfielder, Neis hammered a pitch from Art Reinhart of St. Louis even farther. The ball sailed over the left-field fence and onto the Boston and Albany Railroad tracks. Neis hit only four other home runs that season.

If Snyder and Neis could clear the distant fences, Braves Field, with nearly 11 acres of playing surface, was no longer a paradise for careless pitchers.

Before moving into the Commonwealth Avenue facility, the Braves had played at the South End Grounds, a site used by the four-time champion Red Stockings of the National Association in 1872-75.

In the intervening years, professional clubs had performed at a park on Walpole Street, destroyed by fire, and a park on Congress Street. It was in this park where, on Memorial Day 1894, Bobby Lowe, a 155-pound second baseman, established a major league record by hitting four home runs in a 20-11 victory over Cincinnati.

As they moved and changed ownership, the team also changed names. For years they were the Beaneaters. When they were owned by John Dovey they were the Doves. When they were the property of William Hepburn Russell they were the Rustlers.

In 1912, they were acquired by James Gaffney, a Tammany Hall "Brave," and were rechristened Braves, a name that endured until 1936, when they became the Bees. John Quinn, the new president of the club, sought to remove all traces of losing stigma from the chronic tail-enders and selected the new name in a contest among fans.

Five years later, in 1941, the old name was restored, and Braves they remained from Boston to Milwaukee to Atlanta.

From the time he acquired the club, Gaffney searched for a new playing site. Stymied initially, Gaffney renovated the South End Grounds. In early 1914 he purchased the old Allston Golf Course on Commonwealth Avenue.

To construct the park, it was reported, contractors used 750 tons of steel and more than eight million pounds of cement. At completion, there was a grandstand seating 18,000, two pavilions accommodating 10,000 apiece, and a small bleacher, the famous Jury Box, seating 2,000.

Converting a golf course into a ball park presented numerous problems, not the least of which was the danger of cave-ins. According to legend, a dozen horses and mules were buried alive in a cave-in along the third base line.

During one game, the shortstop area sank an estimated eight inches, chasing Rabbit Maranville into seclusion until the fault was corrected.

But those concerns were years in the future when, on August 18, 1915, Jim Gaffney and Walter Hapgood, his business manager, threw open Braves Field for the first time.

Trolley cars on the Commonwealth Avenue line discharged passengers within the park. When the club tallied up the attendance, they concluded that 56,000 fans had crammed into the 40,000-seat park, with another 6,000 turned away.

Of the 14,000 guests of the club, 10,000 were school children. With Dick Rudolph on the hill, the Braves climaxed a memorable day by defeating the Cardinals, 8-1.

Originally, the scoreboard was located at ground level in left field, so it was not surprising when long drives by Johnny Rawlings and Bill Rariden of New York became home runs when they bounced through openings created by an

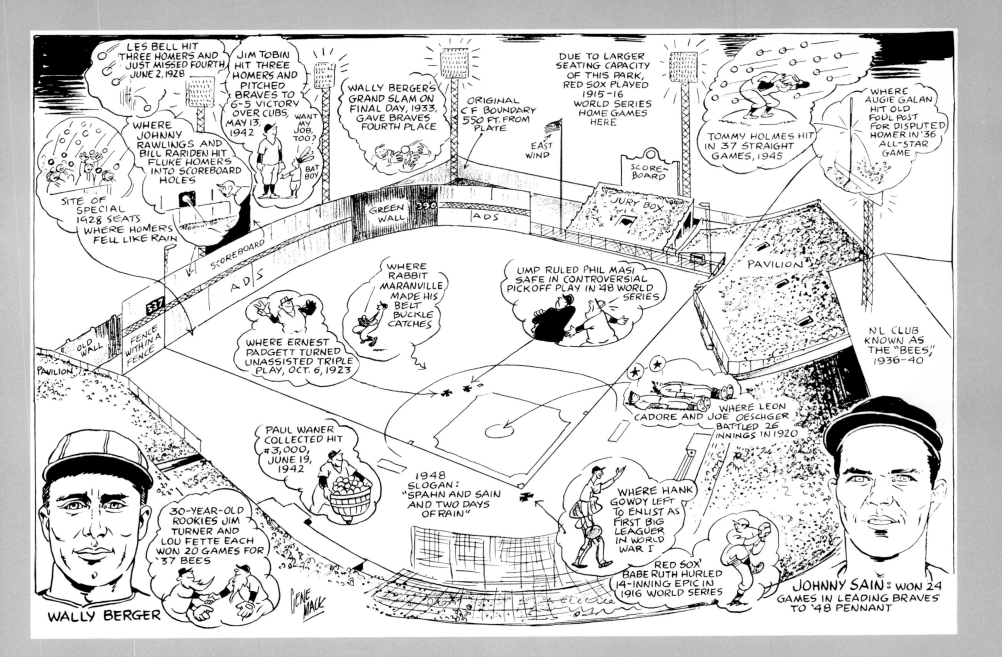

Through the years numerous subtle changes altered home run distances and, in the final years of the park, the distances were 340 feet to left field, 390 to center and 320 to right.

During the reign of the Three Little Steam Shovels—Lou Perini, Guido Rugo and Joe Maney—sky view boxes were installed in 1941 and arc lights in 1946.

A $500,000 facelift revitalized the faded 30-year-old structure in 1946, but more than merely a cosmetic change, the new paint job provided a healthy, surprising boost in goodwill among the customers.

When occupants of one section of stands headed for the exits at the conclusion of the season opener, they found their clothes daubed with green paint, which had been given insufficient time to dry.

Customers took their complaints to the front office. Advertisements in the daily papers expressed the club's apologies and requested fans with legitimate cleaning bills to submit them to the club for payment.

A "Paint Account" was opened at a local bank and two lawyers devoted most of the season to processing claims. More than 18,000 claims—some from California and Florida—arrived at club offices. More than $6,000 was paid to 5,000 claimants.

Less than two months after it opened, Braves Field was the scene of the World Series, although the Braves were not among the participants. In the interest of a larger gate, the Red Sox switched their three games with Philadelphia to the new park.

As a result, more than 40,000 fans watched the Red Sox wrap up the world championship with 2-1, 2-1 and 5-4 victories.

inattentive scoreboard boy.

The first alteration in park design occurred before the 1928 season. In an effort to increase the home run productivity of catcher Frank (Shanty) Hogan, management installed seats in left and center field, reducing home run distances from 402 feet to 353 feet in left and from 550 feet to 387 feet in center.

But by season's opening, Hogan had been traded to New York in a deal that brought Rogers Hornsby to Boston.

The new seats provided one glorious afternoon for third baseman Lester Bell who, on June 2, clouted three home runs into the area and barely missed a fourth that went for a triple.

Otherwise, the new sections spelled only heartache for the home team. By mid-June, 47 home runs had fallen into the new area, most of them off the bats of visitors. Management decided to dismantle the 6,000 seats.

Demolition dragged on slowly, however, and for most of the remainder of the season concrete stringers designated the area for ground-rule doubles.

Braves Field (above), home for Boston's National League club from August 18, 1915, through 1952, was a busy place when bleacher seats went on sale (right).

A similar arrangement existed the next season. Large crowds were on hand to see Ernie Shore win the opening game, 6-5, and Babe Ruth pitch a 14-inning, 2-1 victory in Game 2 as the Red Sox eliminated Brooklyn in five games.

Braves Field will long be remembered for its spectacular pitching performances, the greatest of which occurred on May 1, 1920. On a cool, overcast day, Joe Oeschger of Boston and Leon Cadore of Brooklyn battled 26 innings to a 1-1 tie that was halted by darkness.

Jim Tobin utilized the vastness of Braves Field to pitch two no-hitters in 1944. In his first epic on April 27, the righthander with the baffling knuckleball blanked Brooklyn, 2-0. On June 22, in the nightcap of a doubleheader, Tobin held Philadelphia hitless for five innings before darkness halted action.

In addition to his pitching prowess, Tobin also wrote hitting history at Braves Field by clouting three home runs in a 6-5 victory over the Cubs on May 13, 1942. He thereby became the first pitcher to turn the trick since 1886.

Another slugger received a hero's acclaim on opening day 1935. Babe Ruth, swapping his Yankee flannels for a vice president's portfolio and an outfield position with the Braves, returned to the field where he had starred as a World Series pitcher 19 years earlier. Ever the showman, The Bambino touched Carl Hubbell of the Giants for a home run and single and made a spectacular catch of a foul ball to spark a 4-2 Boston triumph.

Within two months, however, The Babe was gone, no longer able to produce in the grand style to which he was accustomed.

In 1929, Judge Emil Fuchs, owner of the club, assumed the managerial reins, thereby effecting a

sizable savings to a club already seriously strapped financially.

"A manager must no longer chew tobacco and talk out of the side of his mouth," declared the Judge. "The club can't do any worse with me as manager than it has done the past few years."

The pronouncement was not among the Judge's best. For the first time in five years, the Braves finished last.

But the year rolled with laughter. Players recognized his shortcomings early and it wasn't long before all of Boston tittered over the Fuchs funnies.

One day, with the bases full of Braves and none out, he turned to players on the bench and asked, "What shall we try for now, boys?"

"What about a squeeze play?" somebody suggested.

"A squeeze play?" repeated the Judge, his judicial temper rising. "No, let's score in an honorable way."

When Joe Dugan, ex-third baseman of the Yankees, was told to play shortstop, Jumping Joe asked with a wink, "Where's shortstop?"

Braves Field, as it appeared down the left-field foul line (above) for a regular-season game, was the site of three World Series—but only one involved the Braves.

to fine West, or fine and suspend him for his inexcusable charity. As he pondered, West stooped over the water cooler, where he was struck by a foul ball that shattered several teeth.

Under the circumstances, West had been punished sufficiently for his indiscretion, concluded Stengel, who shrugged his shoulders and tried to think of something funny.

Between the Fuchs and Stengel comedy skits, Braves Field patrons were treated to a no-nonsense act that raised hopes of better days to come.

Bill McKechnie, known variously as Deacon Bill or Wilkinsburg Will or the Canny Scot, had played one game for the 1913 Braves before moving to New York in the American League. He managed Pittsburgh to the 1925 world championship and the St. Louis Cardinals to the 1928 National League pennant and he would later pilot the Cincinnati Reds to a couple of flags en route to the Hall of Fame.

McKechnie and Wally Berger arrived in Boston simultaneously, to the mutual advantage of each.

As a rookie, Berger walloped 38 homers, 27 doubles and 14 triples, in addition to driving in 119 runs.

The Braves climbed two notches, to sixth place, in McKechnie's first season, sank to seventh in 1931, finished fifth in 1932 and then came home fourth in 1933 on the strength of a dramatic Berger homer.

Idled for three weeks by an attack of the flu, Wally pinch-hit a grand-slam homer in the ninth inning of the final game to defeat the Phillies, 4-1. That smash produced the Braves' initial first-division finish since 1921.

The Braves finished fourth again in 1934, sank to eighth, climbed to sixth and came in fifth in

Retorted the Judge, "Show Mr. Dugan where the clubhouse is and how to take off his uniform."

The Judge's one season of managerial mirth was prologue to another era, 1938-43, when Braves Field took on the appearance of an Olsen and Johnson thigh-slapper.

These were the years of Casey Stengel's stewardship, when second-division finishes gave little hint of the managerial genius that would carry The Perfessor to the Hall of Fame after an illustrious career with the Yankees.

With the Braves, Casey was the frustrated clown, the rubber-faced mimic who resorted to comedy when his best-laid plans went askew.

One illustration will suffice. Max West, returning to the dugout after being retired at first base, spied a baseball rolling in his path. Thinking it was a foul tip, West picked up the ball and tossed it to Philadelphia catcher Mickey Livingston. To West's horror, Livingston tagged out a Boston runner trying to score from third base on a passed ball.

On the Boston bench, Stengel debated whether

The small right-field bleacher section (above) at Braves Field was known as the Jury Box and had a seating capacity of about 2,000.

1937, when McKechnie was named Major League Manager of the Year by The Sporting News.

Following six seasons of incompetence under Stengel and two years of mediocrity under Bob Coleman, the stage was set for an era of prosperity under Billy Southworth, a one-time Braves outfielder who managed the Cardinals to three consecutive pennants, 1942-44.

Attendance at Braves Field more than doubled in 1946, as the Braves just missed the million mark while finishing fourth, one game out of third.

New arc lights helped swell attendance, as did the Troubadours, sometimes referred to as the Three Little Earaches. Mixing music and vaudeville, the Troubadours entertained throughout the season and proved so popular that the Braves invited them on a western trip.

By 1948, the Braves' long drive to the top was climaxed by their first pennant in 34 years, and attendance just missed the 1.5 million mark.

The pitching staff consisted mainly of Warren Spahn and Johnny Sain, leading one press box poet to write that the club's success key was "Spahn and Sain and two days of rain."

Braves Field, idle as a World Series site since the Red Sox played there in 1916, bulged at the seams when Sain opposed Bob Feller and the Cleveland Indians in the first contest. New England pride swelled accordingly when Sain turned in a four-hit, 1-0 victory.

In the eighth inning, one of the most controversial plays in World Series history occurred. Pinch-runner Phil Masi of the Braves was on sec-ond base with one out when Feller suddenly threw to shortstop Lou Boudreau, who obviously had Masi caught on the pickoff. But second base umpire Bill Stewart called the runner safe and a big argument ensued. After order was restored, Sain lined out but Tommy Holmes singled past third to drive home Masi with the game's only run.

Spahn lost a 4-1 decision to Bob Lemon in Game 2 and, although Spahn won an 11-5, fifth-game laugher in Cleveland, forcing the Series back to Boston, the steam was gone from the Three Little Steam Shovels' ball club. The Braves collected nine hits off Lemon and Gene Bearden, but they also left seven runners on base and lost the sixth game, and the Series, 4-3.

After their one taste of glory, the Braves encountered bad times again. As the team struggled, Braves Field turnstiles slowed to a sickening pace. Although rookie third baseman Eddie Mathews struck a home run spark, it wasn't enough.

On the last day of the 1952 home season, 8,822 patrons were in the stands to see the Brooklyn Dodgers score six runs in the eighth inning for an 8-2 victory.

That was all. Season attendance was 281,000. By the next spring, the Braves were gone to richer pastures in Milwaukee.

Braves Field, once the brightest and largest gem in the major leagues, was a ghost park. The park of James Gaffney and Babe Ruth, of Emil Fuchs and Wally Berger, of Bill McKechnie and Casey Stengel, and of Billy Southworth, Spahn and Sain was sold to Boston University. It served as a football field for five years, then yielded to the demolition crew.

On the site was erected a modern sports complex.

Bob Elliott of the Braves (above, second from left) is out as Indians first baseman Eddie Robinson stretches for a throw to complete a double play in Game 2 of the 1948 World Series at Braves Field.

With the Braves having fled to Milwaukee, Braves Field gathered weeds (above) in 1953. Boston fans—well, most of them (right)—had deserted the club in 1952.

FENWAY PARK

Boston

In an era of symmetrical, multi-purpose stadiums, Fenway Park stands as a monument to antiquity, distinguished by its irregular architecture, its infinite charm and its seven decades of memorable baseball.

Seventeen facets and barriers mark its interior design, the "Green Monster" frowns frighteningly in left field and pigeons fly merrily throughout the premises, no longer endangered by rifle shots from the guns of Ted Williams, who decimated the population until halted by the Humane Society.

Oh, those pigeons! In 1945, a throw by Philadelphia outfielder Hal Peck skulled a pigeon in flight. The baseball deflected to the second baseman, who tagged out Skeeter Newsome trying for a double.

The fate of the bird is uncertain. One version insists it was killed. The other maintains that it plunged to earth, shook off its momentary dizziness and took off for safer territory.

The same season, Boston outfielder Tom McBride took a bead on what he felt sure was a long fly off the bat of Philadelphia's Sam Chapman. Too late he discovered his error—he had sighted on a pigeon.

Billy Hunter of the St. Louis Browns once kayoed a pigeon in batting practice, and a high foul off the bat of Willie Horton of Detroit brought down another bird in 1974.

A Fenway Park game once was delayed because of golf balls, hundreds of them tossed onto the field by irate youngsters on Caddy Day. Here, too, a game was interrupted four times by fog, and Red Sox first baseman Dick Stuart, showing rare defensive talents, received a standing ovation for making a clean catch of a wind-blown hot dog wrapper.

Also within this storied structure the Red Sox

scored 17 runs in one inning, 49 runs in two consecutive games, Ted Williams pitched two innings in an American League game and Lou Boudreau unveiled a revolutionary defensive deployment to muffle the rampaging bat of the same Williams.

For 70 years the misshapen ball park at the intersection of Lansdowne and Jersey streets has presented the good and the bad, the humorous and the humdrum of baseball.

Prior to the construction of Fenway Park in 1912, the club, known as the Pilgrims, played at the Huntington Avenue Grounds, a 9,000-seat facility built on an old carnival site in 1901, when Ban Johnson awarded Boston a franchise in his fledgling American League.

The first game of the modern World Series was contested here on October 1, 1903, with the Pittsburgh Pirates defeating the Pilgrims, 7-3.

Twelve days later, on October 13, Bill Dinneen completed the American League club's drive to the championship by pitching his second shutout and third victory in eight games, a 3-0 decision before 7,400.

The first perfect game in modern major league history (since 1900) was recorded on the Hunt-

Boston fans ring the infield and outfield areas and swarm the rest of the field at Huntington Avenue Grounds (above) after watching their A.L. club win the first World Series in 1903.

ington Avenue Grounds on May 5, 1904, by Cy Young, who shut out Philadelphia, 3-0.

One of baseball's most unusual home runs was smacked here on June 27, 1911. In an effort to speed up games, Ban Johnson had ruled out warmup pitches between innings. In a game against Philadelphia, however, Ed Karger, noting that Boston outfielders were not yet in position, started lobbing pitches to his catcher.

On the second pitch, Stuffy McInnis lined a drive to right-center field and, at the urging of his teammates, circled the bases while Boston outfielders failed to chase the ball.

The league president turned a deaf ear to the protests of the Red Sox, who maintained that not all Philadelphia players had left the field when McInnis hit the ball.

Construction of Fenway Park, named by club President John I. Taylor because it was located in "The Fens," a marshy area of the city, commenced in 1911. The inaugural game, scheduled for April 18, 1912, was rained out as was the doubleheader the next day, Patriots Day.

When the elements relented on April 20, 27,000 jammed the facility, gazing admiringly at a steel and concrete park that featured a single-deck grandstand, wooden bleachers in left field, a wooden pavilion in right and wooden bleachers in extreme right and center fields.

In addition to the park's irregular contour, adhering to the plot of ground on which it was built, there was a 10-foot embankment in front of the left-field fence. In time the incline became known as "Duffy's Cliff" in tribute to Duffy Lewis, who raced up and down the embankment with equal agility.

Years later, the Cliff gave to baseball one of its more humorous incidents. Smead Jolley, more

gifted as a hitter than as a fielder, fell flat on his anterior while chasing a carom off the wall. Returning to the dugout at the end of the inning, Jolley accosted snickering teammates with: "You smart guys taught me how to go up the hill, but nobody taught me how to come down."

After viewing the wonders of modern ball park construction, the opening-day customers enjoyed an 11-inning, 7-6 victory over New York as Buck O'Brien and Charley (Sea Lion) Hall outpitched Jim (Hippo) Vaughn.

Because the workmen were unable to put the finishing touches on the park in time for opening day, formal dedication was delayed until May 17, when 17,000 watched the Sox bow to Ed Walsh of the Chicago White Sox, 5-4.

To Mayor John F. (Honey Fitz) Fitzgerald went the honor of making the first pitch. A half century later, his grandson, John F. Kennedy, President of the United States, would make the ceremonial first pitch that ushered in the season in Washington, D.C.

By mid-June, 1912, the Red Sox had gained first place and at season's end enjoyed a 14-game margin over the Washington Senators. Tris Speaker batted .383, third highest in the American League, and Joe Wood fashioned a 34-5 pitching record.

The New York Giants, who had refused to meet the Red Sox in a postseason series in 1904 because, said Manager John McGraw, "We don't play minor leaguers," now, eight years later, were required to face the A.L. champions under the World Series format.

The Giants lost the opening game in their own park, played an 11-inning, 6-6 tie halted by darkness and won three of the next five games to force the Series into a one-game shootout for the championship at Fenway Park on October 16.

After nine innings the teams were tied, 1-1, and when the Giants presented 23-game winner Christy Mathewson with a one-run lead in the 10th, the die for a Boston defeat was all but cast.

But in a sequence of events unmatched in World Series annals, the Red Sox rolled back the tide. First, pinch-hitter Clyde Engle lifted a routine fly to center field where Fred Snodgrass, after moving about 10 feet, let the ball trickle through his fingers.

Snodgrass then made a near-miraculous catch of a line drive by Harry Hooper and Steve Yerkes worked Matty for a base on balls.

When Tris Speaker hit a high pop foul to the right side, first baseman Fred Merkle, catcher

With the stands bulging at Fenway Park, resourceful fans (above) get a bird's-eye view of a Red Sox game from atop a nearby building beyond the right-field corner.

year-old lefthander just acquired from the International League for $2,500.

The kid failed to go the route, but he did receive credit for a 4-3 victory over Cleveland. The youngster would leave an indelible impression on the game, first as a pitcher, then as a hitter whose gargantuan clouts and dramatic lifestyle would dominate the American sports scene in the Golden Twenties. Babe Ruth was in the majors to stay for 22 years.

Although the Red Sox did not win the pennant in 1914, Fenway Park hosted two World Series games. When the Boston Braves, completing their historic rush from last place on the Fourth of July to a National League pennant, decided that their 11,000-seat South End Grounds was inadequate for the World Series crowds, the third and fourth games were played in Fenway Park.

The switch paid off handsomely. More than 30,000 responded daily as George Stallings' Miracle Braves defeated the supposedly invincible Philadelphia Athletics, 5-4 and 3-1, to complete the first four-game sweep in Series history.

When the Red Sox won pennants in 1915 and 1916, the Braves returned the favor of 1914 and turned their new 40,000-seat field over to the Red Sox. On each occasion, the Sox won a world championship, beating Philadelphia and Brooklyn in five-game Series.

By the summer of 1917, Babe Ruth was on his way to 24 victories and a .325 batting average. On June 23, the lefthander started a game against Washington at Fenway Park. When plate umpire Brick Owens called ball four on leadoff batter Ray Morgan, the Babe flew into a rage, rushed to the plate, gave the arbiter an ungentle shove and was ejected from the game.

Chief Meyers and Matty converged on the ball, Mathewson shouting, "Chief, Chief, Chief."

Matty's shouts were lost among the screams of the multitudes and, as Merkle and Meyers glanced helplessly at each other, the ball fell untouched.

Reprieved, Speaker lined the next pitch to right field for a single and raced to second as Engle scored and Yerkes advanced to third. McGraw had no choice but to walk Duffy Lewis intentionally, setting up a force play at every base.

The strategy backfired, however, when Larry Gardner stroked a long fly to right field and Yerkes scampered home after the catch. McGraw

had lost to the "minor leaguers."

The game was witnessed by only 17,000, the result of a management blunder the previous day when 32,000 jammed the stands.

In a thoughtless moment, a club executive decided to sell to the public a section of seats normally occupied by the Royal Rooters, a vociferous and loyal group of partisans. When the Rooters discovered the situation, 300 staged a protest march around the field before they were herded toward the exits by mounted police. An effective boycott by fans helped keep attendance down for the finale the next day.

A baseball legend was born in Fenway Park on

Fenway Park's Jersey Street entrances (above) were busier than usual in 1946. Not only was Fenway the site of that season's All-Star Game, it played host to three games of the '46 World Series.

On the bench Ernie Shore was roused from a reverie by Manager Jack Barry shouting from second base: "Shore, go in there and stall around until I can get somebody warmed up."

The righthander took five warmup pitches, the limit under existing rules, and faced the next batter. On the first pitch, Morgan was thrown out stealing. Shore continued to pitch and continued to retire batters, all that he faced, as the Red Sox won, 4-0.

For years the game was listed in the record books as just another no-hitter until it was decided that, in fairness to Shore, he should receive credit for a perfect game, even if with an asterisk.

Fenway Park was the scene of a threatened strike during the 1918 World Series. Boston and Chicago players, irked by the small individual shares, remained in the clubhouse long after the scheduled start of the September 10 game. Because crowds had averaged barely 23,000, because ticket prices had not been increased for the Series and because the second, third and fourth-place teams were to share in the World Series pool for the first time, a winner's cut could come to about $1,000, a loser's share to $500.

While a band entertained the uneasy crowd with patriotic airs, a reminder of the sacrifices being made in World War I, members of the three-man National Commission that governed baseball parleyed with the athletes. Eventually, an hour after the scheduled start, the players agreed to take the field for Game 5, which the Cubs won, 3-0, behind Hippo Vaughn. The Red Sox wrapped up the championship the next day, winning 2-1 behind Carl Mays.

Post-war prosperity was sweeping the country in the early 1920s, but while the Golden Era of Sports was swelling the coffers of other major league clubs, Fenway Park resembled an alms house. Harry Frazee, the theatrical producer-owner, fell on evil times with a succession of money losers. To remain solvent, he started to sell Red Sox stars, including Ruth, who brought $125,000.

As the Yankees profited with ex-Red Sox luminaries, Fenway fans suffered and damned the name of Frazee as they entered the park and read posters advertising his latest production.

In July of 1923, Frazee sold the Red Sox to Bob Quinn, vice president and business manager of the St. Louis Browns. But conditions remained unchanged. When the bleachers along the left-field foul line burned down in 1926, charred timbers were removed but the section was not rebuilt and fielders chased foul flies into the area behind third base.

A modest budget, followed by the Great Depression, haunted Fenway Park until February 25, 1933, when Quinn sold the club to Thomas Austin Yawkey, lumberman-sportsman who inaugurated park improvements the next season.

A four-alarm fire destroyed virtually all the new construction in January of 1934, but when the season opened on April 17, there were concrete bleachers in center field, replacing the old wooden seats. In addition, Duffy's Cliff had disappeared in left field and the wooden wall behind it had been replaced by a metal barrier.

Continued improvements added a 23-foot screen on top of the 37-foot left-field wall to protect the shop windows on Lansdowne Street in 1936, and, in 1940, bullpens were constructed behind the right and right-center field walls.

The new area was named "Williamsburg," in tribute to the club's young slugger, Ted Williams,

Duffy Lewis (of "Duffy's Cliff" fame), Tris Speaker and Harry Hooper (left to right, top photo) meet in 1930. Ernie Shore (below left) made history in 1917 while relieving the man alongside, Babe Ruth.

P		1	2	3	4	5	6	7	8	9	H
24	ST. LOUIS	0	0	3	0	0	0	0	0		6
22	BOSTON	0	8	5	7	2	0	2	5		28
	DETROIT										
	NEW YORK				N	I	T	E			

Ted Williams (above) may have been bored on June 8, 1950, when the Red Sox, outhitting St. Louis 28-6, led 29-3 entering the ninth inning. Boston won, 29-4.

who had hit 14 of his 31 homers in 1939 into the distant reaches of right field. Given an easier target in 1940, Williams hit only 23.

Skyview boxes were constructed on both sides of the rooftop press box in 1946, lights were installed in 1947, advertisements were removed from the left-field wall the same year, creating the famed "Green Monster," and, in 1952, a runway was built between the visitors' dugout and clubhouse, thereby eliminating the necessity of all players exiting the field by the same route.

A $1.3 million scoreboard, measuring 24 feet by 40 feet, was erected behind the center-field bleachers between the 1975-76 seasons. In addition, the press box was enlarged, enclosed in glass and air-conditioned.

For more than 20 years, including two terms of military service, Fenway Park was home to Ted Williams, and dozens of keepsakes abound for legions of admirers.

Among Williams' lesser-known but highly cherished achievements was his two-inning pitching performance on August 24, 1940. Manager Joe Cronin, seeking to give his overworked bullpen some rest and also silence Ted's extravagant boasts of his pitching prowess, summoned the big fellow to the mound while inserting pitcher Jim Bagby in left field for the last two innings of a 12-1 loss to the pennant-bound Detroit Tigers.

Williams yielded three hits and one run and struck out Rudy York, the feared slugger standing motionless as a sweeping curve broke across the plate for strike three.

Best remembered of Williams' hitting achievements were two homers, two singles, four runs and five runs batted in during the American League All-Stars' 12-0 victory, July 9, 1946, and his farewell home run on September 28, 1960. On his final at-bat in an illustrious career, Teddy Ballgame homered into the Red Sox bullpen. It was No. 521.

The famed slugger also bunted once at Fenway. It happened in Game 3 of the 1946 World Series to take advantage of a right-side shift that left only one St. Louis player on the left side of the diamond.

The widely imitated defense was introduced by Lou Boudreau, manager of the Cleveland Indians, on July 14, 1946, after watching Williams hit three homers and drive in eight runs in the first game of a doubleheader.

Accepting the challenge and disdaining a sure hit to the third-base side, Williams swung away, grounding out to Boudreau in short right field.

One of the most dramatic home runs in historic Fenway was delivered at 12:30 a.m. on October 22, 1975 by Carlton Fisk. With the Red Sox and Cincinnati Reds deadlocked, 6-6, in the sixth game of the World Series, the Boston catcher hoisted a fly off the left-field foul pole to produce a 12-inning Boston victory.

Before the day was over, however, the Red Sox, after leading 3-0, dropped a 4-3 decision, ending their dream of world conquest again. It was getting to be a painfully familiar experience for the Red Sox. Eight years earlier, Bob Gibson hurled the St. Louis Cardinals to a 7-2 triumph in the seventh game of the 1967 Series.

A view from the right-field corner (above) offers a different perspective to Boston's Fenway Park—and it's a sight that even a pigeon might appreciate.

As Ted Williams walks toward the Green Monster (above) while taking his position in the 1946 World Series, the irregular contour of the rest of Fenway's outfield is obvious.

EBBETS FIELD

Brooklyn

It died much too young, at age 46, and when the two-ton headache ball, painted white with stitches to resemble a baseball, crashed into the roof of the dugout near third base, there was a collective sigh, not unlike a sob, from the 200 who had gathered for the last rites.

From April 9, 1913, until February 23, 1960, Ebbets Field stood as a monument to comedy and compassion, to the best and worst of baseball, to Dazzy Vance, Babe Herman and Wilbert Robinson, to Dixie Walker, Dolph Camilli and Pee Wee Reese, to Jackie Robinson, Roy Campanella and Duke Snider.

Here roamed the Daffiness Boys of the 1920s and '30s, Leo Durocher's battlers who captivated a nation in the early 1940s and the methodical maulers of Burt Shotton, Chuck Dressen and Walter Alston in the '40s and '50s.

From the day of its birth there seemed little doubt that Ebbets Field would be different. It would be set apart from other major league baseball parks. On that historic first day, bleacherites were kept waiting outside the gates because somebody had forgotten to bring the key.

On the march to the center-field flagpole for the ceremonial raising of the flag, proceedings were interrupted because somebody had neglected to bring Old Glory.

Those events established the tempo, which was sometimes rapid and sometimes creepy, but always entertaining.

Brooklyn had been a baseball hotbed long before the twentieth century, dating to pre-Civil War days when games were played on open fields. An early demonstration of the city's affection for baseball occurred on June 5, 1871, when 6,500 jammed into enclosed Union Grounds for a game between the Mutuals of New York and the Chicago club. Another 5,000 watched the contest from rooftops and from atop vehicles outside the park. The Mutuals won the game, 8-5.

In 1872 the Atlantics joined the National Association and played in the Capitoline Grounds. When the N.A. folded after the 1875 season, the Atlantics collapsed also. And when the Mutuals were expelled from the National League for failing to make a western trip in 1876, Brooklyn dropped out of professional baseball.

On May 12, 1883, the city welcomed a new team, a member of the Interstate League, a minor circuit that opened its season at new Washington Park, so named because it was in an area in which George Washington's Continental Army fought the battle of Long Island.

After one season, Owner Charley Byrne, encouraged by capacity crowds, moved his club into the American Association. In its inaugural appearance, Brooklyn defeated Washington, 11-3, making the most of 10 Washington errors.

Mary Ebbets (above), daughter of the Dodgers' owner, handled the curtain-raising duties when Ebbets Field officially opened on April 9, 1913. Philadelphia defeated Brooklyn, 1-0.

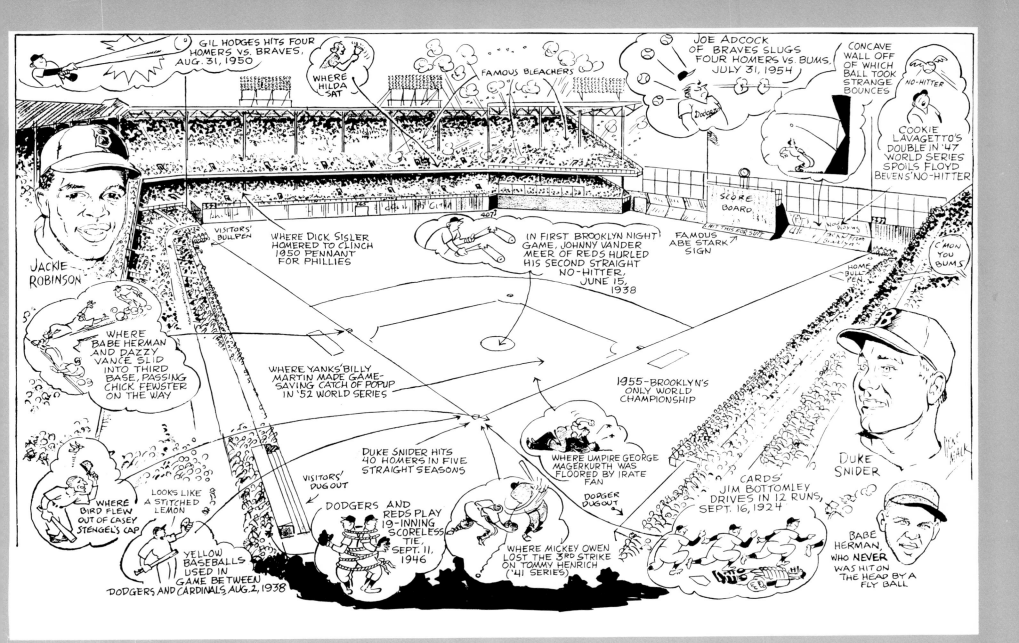

57

On May 23, 1889, fire of mysterious origin destroyed the grandstand. Although insurance covered less than half of the damage, Byrne ordered reconstruction to begin immediately. By Memorial Day, the 3,000-seat grandstand, 1,000 seats larger than previously, was ready for a holiday doubleheader.

Despite the fire, the club drew 355,690 fans during the season. The four-time champion St. Louis club attracted 95,383 of that total for eight games.

It was during this period that the team was first called the Dodgers, or Trolley Dodgers, a name applied to the borough inhabitants because of the hazardous conditions created by the new-fangled public conveyances.

When the Dodgers met the New York Giants, champions of the National League, in a post-season series, Byrne was convinced that the huge crowds dictated a move to larger quarters. Despite the fact that his lease on Washington Park had several years remaining, Byrne decided to move his club to Eastern Park in the eastern section of New York, and jumped to the National League.

Fellow A.A. owners, infuriated that Byrne would defect with a championship club, organized another A.A. team for Brooklyn and arranged to play games at Ridgewood Park, where Byrne had played some Sunday games when blue laws prohibited Sabbath games in Brooklyn.

Meanwhile, the Players League was born and the Brooklyn entry beat Byrne to a lease on Eastern Park. The N.L. club owner had no choice but to remain at Washington Park, where the club won its first pennant in the National League.

For the 1890 season, the Brooklyn N.L. club was known as the Bridegrooms in tribute to the

six players who had married during the off-season. Following the season, the Players League collapsed and the A.A. club, known as the Gladiators, also succumbed, leaving the major league market to Byrne and his club, which by this time played in Eastern Park.

Even with numerous improvements, Eastern Park was not the popular baseball rendezvous that Washington Park had been. In 1898, after the death of Byrne, his secretary, Charles H. Ebbets, returned the Dodgers to their former habitat, partly because of the inviting $7,500 annual rent and partly because of dwindling attendance at Eastern Park.

At this site, between Third and Fifth streets, between Fourth and Fifth avenues, Ebbets introduced a new manager. He was Ned Hanlon, who had managed the famous Baltimore Orioles to N.L. pennants in the early years of the decade. Hanlon brought several of his Baltimore stars with him, transforming a 10th-place aggregation of 1898 into a pennant winner the next two years.

At that time a troupe of actors, known as Hanlon's Superbas, was playing the vaudeville circuit. What could be more natural than for the Trolley Dodgers to be known as the Superbas? The name caught on quickly and, even in the 1950s, oldtimers still liked to refer to the Dodgers as the Superbas.

Charles Ebbets eventually grew dissatisfied with Washington Park. Sporting fans with money to spend were being denied their pleasure by the limited capacity of the antiquated structure. A modern park with plenty of seats was the only solution.

In his idle hours, Ebbets started to canvass the city. Taking into consideration improved service by the Brooklyn Rapid Transit Company in a burgeoning community, Ebbets made his choice for a new park site: a 4½-acre plot bordered by Bedford Avenue, Sullivan Street, Franklin Avenue and Montgomery Street.

To those with limited vision, Ebbets had blundered badly. They could not see past the hovels and shanties that dotted the area, the crags from which the squatters dumped garbage and refuse. Ebbets ignored his detractors. He formed a corporation and, secretly, parcel by parcel, he bought up the claims until only one remained. The owner of the last lot was out of town, he was told.

Hilda Chester (above), a bleacherite with an ever-present cowbell, was just one of the many characters who inhabited Ebbets Field and cheered on the Dodgers.

Ebbets dispatched agents. The trail led to California, then Berlin, to Paris and from there no Parisian knew where. The agents returned to the United States and found the quarry in Montclair, N.J., where he had been all the time.

Would he sell his plot of ground? If so, did he have a price?

"Would five hundred dollars be too much?"

Quickly, the agent produced pen and contract. The search was over. Charles Ebbets had the ground for his ball park.

On March 14, 1912, Ebbets turned the first spadeful of earth for the new park. Among the spectators were the sports editors of the four Brooklyn dailies, referred to by Ebbets as "The Four Kings."

"What are you gonna call your park?" one of them wanted to know.

"Why, I hadn't even thought about it," Ebbets replied.

"Why don't you call it Ebbets Field? It was your idea. You've put yourself into hock to build it."

"All right," agreed Ebbets. "That's what we'll call it."

While the park was under construction, Ebbets encountered rough financial sledding. To solve his problem, he offered a half interest in the club to the McKeever brothers, Steve and Ed, local contractors, in exchange for $100,000.

The first game in Ebbets' showplace was an exhibition between the Dodgers and the New York Highlanders, forerunners of the Yankees, on a raw, wintry day.

When newspapermen arrived for the official opening on April 9, they discovered that, although the local editors had approved the park design, they had overlooked one glaring deficiency—

Photos of pregame ceremonies at Ebbets Field show the contour of the Brooklyn ball park in left field (above right) and in right field (below right).

there was no provision for a press box. The problem was corrected by removing two rows of seats from the front of the upper deck. A full-scale press box was not constructed until 1929.

The 25,000 who jammed the park for the inaugural saw a double-decked stand from the right-field wall to just beyond third base. Beyond that a single-deck concrete bleacher section extended to the left-field wall, 419 feet from home plate. The right-field wall, rising nine feet, was 301 feet distant.

The erection of left-field stands, and additional improvements and renovations, reduced the left-field distance to 348 feet.

In later years, too, the right-field wall was raised to 20 feet and was topped by a screen. The wall contained a break in the middle so that baseballs hit against it caromed erratically past unwary outfielders.

Signs added to the park's character. Prominent were those of Abe Stark—"Hit Sign, Win Suit"—and the Schaefer Beer sign in which the "h" and "e" of Schaefer could be illuminated to designate a hit or error.

Characters inhabited Ebbets Field in abundance. None was more easily recognized than Hilda Chester, the bleacherite who, with her cowbell, could make more noise, it was said, than four male hog callers.

Hilda was not alone, however, in the art of cacophony. There was the Dodger Sym-Phony Band which for years entertained with loud and brassy selections that assailed the ears of music lovers but charmed the hearts of Flatbush faithful.

Ebbets Field may be best remembered as the scene of Mickey Owen's passed ball, or where a fan slugged umpire George Magerkurth, or where

Cookie Lavagetto shattered a World Series no-hit bid with two outs in the ninth inning, or where Gil Hodges and Joe Adcock slugged four home runs in a nine-inning game or where. . . . Casey Stengel, the master of mirth and merriment, set the tone for wackiness in 1918 when, following his trade to Pittsburgh, he returned to Ebbets Field as a member of the Pirates.

On his first at-bat, the fans howled wildly in salute to an old favorite. Equal to the occasion, Casey bowed nimbly and doffed his cap, whereupon a bird flew off the top of his head and winged majestically out of the park.

"Where did Casey find the bird?" a reporter inquired.

In a typical rambling dissertation, Stengel explained:

"When I went to right field in the last half of the first inning, I saw it stumbling along the base of the wall. I guess it wasn't looking where it was

Hot dogs and lemonade were available to fans outside Ebbets Field (above) on October 6, 1920, the day of Game 2 of the World Series between Brooklyn and Cleveland.

Vance on second and Chick Fewster on first. Herman lined safely to right field, and then things started to happen.

DeBerry scored. Vance held up, thinking the ball might be caught, then advanced only as far as third. Fewster, certain that the ball would fall safely, rounded second base and headed full sail for third. Herman, confident that he could stretch the hit into a triple, raced past second head down. As he slid into third he was greeted, none too warmly, by Vance and Fewster.

Fewster, believing he was out, stepped off the base and was tagged out. Herman, trying to retrace his steps, was tagged out by the second baseman.

In the press box a critic typed: "Being tagged out was much too good for Herman."

Such baseline blunders spawned such vaudeville jokes as: "The Dodgers have three on base."

"Yeah, which base?"

Such incidents also gave birth to "dem Bums," a favorite Flatbush fan derogation that cartoonist Willard Mullin converted into a popular team nickname.

But there was gilt-edged baseball in Ebbets Field, too. Twenty-eight World Series games were contested in Flatbush, 14 of them victories for the Dodgers, 14 defeats. The most memorable triumph occurred on October 3, 1947.

For 8⅔ innings, Yankees righthander Floyd (Bill) Bevens held the Dodgers hitless, although issuing 10 bases on balls.

Two walks, a sacrifice and an infield out netted one run for the Dodgers in the fifth inning, but they still trailed 2-1 with two out in the ninth inning and runners on first and second. With Eddie Stanky due at the plate, Manager Burt Shotton inserted Cookie Lavagetto to pinch-hit.

flying and hit the wall and was stunned. I picked it up, figuring I would take it into the dugout and give it some water or something and I didn't know what to do with it, so I put it in my hat. Then I forgot about it when I was coming in because I was first up to the plate. Honest, I was as surprised as anyone when it flew off my head."

And then there was Floyd Caves (Babe) Herman, the redoubtable slugger whose fielding and base-running did not always measure up to major league standards. Stoutly denying that he had ever been hit on the head by a fly ball, as had been alleged, he did concede that he had, on occasion, been struck on the shoulder.

One misadventure that Babe could not deny was his feat of doubling into a double play. The date was August 15, 1926, and the Dodgers were playing the Boston Braves. It was the seventh inning of the first game and the bases were full of Dodgers—Hank DeBerry on third base, Dazzy

The front entrance to Ebbets Field (above) was a busy place, as usual, in July of 1949 as the Flatbush faithful headed for the turnstiles.

As Carl Furillo (6) looks on, a park attendant (above left) retrieves a ball that Stan Musial hit into the right-field screen for a ground-rule double at Ebbets Field (shown, above right, from center field).

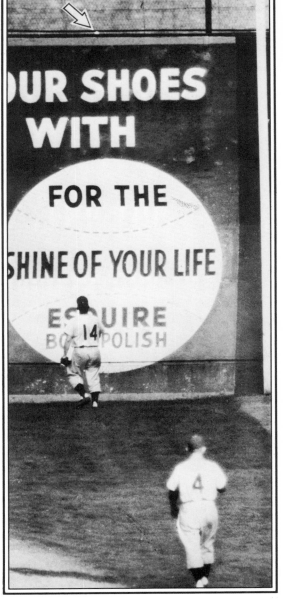

Although Brooklyn's Pee Wee Reese homered to right field (above right, with arrow pointing to the ball resting on a narrow ledge) on October 1, 1950, the Phillies beat the Dodgers to clinch the pennant.

The move seemed of minor significance, inasmuch as Lavagetto was a righthanded batter like Stanky. But Cookie sliced a drive off the right-field wall, costing Bevens his no-hitter as well as a 3-2 loss.

The story was different on October 5, 1941, when the Dodgers led the Yankees, 4-3, with two out in the ninth and the bases empty in the fourth game of the World Series.

On a 3-and-2 pitch from Hugh Casey, Tommy Henrich swung and missed. The game should have been over and the Series deadlocked at two victories apiece. But the breaking pitch ricocheted off catcher Mickey Owen's mitt and rolled to the stands as Henrich raced safely to first base.

Before Casey could recover from the shock, Joe DiMaggio singled, Charlie Keller doubled, Bill Dickey walked and Joe Gordon doubled. The Yankees scored four runs for a 7-4 victory and led three games to one in the Series, which they wrapped up the next day.

Emotion usually ran high at Ebbets Field, but never as high as on September 16, 1940, when spectators, taking their cue from the bickering Dodgers, heaped game-long scorn upon umpire George Magerkurth. At game's end, a burly fan attacked the 6-3, 240-pound arbiter before he could leave the field, knocking him to the ground while pummeling him from on top.

Bill Stewart, a fellow umpire, freed Magerkurth from the grip of his assailant, who was hauled off to the station house where he was identified as a parole violator and escorted back to his detention cell.

Johnny Vander Meer of Cincinnati hurled his second consecutive no-hitter at Ebbets Field on June 15, 1938—the first night game in Brooklyn. Brooklyn first baseman Gil Hodges slammed four

The Sym-Phony Band (above) entertained Ebbets Field fans with loud and brassy selections that assailed the ears of music lovers but charmed the hearts of Dodger fans.

home runs there on August 31, 1950, and his Milwaukee counterpart, Joe Adcock, duplicated the accomplishment on July 31, 1954.

Here, too, Larry MacPhail and Leo Durocher created a "reign of terror" in the late 1930s and early '40s, Dixie Walker was the People's Cherce and Jackie Robinson broke the major league color line in 1947.

After Larry MacPhail gave way to Branch Rickey as the Ebbets Field major domo and The Mahatma yielded the scepter to Walter O'Malley, the Dodgers won their only world championship in Brooklyn in 1955.

After losing the first two World Series games at Yankee Stadium, the Flatbush Flock swept three in a row at home before returning to the Bronx where, after losing Game 6, Johnny Podres copped the finale, 2-0.

For years, Walter O'Malley had insisted that the Dodgers were unable to compete with more affluent clubs because of smaller revenues resulting from a small park. Reports that City Hall would throw its influence into a search for a suitable site for a larger park came to naught and by the close of the 1957 season, it was fairly well established that the Dodgers were bound for Los Angeles and the promise of untold riches.

On September 24, 1957, Ebbets Field breathed its last as a major league ball park. It expired in style, with a 2-0 victory over the Pittsburgh Pirates before 6,702 curiosity seekers.

After the game, the players and media persons enjoyed a beer and crab fingers farewell party, courtesy of catcher Roy Campanella.

On February 23, 1960, the demolition crew, attired in blue and white windbreakers like those of the Dodgers, moved in. The last rites at Charles Ebbets' once-magnificent monument, only 46 years old, were about to begin.

The obsequies attracted approximately 200 persons. Lucy Monroe sang the National Anthem just as she had during the glory days. James and Dearie McKeever Mulvey, part of the Dodgers, were present as were oldtime favorites Ralph Branca and Carl Erskine.

Weeks later, when souvenir items went on sale —gold-plated bricks for $1, flower pots with infield soil for 25 cents—the cornerstone was disposed of for $500 in a sealed bid from Warren Giles, National League president. That, too, went to the Hall of Fame.

In time, a middle-income housing development arose on the site where Dodger heroes once rose and fell.

The Dodgers played a total of 15 games at Jersey City's Roosevelt Stadium (above left) in 1956 and 1957 before moving to Los Angeles in 1958. Ebbets Field came tumbling down (above right) in 1960.

COMISKEY PARK

Chicago

When Charles A. Comiskey tossed a party, friends came from far and farther, confident that the Old Roman would greet them with elegant food, imported wines and camaraderie beyond compare.

That was the situation on July 1, 1910, when Commy hosted a giant bash in the vicinity of 35th Street and Shields Avenue on the South Side of Chicago.

It was, said the editor of the Reach Baseball Guide, "a gala day in the city of Chicago, and a red-letter day in the eventful life of the white-haired chief of the Chicago American League club. The afternoon witnessed the formal opening and dedication of the White Sox's new ball park and the evening was devoted to official celebration of the historical event by a great banquet at which a host of notables, including most of the grandees of the baseball world, were the guests of Comiskey. A record-breaking crowd witnessed the opening game at the new park between the White Sox and the St. Louis Browns at what may be without hesitation, and without invidious comparison, declared to be the finest ball park in the United States."

For the grand inaugural of White Sox Park, the self-styled "Baseball Palace of the World," approximately 28,000 jammed into the steel and concrete facility, 6,000 of them guests of the Old Roman. Four bands entertained the customers and a military unit demonstrated its precision marching skills.

One account reported that "hundreds of auto-

mobiles" transported fans to the park. One fan who shunned the motor vehicle was Amos Alonzo Stagg. The famous University of Chicago football coach walked 15-20 blocks from the campus to the park, where he occupied a place of honor in Comiskey's private box.

Mayor Fred Busse delivered an address of welcome and the local nine took the field, dressed smartly in their new uniforms with blue trim.

The Browns, however, spoiled the party as Barney Pelty outpitched Ed Walsh, 2-0. But good times rolled again that evening when Comiskey displayed his transcendent talents as a party host.

It was generally agreed that Comiskey's new park, built at an estimated cost of $750,000, was designed and built only after extensive planning. Compliments showered on Comiskey, who approved plans only after Zachary Taylor Davis, the architect, and Ed Walsh, a Chicago pitcher, toured major league parks, seeking out the best features in each.

Symmetrical in design, the park showed foul lines measuring 363 feet, with the center-field wall 420 feet away.

The park, with its single-deck grandstand extending from right field to left field, was constructed in less than five months. Ground was broken on February 15. The cornerstone was laid on St. Patrick's Day and, in recognition of the area's large Irish colony, it was green. Nearly 40 years later the green stone disappeared under a coat of white paint.

Originally christened White Sox Park, the enclosure quickly became Comiskey Park in the minds of the sporting public and, although efforts were made in later years to restore the original designation, the park retains the name of its builder. As such, it is the oldest major league park.

The handsome structure at 35th and Shields was the second playing field for the White Sox.

South Side Park, pictured (above) during a 1904 game between Boston and Chicago, served as the White Sox's home until Comiskey Park opened in 1910.

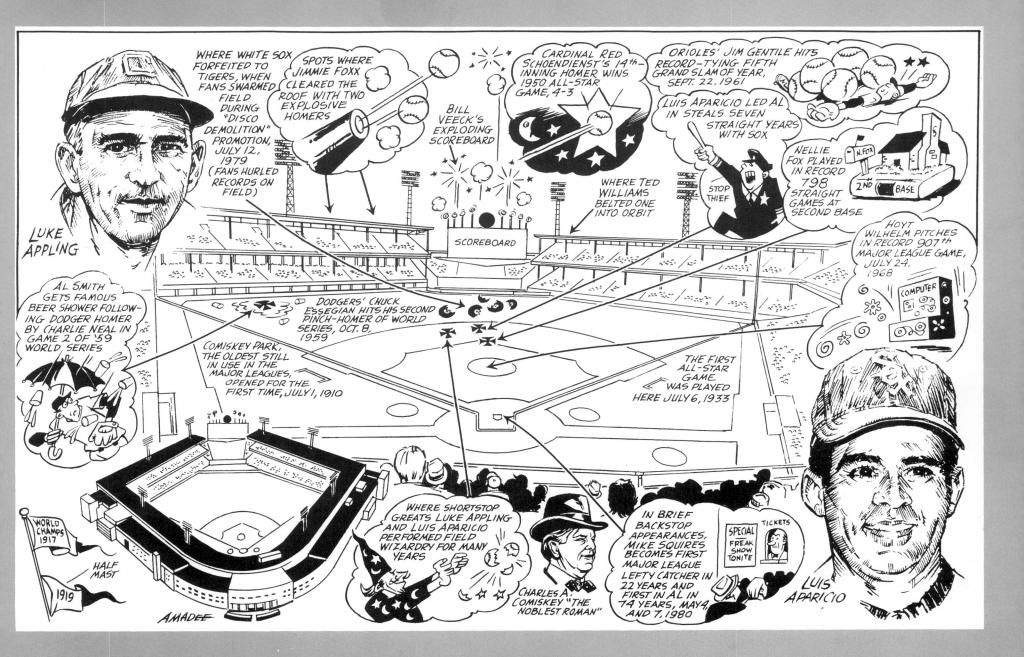

When Comiskey transferred his St. Paul Western League club to Chicago, where it became the White Stockings of Ban Johnson's newly proclaimed major league—the American—he had hoped to play his games at a park at 39th and Wentworth. He had remembered the park from his days with the Chicago entry in the Players League in 1890.

To his disappointment, Comiskey discovered that the park had been dismantled, so he leased the grounds of the Chicago Cricket Club on 39th Street between Wentworth and Princeton, where he built a single-deck wooden grandstand seating about 15,000.

South Side Park was the home of the White Sox for nearly 10 years and, after abandonment by the Sox, served semi-pro and Negro clubs for 30 years. It was destroyed by fire on Christmas night, 1940.

The White Sox brought the first American League pennant to South Side Park in 1901 and reigned there as the kings of baseball in 1906 when, as the Hitless Wonders, they overthrew the powerful Cubs in the crosstown World Series.

The White Stockings, a name first used by the city's entry in the National Association in 1871, batted only .228 as a team in the regular season. The Cubs, meanwhile, won 116 games and finished 20 games ahead of runner-up New York.

In addition to its single-deck grandstand, Comiskey Park, in its original state, contained bleachers except for an area in center field.

After the 1926 season, Comiskey authorized a $1 million renovation that added a second deck to the grandstand, leaving only a small uncovered bleacher section in the outfield. The foul lines, as

Cars jammed the parking lot and fans clogged the turnstiles (above) in the early 1930s for an American League game at 35th Street and Shields Avenue.

a result of the project, measured 352 feet.

Comiskey had hoped to increase the seating capacity to 55,000 but the Chicago fire code limited it to 52,000.

Comiskey Park underwent further change in 1934 following the acquisition of Al Simmons from the Philadelphia A's. In an effort to swell the slugger's home run production, the infield was moved out 14 feet.

The tactic failed in its mission, however, as Bucketfoot Al failed to regain his home run stroke, and the diamond was restored to its original position.

On several occasions management experimented with inside fences. In 1949 and 1969-70, fences were installed in left and right fields, and then removed when Chicago hitters couldn't take advantage of the more inviting targets. A center-field fence, also installed in 1949, was removed in 1976.

In 1950, the bullpens were switched from the left and right-field foul areas to center field behind a five-foot high fence.

Arc lights were installed in 1939. The first night game was played against St. Louis on August 14, with 30,000 watching the White Sox win, 5-2, behind the three-hit pitching of John Rigney.

To afford a better background for batters, the center-field bleachers were closed in 1947 and the movable box seats were replaced by permanent seats the same year, reducing the seating capacity to its present total of 44,492.

In 1959, Bill Veeck, new owner of the club, installed a picnic area in left field and his wife, Mary Frances, supervised the renovation of the ladies' rest rooms, making them the "prettiest in

Night baseball came to Comiskey Park on August 14, 1939, when the White Sox played the St. Louis Browns (above). John Rigney pitched a three-hitter as Chicago won, 5-2.

baseball."

The first electric scoreboard was erected on top of the center-field bleachers in 1951 and Veeck's "Exploding Scoreboard" first roared its home run salute in 1960.

In addition to fireworks and aerial bombs, there were 35 tapes, 32 seconds in length, that combined the best in shrieks, crashes, roars and howls. Fans delighted to the weird cacophony of train wrecks, live battles, diving planes and a circus caliope.

While Chicagoans waxed ecstatic over "The Monster," visitors grimaced noticeably. "What is this, Disneyland?" snorted Jimmie Dykes, Detroit manager and former White Sox skipper, after a home run off his ace righthander, Jim Bunning.

Three consecutive World Series were played in Comiskey Park, starting with the Sox games against the New York Giants in 1917.

The American Leaguers, managed by Clarence (Pants) Rowland, won the first two games in their home park as Eddie Cicotte took the opener, 2-1, and Red Faber followed with a 7-2 victory.

The Giants knotted the Series at the Polo Grounds, winning 2-0 and 5-0. But the Sox pulled out an 8-5 victory in Chicago and wrapped up the championship in New York with a 4-2 win behind Faber.

When the Chicago Cubs won the National League pennant in 1918, they arranged to play their home World Series games in Comiskey Park because of its larger seating capacity. But the fans, deeply concerned with overseas developments in World War I, did not respond as expected.

To reduce travel, the first three games were played at Comiskey Park. Babe Ruth won the opener for Boston, 1-0; George (Lefty) Tyler tied it up for the Cubs, 3-1, and Carl Mays put the Red Sox ahead again, outdueling Jim (Hippo) Vaughn, 2-1. In Boston, the Red Sox won, 3-2, lost 3-0, and won again, 2-1.

The 1919 White Sox, universally regarded as one of the strongest teams ever assembled, won the pennant by 3½ games over Cleveland. Their team batting average of .287 was the highest in the majors. Joe Jackson, with a .351 average, was reputed to have the most natural batting stroke seen up to that time.

The pitching staff was led by Cicotte, who won 29 games while losing seven, and posted an earned-run average of 1.82.

Great as they were, the White Sox also were the worst. On baseball's pages, they are the "Black Sox," a team that had eight players who conspired with gamblers to fix the outcome of the 1919 World Series.

Although the players were acquitted by the Chicago courts, they were banned from baseball by the first commissioner, Judge Kenesaw M. Landis, who had recently replaced the National Commission as the game's top authority.

Protests of innocence by some of the players and campaigns in their behalf by high-minded friends fell on deaf ears. The Judge was inflexible. Pitchers Cicotte and Claude (Lefty) Williams, first baseman Chick Gandil, shortstop Swede Risberg, third baseman Buck Weaver, outfielders Jackson and Oscar (Happy) Felsch and utilityman Fred McMullin felt the impact of the Judge's iron hand.

Gamblers who engineered the fix were reported to have made $500,000. According to testimony, Jackson asked for $20,000, but was paid only $5,000, and Cicotte found $10,000 under his hotel pillow before the first game in Cincinnati.

Gandil, ringleader of the players, reportedly received $20,000. He did not return to baseball after the 1919 season.

Comiskey grew suspicious of mischief in the first game when shoddy play by the customarily tidy Pale Hose permitted the Reds to win, 9-1. A five-run fourth inning, featuring the first of two triples by pitcher Walter (Dutch) Ruether, pinned the loss on Cicotte.

When Comiskey voiced his suspicions to John Heydler, the National League president tried to allay his fears.

Comiskey's reasons for contacting Heydler, rather than Ban Johnson, president of his own league and longtime confidant, were explained by the White Sox owner during a grand jury investigation in 1920.

"I told Heydler," said Commy, "that I was sending for him, and not for Johnson, because I had no confidence in Johnson.

"I employed a large force of detectives to run down every clue and paid them over $4,000 for their services.

"Johnson now says that an official investigation was made. If so, it was made unbeknown to me, my manager or my ball players. The result of such an alleged investigation has never been communicated to me, nor to the league.

"If any of my players are not honest, I'll fire them no matter who they are. If I can't get honest players to fill their places, I'll close the gates of the park that I have spent a lifetime to build and in which in the declining years of my life, I take the greatest measure of pride and pleasure."

Commy's anxiety about his players' honesty mounted in the second game of the Series when Williams, who had walked only 58 batters in 297 innings during the regular season, issued three

Lou Gehrig (ball in hand, above) and Babe Ruth (right of Gehrig) are
among the American Leaguers awaiting the start of the first All-Star
Game, played July 6, 1933, at Comiskey Park.

passes in one inning, helping the Reds win, 4-2.

When the Series shifted to Comiskey Park, Dickie Kerr, a nonconspirator, shut out the Reds on three hits, 3-0. Jimmy Ring held the Sox to three hits in Game 4 and, while Cicotte yielded only five, two safeties came in the fifth inning. Combined with two Cicotte errors, the hits produced two runs, good for a 2-0 Cincinnati victory.

Although held to four hits, the Reds won the fifth game, 5-0, as Hod Eller spaced three hits before 34,379 fans, the largest throng in the best-of-nine Series.

Kerr kept Chicago hopes alive with a 10-inning, 5-4 victory at Cincinnati and Cicotte followed with a seven-hit, 4-1 win before the Series returned to Chicago. Williams, drawing his third starting assignment, failed to survive the first inning of the game. The Reds scored four runs and coasted to a 10-5 decision.

Four White Sox pitchers—Faber, Williams, Kerr and Cicotte—won 20 or more games in 1920. But as hopes mounted for another World Series in Comiskey Park, investigation into fix allegations of the 1919 Series escalated as well.

Deprived of the late-season services of the eight miscreants, the White Sox fell short in their pennant drive. The Cleveland Indians finished first and it was 40 years, long after the Old Roman died, before the White Sox won another pennant.

Comiskey Park returned to the national spotlight in 1933, less than two years after Comiskey's death, through the drive and vision of Arch Ward, sports editor of the Chicago Tribune. Searching for a sports adjunct to Chicago's Century of Progress Exposition, Ward hit upon the idea of a major league All-Star game, matching the top players in the two circuits. Obtaining approval of league presidents and club owners pre-

sented the major obstacle, but Ward surmounted that hurdle. The game was scheduled for Comiskey Park on July 6, 1933.

The teams, selected by league presidents and managers, were managed by Connie Mack, legendary pilot of the Philadelphia Athletics, and John McGraw, who had terminated his lengthy career as skipper of the New York Giants in 1932.

The game attracted 47,595 and raised $45,000 for the Association of Professional Ball Players, the game's benevolent society.

Babe Ruth clouted a two-run homer for the A.L. and Frank Frisch socked a solo homer for the N.L. Lefty Gomez, a notoriously weak-hitting pitcher, received credit for the Americans' 4-2 victory and also accounted for the first run batted in with a second-inning single that plated Jimmie Dykes.

Comiskey Park was the scene of a second All-Star Game on July 11, 1950, when 46,127 saw

Fans in the left-field stands at Chicago's Comiskey Park, obviously in search of a souvenir as well as runs, urge on the White Sox.

just one win away from the world championship when action returned to Comiskey Park. The Dodgers amassed an 8-0 lead in the first four innings, but Podres failed to survive the Sox's three-run uprising in the fourth and Larry Sherry, appearing in his fourth game, picked up the 9-3 win. Batting for Duke Snider in the ninth inning, Essegian set a World Series record by smacking his second pinch home run.

In his two terms as chief executive officer at Comiskey Park, Bill Veeck was constantly alert to new and different methods to swell attendance. Unintentionally, Sportshirt Bill gave the Chicago gate one of its biggest boosts in 1948, when he was the big chief of the Cleveland Indians.

On August 13, Satchel Paige, the legendary star of the Negro leagues and lately signed by the Indians, started a game at Comiskey Park.

Even though the event had received advanced billing, Veeck expressed surprise when 51,013, then a record for Comiskey Park, watched Paige, at age 42, shut out the White Sox.

Thirty-one years after the Paige game, another 50,000 crowd turned out for "Disco Demolition Night," a promotion arranged by the White Sox and a local radio station.

Young rock fans were urged to bring disco records to Comiskey Park where they would be admitted to a doubleheader with the Detroit Tigers. Between games, it was announced, the records would be tossed into a huge bonfire, thereby demonstrating the rock fans' hostility toward disco fans for invading their musical turf.

The program went askew when 7,000-8,000 teen-agers stormed onto the field, ripping up sod so extensively that the second game of the twin bill had to be forfeited. The whole promotion "was a mistake," Veeck conceded.

the N.L. win a 14-inning struggle, 4-3. Red Schoendienst's home run off Ted Gray provided the N.L. with its first victory since 1944.

The White Sox's extended pennant drought climaxed in 1959 when the Pale Hose beat out the Cleveland Indians by five games. Al Lopez's Go-Go Sox, featuring speed on the bases and a tight defense, captured the flag in the first year of ownership by a Bill Veeck syndicate that bought the club from Comiskey heirs.

Early Wynn and Gerry Staley got the Sox off to a rousing start in the World Series, combining in an 11-0 shutout at Comiskey Park. Johnny Podres received credit for the Los Angeles Dodgers' 4-3 second-game victory, but only because Chuck Essegian, batting for Podres, smacked a seventh-inning homer and Charley Neal belted a two-run homer in the same inning.

By winning two of the next three games in the Los Angeles Memorial Coliseum, the Dodgers were

Comiskey Park as it appeared in 1960 (above), 50 years after the stadium opened and one season after the White Sox ended a long pennant drought.

WRIGLEY FIELD
Chicago

As a major league baseball park, Wrigley Field ranks high in homey atmosphere, spectator comfort and rich tradition. Its claim as Parlor Park USA is well substantiated.

Ivy vines adorn the outfield walls and natural grass covers the playing surface. Without light towers to disturb the design, Wrigley Field resembles a well-preserved relic from a long-gone era. In many respects, it is.

Wrigley Field has served as the home of the Chicago Cubs since 1916 and, in all probability, will remain so far into the future, drawing a million fans annually to its attractive acres.

The only National League charter club still operating in its original city, the Cubs, first known as the White Stockings, made their N.L. home debut on May 10, 1876, in a rickety wooden park on the west side of Dearborn Street between 23rd and 24th streets.

A Chicago team had performed in the Union Association in 1871, but disbanded after one season when its park was destroyed by the Chicago fire.

The White Stockings felt the need for a new

stadium in 1887 and constructed Lakefront Park, located south of Randolph Street between Michigan Avenue and the Illinois Central Railroad tracks. The team won pennants there in 1880, '81, and '82, featuring such popular favorites as Adrian (Cap) Anson and Mike (King) Kelly.

Flush with three consecutive pennants, the White Stockings in 1883 enlarged Lakefront Park to 10,000 seats, more than any other park in

baseball. Eighteen rows of private boxes, with curtains and arm chairs, were the rage of the local sports scene.

Lawrence Corcoran, pitching mainstay of the redoubtable champions, hurled three no-hitters in Lakefront Park, and Ed Williamson, taking advantage of an inviting left-field wall, slammed 25 homers at the park in 1884. Combined with two he clouted at Buffalo, it gave him an unheard of total of 27 for the season, an N.L. record that stood until 1922 when Rogers Hornsby hit 42 for St. Louis.

Baseball's exploding popularity forced the White Stockings to make still another move, to West Side Park at Congress and Throop Streets. The club, managed by Cap Anson and now known as the Colts, won pennants in 1885 and '86 at this location. It remained home until 1893, when they were required to pull up stakes because of the Columbian Exposition.

The next stop was at Polk and Lincoln (now Wolcott), site of the West Side Grounds, which had a double-decked grandstand that accommodated 16,000 and featured small balcony boxes

The back of Wrigley Field's scoreboard and the bleacher-seats entrance to the ball park (above) have been familiar sights to Cub fans for many years.

75

atop the grandstand between first and third bases.

Big Ed Delahanty of Philadelphia achieved his foremost batting feat at West Side Grounds on July 13, 1896, smashing a record-tying four home runs.

During a brief period following the resignation of Manager "Pop" Anson in 1897, the club was known as the Orphans—the players missed their Pop, it was alleged—and in 1900 they adopted the name of Cubs.

At West Side Grounds, the Cubs developed into the terrors of the National League. With the immortal Tinker-to-Evers-to-Chance double play combination, the Cubs won four pennants (1906, '07, '08 and '10) in five years.

In the first year, the Cubs lost all three World Series games played in their home park, one a shutout, as the "Hitless Wonders," the crosstown White Sox, startled the baseball fraternity by upsetting the 116-game regular-season winners in six games.

The Cubs came back to defeat the Detroit Tigers in the Series of 1907-'08, but fell to the fast-rising Philadelphia Athletics in 1910.

The loss to the A's signaled the Cubs' fall from glory, as the New York Giants ran off with three consecutive pennants.

By 1914, the Cubs were battling the White Sox and the Whales of the Federal League, a self-proclaimed major circuit, for the Chicago sports dollar. When the Feds gave up, Whales Owner Charles Weeghman acquired the Cubs as part of the peace settlement. In 1916, the club was moved into Weeghman Park at Clark and Addison streets. The park soon was renamed Cubs Park and, after William Wrigley Jr., gained control of the club in the 1920s, it was renamed Wrigley

Field.

The Cubs played their first game in their new home on April 20, 1916. Vic Saier's 11th-inning single produced a 7-6 victory over Cincinnati. Chicago catcher Bill Fischer led a 15-hit attack with four safeties.

Park renovations, designed to provide the best in comfort and beauty, commenced in 1922-23 when Wrigley moved back the stands several feet so that the seating capacity could be increased to 20,000.

In 1926-27 the stands were double-decked, raising the capacity to 40,000, and the playing area was lowered several feet.

One of Philip K. Wrigley's early moves was construction of bleachers in 1937. The following year, wider chairs were installed in the boxes and grandstand. While the move added to customer comfort, it reduced the park capacity by several thousand seats.

Shortly before World War II, the tiers in the left-field stands were circled so that all seats

out of the infield.

The Reds scored the game's only run in the 10th inning. With one out, Larry Kopf singled. Hal Chase followed with a fly ball which Cubs center fielder Cy Williams dropped, and Jim Thorpe beat out a dribbler in front of the plate to drive in Kopf.

After winning a pennant in the war-shortened 1918 season and playing their home World Series games in Comiskey Park, the Cubs suffered through an 11-year flag drouth until winning their sixth modern N.L. championship in 1929.

Pennant fever ran high on the near North Side as the Cubs prepared to take on the Philadelphia Athletics. To accommodate the greatest number of fans possible, the club obtained city permission to build bleacher seats beyond the outfield walls. The crowd totaled 50,740, most of whom were sitting knee to knee, when the starting pitchers began to warm up for the first game.

A glance at the Chicago bullpen showed Charley Root taking his preliminary tosses. That was expected. The righthanded Root had won 19 games for the Cubs and was the logical choice.

But the righthander in the Philadelphia bullpen did not resemble George Earnshaw, Connie Mack's righthanded ace, nor any of the other familiar righthanders.

Suddenly, like a prairie fire, word swept through the stands. Connie Mack had nominated Howard Ehmke to start the first game. Ehmke, a 35-year-old veteran, had pitched only 55 innings during the season. He had won seven games and lost two, but had not been with the club in the closing weeks of the season.

Under orders from Mack, Ehmke spent those weeks scouting the Cubs, compiling a book on Rogers Hornsby, Kiki Cuyler, Hack Wilson, Riggs

faced home plate. Later, the box seat deck extending from left field to first base was torn down and replaced with a new box seat deck of monolithic reinforced concrete.

Work on the right-field wall was completed during the winter of 1950-51, with the box seat tiers in right field circled so that the seats faced home plate. In addition, new chairs, wider and more comfortable, were installed in the upper box seat deck. When all the renovations were completed, park capacity was 36,755. Distances to

the fences were 355 feet to left, 353 to right and 400 to center.

The most extraordinary pitching duel in the major leagues took place at Wrigley Field on May 2, 1917, when Jim (Hippo) Vaughn of the Cubs and Fred Toney of the Cincinnati Reds hooked up in a remarkable struggle that lasted nine hitless innings.

In the first nine innings each pitcher walked only two batters. Vaughn pitched so effectively that only one batter, Greasy Neale, hit the ball

George Rohe of the White Sox heads for first base (above) en route to a bases-loaded triple against the Cubs in Game 3 of the 1906 World Series at West Side Grounds.

Stephenson and Charley Grimm.

Even in the A's camp there was disbelief. A number of players, having expected the first-game assignment to go to Lefty Grove, were openly critical of their manager.

Dissatisfaction did not endure long, however. Ehmke had scouted the Cubs well. He established a Series record by fanning 13 batters and pitched eight shutout innings before the Cubs pushed across a run in a 3-1 A's victory.

Earnshaw and Grove collaborated on an 9-3 second-game victory before nearly 50,000. When the action shifted to Philadelphia, Guy Bush handcuffed the A's, 3-1, in the third game. But the A.L. champions won the next two games, 10-8 and 3-2, for the club's first world title since 1913.

Of all the home runs hit out of Wrigley Field, none created as much initial excitement nor inspired as much lingering controversy as one clouted by Babe Ruth in the 1932 World Series.

The Yankees won the first two games at New York and were tied with the Cubs, 4-4, when The Bambino batted in the fifth inning of the third game.

What happened next is described by Warren Brown in his history of the Cubs:

"Root fired a strike past him. The Babe held up one finger. Root let fly with another pitch. Another strike. Again The Babe held up a finger.

"There are those who will always contend that what The Babe did this time was point out toward the center-field corner, as Root prepared to pitch.

"They will contend further that as the pitch came up to him (and this cannot be contradicted) that Ruth whaled away at it, and the last glimpse anyone in the park had of that baseball was when it dropped over the fence just beyond where The Babe had pointed.

"That's the legend and there are those who can add all sorts of flourishes to it.

"Whether Ruth pointed at Root, pointed at the fence or whether he remembered his manners and did not point at all, but merely indicated that there were two strikes on him and that he still had the big one left, is something that will not be debated here."

When Lou Gehrig followed with another homer, the Yankees had a two-run inning, on their way to a 7-5 victory.

It was all over the next day when the Yankees, unleashing a 19-hit attack that included two homers by Tony Lazzeri, defeated the Cubs, 13-6.

The World Series returned to Wrigley Field in 1935 when the Cubs, on the strength of a 21-game winning streak, edged out the St. Louis Cardinals' Gashouse Gang for the pennant and earned the right to meet the Detroit Tigers for the world championship.

In the first two games, which the teams split in Detroit, Chicago bench jockeys turned the atmosphere blue with their salty jibes at the Tigers and George Moriarty, an American League umpire behind the plate.

Moriarty, a former Detroit player and manager, was no slouch himself in stinging oratory. He gave as well as he received.

From his box seat, Commissioner Kenesaw M. Landis listened and winced. Before the third game, he summoned the principals to his Chicago office and issued a cease-and-desist order.

"I have always prided myself on a command of lurid expressions," the Judge conceded. "I must confess that I learned from these young fellows some variations of the language even I didn't know existed."

Subdued and handicapped by the Commission-

An overflow throng (above)—including fans inside the brick wall in left field and others perched atop the fences—watches the action in a 1938 Cubs-Pirates game at Wrigley Field.

Trying for a strikeout, Brown achieved only a knockout, that of the Pirates.

The Cubs now enjoyed a one-half game lead. And when Bill Lee defeated the Pirates, 10-1, the next day, it was apparent that the Buccos had fired their last volley.

The Cubs fared no better against the Yankees in the World Series than they had six years earlier. Lee lost the opener at Wrigley Field, 3-1, and Dean, less successful with his "nothing ball" than he had been against the Pirates, dropped the second game, 6-3. The Cubs then succumbed weakly in New York, 5-2 and 8-3.

Wrigley Field's next, and most recent, brush with World Series hoopla occurred in 1945. It was the last season of World War II and, while baseball retained the major league stamp, it was an inferior grade.

To cut down on wartime travel, the first three games were scheduled for Detroit, the remainder for Chicago. The Cubs won the opener, 9-0, lost the second, 4-1, and took the lead again when Claude Passeau won Game 3 with a one-hit, 3-0 shutout. The righthander was touched for a second-inning single by Rudy York and issued one walk, to Bob Swift in the sixth.

Dizzy Trout deadlocked the Series at two games apiece when action shifted to Chicago, turning in a 4-1 victory, and the Tigers went one up the next day as Hal Newhouser beat the Cubs, 8-4.

For the third time the Series was squared after the Cubs won Game 6, 8-7, a slightly wacky demonstration in which Managers Charley Grimm and Steve O'Neill used 19 players each in the three-hour, 28-minute marathon.

The Cubs led, 7-3, after seven innings, but a four-run Detroit rally, climaxed by Hank Green-

er's gag rule, the Cubs lost two games at home, 6-5 in 11 innings and 2-1 as Alvin Crowder allowed only five hits. Down three games to one, the Cubs stalled disaster in the fifth contest when Lon Warneke defeated Schoolboy Rowe, 3-1. But Tommy Bridges, winning his second game of the Series, turned back the Cubs, 4-3 in Detroit, for the Tigers' first world championship.

For the fourth time in 10 years the Cubs returned to the World Series in 1938, riding the wings of a dramatic blow that has been remembered ever since as Gabby Hartnett's "Homer in the Gloamin'."

The Pittsburgh Pirates, leading the race for most of the season, held a 1½-game lead when they arrived in Chicago for a critical three-game series on September 27. It was imperative that the Cubs sweep the three games from the faltering Buccos.

Dizzy Dean, the lame-armed, $185,000 acquisition from the St. Louis Cardinals, defeated the Buccos, 2-1, in the opening game, combining his "nothing ball" with an overabundance of guile. The Cubs were now within one-half game of the top.

In the second game, the contenders were tied, 5-5, entering the last of the ninth. Darkness already had a grip on Wrigley Field and the umpires had agreed that this would be the final inning.

Mace Brown, a tight-fisted righthanded relief ace of the Pirates, retired the first two batters and quickly slipped two strikes past Hartnett, who had replaced Grimm as manager in July when the Cubs trailed the Pirates by 6½ games.

Disdaining the usual strategy of wasting a pitch or two, Brown grooved the next pitch and Old Tomato Face was ready. The crack of bat against ball left no doubts—the ball was gone.

By the 1940s, Wrigley Field had taken on a different look (above), with expanded seating and ivy-covered walls dominating the view.

by shortstop Ernie Banks, who had caught the second ball. Musial was called out, but fortunately for the Cards, and for Delmore, the Redbirds won the game.

Keeping fans informed has long been a Wrigley Field trademark. The scoreboard, situated atop the center-field bleachers, was constructed in 1935 under the direction of a young Cub executive named Bill Veeck, who was to introduce an exploding scoreboard years later at Comiskey Park.

The Wrigley Field scoreboard, 27 feet high and 75 feet long, is operated by hand and provides inning-by-inning scores of all major league games, as well as pitching changes. In 1982 an electronic message board was placed under the scoreboard in center field.

After a game, passers-by outside the stadium can determine if the Cubs won or lost, depending on the flag that flies from a center-field pole. A victory is denoted by a blue flag with a white "W." A white flag with a blue "L" denotes a loss.

Ever since arc lights became a way of life in major league baseball, Wrigley Field has been noted, sometimes disparagingly, as the only ball park devoted exclusively to daytime baseball.

When the Tribune Company purchased the Cubs from the Wrigley interests in 1981, one of the first announcements was that there was no plan to install lights.

There was a time, in 1941, when all was in readiness for lights at the park. Equipment had been purchased and towers were about to be erected. Then the Japanese attacked Pearl Harbor. The next day, the Cubs gave the towers, the lights and the cables to the United States Government, which used the material in rapidly booming shipyards.

berg's homer, tied the score in the eighth and sent the contest into extra innings.

Frank Secory, later a National League umpire, launched the winning run in the 12th with a single, and gave way to pinch-runner Bill Schuster. When Stan Hack singled to left field for his fourth hit of the game, the ball bounced crazily over Greenberg's shoulder and Schuster scampered home.

After a day off to sell tickets, which were virtually non-existent, the Tigers nailed down the championship, 9-3.

With that defeat, World Series action took leave of Wrigley Field for more than 3½ decades, although two All-Star Games gave the historic site a touch of pomp and splendor.

On July 8, 1947, the American League squeezed out a 2-1 victory as Stan Spence drove home Bobby Doerr with the deciding run in the seventh inning. Frank Shea of New York received credit for the win, the first rookie to gain that distinction.

On July 30, 1962, the A.L. won again, scoring a 9-4 win behind home runs by Pete Runnels, Leon Wagner and Rocky Colavito.

The Cardinals were involved in a bizarre play at Wrigley Field on June 30, 1959. The incident started innocently enough when Umpire Vic Delmore called ball four on Stan Musial. As the baseball rolled to the screen, catcher Sammy Taylor insisted that the ball had ticked Musial's bat and extended his hand to receive another ball.

The Cubs commenced to argue with Delmore. Musial rounded first base and set out for second, where he slid in safely.

In the meantime, pitcher Bob Anderson grabbed a ball out of Delmore's hand and fired it toward second base at the same time third baseman Alvin Dark retrieved the original ball and also threw toward second base.

Musial, seeing one baseball sail into the outfield, started for third base, only to be tagged out

Eager fans awaiting entry into the ball park at Clark and Addison streets are greeted by the stadium sign acknowledging the Cubs' 1945 National League championship (above).

80

In a 1982 game, Joel Youngblood (18) and Mookie Wilson (1) of the Mets and umpire Lanny Harris searched the vines (above) and finally found a ball hit by Bill Buckner.

CROSLEY FIELD

Cincinnati

Crosley Field was not the first ball park in Cincinnati, but it did not miss that distinction by many years. The park at Findlay and Western avenues was known variously as Palace of the Fans, Redland Field and Crosley Field, from 1884 to 1970.

The 1869 Red Stockings, famed as the first professional baseball team, played on the field adjacent to Lincoln Park. This was the team's home field when it was not touring the nation in an undefeated season.

When the National League was founded in 1876, it was only natural that Cincinnati should be a charter member. However, the city's dominance of seven years earlier evaporated quickly in league competition. The Red Stockings won only nine games while losing 56. They finished dead last.

Curiously, the tail-enders received excellent support at the gate despite their poor record and despite the fact that fans were required to ride special trains or carriages to reach the park, located in an area that became known as Chester Park. Crowds of 3,000 were not uncommon, although the devotees, after arriving at the field, were assessed a 50-cent admission fee.

The ignominious start did not discourage the club owners. Two years later, the team won the N.L. pennant and the owners were anticipating remaining in the circuit indefinitely until attending a league meeting in the winter of 1880-81.

When Cincinnati officials informed fellow magnates that the team would continue to play games on Sunday and, moreover, would continue to sell beer as well, the horrified moguls kicked the Ohioans out of the league.

One season without a professional ball club was enough for Cincinnati townfolk. Petitions were circulated crying for another team. The cries were answered when the city was granted a franchise in the new American Association, a major league rival of the established N.L.

The A.A. team leased the Bank Street Grounds for its home games and doubtless would have remained there ever after if it had not been for the Union Association, which placed a franchise in Cincinnati in 1884.

While the A.A. club owners were trying to ignore the upstarts, the newcomers arranged a lease on the Bank Street premises.

Forced to find a new playing site in a hurry, club President Aaron Stein selected a brickyard at Findlay and Western Avenues, a half mile from the Bank Street park.

Opening day for the A.A. Reds closed in tragedy. The hastily constructed stands collapsed, killing one spectator and injuring countless others. The Union Reds immediately asked the city mayor to declare the A.A. park unsafe. The mayor rejected the request.

By 1890, National League fathers were ready to readmit the Reds, even with their beer and Sunday ball. Four years later the grandstands were rebuilt and the diamond relocated so that Western Avenue bordered the right and center-

By 1941, the park at the corner of Findlay and Western avenues was known as Crosley Field, home of the world champion Cincinnati Reds.

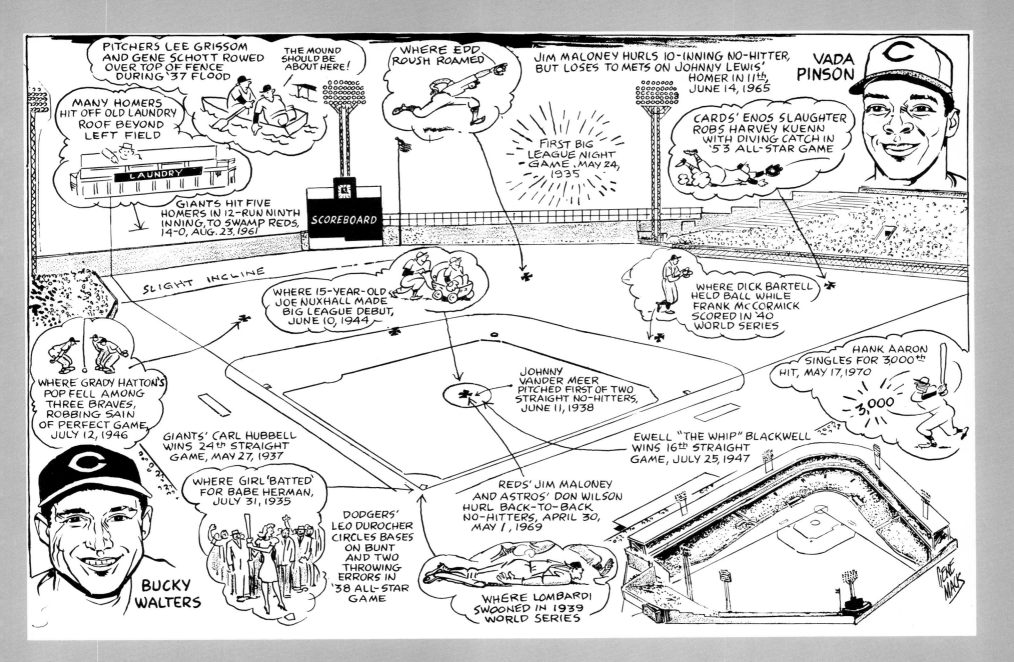

 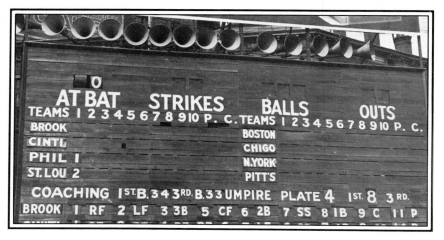

field fences. The change was made so that the late afternoon sun would be behind the batter, instead of in his eyes.

Ohio Governor William McKinley was scheduled to throw out the first ball at the 1894 opener, but the gala occasion was washed out by rain. When the inaugural was rescheduled for a day later, the future 25th President of the United States was unable to attend.

At the time, the Reds' home park was known as Redland Field, a name it retained until it was rebuilt in 1902 following a disastrous fire. At that time it was christened, somewhat grandly, Palace of the Fans.

Opening day patrons in 1902 gazed in wonderment at the new structure featuring pillars and columns much like those that caught tourists' eyes at the Columbian Exposition in Chicago nearly a decade earlier.

One feature of the rebuilt park was Rooters Row, a down-front section along the first and third-base lines. From this preferred location, and from behind protective screening, the townspeo-

ple swilled their beer (12 glasses for one dollar) and showered abuse on the players, both home and visiting. For 10 years Rooters Row provided brisk business for the beer vendors and headaches for the players.

In the same year that the Palace of the Fans was dedicated, 1902, John T. Brush sold the Reds to Julius and Max Fleischmann of the gin and yeast family. The brothers' choice for chief executive officer of the club was August (Garry) Herrmann, previously the president of the board of the city water commission.

During his years with the Reds, Herrmann also served as chairman of the National Commission, the ruling body of baseball until Judge K. M. Landis assumed the role of commissioner in 1920.

The Cincinnati ball park was partially ravaged by fire again in 1911. When the new field opened for the 1912 season, the pillars and columns, so popular a decade earlier, were gone. The reconstructed park resembled the park of later years and again it was called Redland Field, with a

capacity of about 25,000.

Although opened on April 11, the park was formally dedicated on May 18, 1912. Among the celebrities in attendance were two gentlemen prominent for years in Cincinnati baseball circles. They were Ban Johnson, a former Cincinnati sportswriter and now president of the American League, and Chicago White Sox Owner Charles A. Comiskey, manager of the Reds in the 1890s.

Dimensions of the new field were 360 feet down the foul lines and 420 feet to center field. A double-deck stand rose behind home plate. There were single-deck pavilions along the outfield foul lines and a bleacher section in right field. Unlike earlier parks, new Redland Field also contained clubhouses for home and visiting players. Visiting teams would no longer be required to ride public conveyances to the ball park while in full uniform, thereby exposing themselves as fair game for young boys seeking to test their aims with mudballs.

After 27 years of trying, the Reds captured their first N.L. pennant in 1919. Then, to the

Redland Field (above left), the early version of Crosley Field, featured a wooden scoreboard (above right) with a public address system that consisted of loudspeaker horns.

dismay of just about everybody outside of Cincinnati, the team defeated the heavily favored Chicago White Sox in the first two games of the World Series, 9-1 and 4-2.

From that auspicious—and perhaps suspicious—start, the Reds went on to win the world championship, five games to three. A shadow fell over the title a year later when it was disclosed that eight Chicago players had conspired with gamblers to fix the Series.

But the venerable ball park at Findlay and Western rang to the cheers of World Series crowds three more times before yielding to the demolition crews.

In 1939, under Manager Bill McKechnie, the Reds beat out the St. Louis Cardinals, but then capitulated to the New York Yankees in a four-game sweep that is best remembered for Ernie (Schnozz) Lombardi's snooze at home plate.

Lombardi, the hulking Cincinnati backstop, lay dazed after a collision with Charlie Keller, a muscular New York outfielder, in the fourth game, enabling Joe DiMaggio to score the final run in a three-run 10th-inning rally which gave the Yankees the World Championship.

The World Series scenario played out to a more pleasing climax for Cincinnati partisans in 1940, when the Reds eliminated the Detroit Tigers in seven games.

Crosley Field's final brush with World Series hoopla occurred in 1961. Once more the Reds' antagonists were the Yankees. After dividing two contests in the Bronx, the Reds lost three games at Findlay and Western, including a 13-5 humiliation in the finale.

In the years between its dedication in 1912 and auld lang syne in 1970, the Cincinnati park underwent probably more changes than any other

The first major league night game, played May 24, 1935, at Crosley Field (above), presented as many problems for photographers as pitchers and hitters.

major league facility.

Chronologically, they were:

- 1919—Portable field seats were installed in front of the double-deck stands.
- 1927—Portable seats were replaced by permanent boxes. The park was remodeled and 5,000 seats were added. Home plate was moved toward the outfield, creating measurements of 339 feet to left field, 407 to center and 377 to right.
- 1935—The park, now known as Crosley Field following Powel Crosley's purchase of the club from Sidney Weil, took on a new look with concrete stands from first and third bases to the outfield walls.
- 1938—Home plate was relocated once more. New measurements were 328 feet to left field, 387 to center and 366 to right. A press box was erected on the roof, removing the scribes from the unprotected front row of the second deck.
- 1939—A second deck was added to the right and left-field wings, raising the park capacity by 3,000 seats.
- 1946—A screen was erected in right field, reducing the distance from home plate to 342 feet.
- 1950—An elevator was installed and on June 30 the right-field screen was removed, restoring the distance to 366 feet.
- 1953—The right-field screen went up again. The distance was shortened to 342 feet.
- 1957—A scoreboard was installed in left-center field. The board, 65 feet wide, measured 50 feet, two inches in height, with the clock adding another seven feet, 10 inches.
- 1959—The right-field screen disappeared again. Distance: 366 feet to home plate.

In its final years, Crosley Field's capacity was 29,603.

Historically, the most significant change in the park's design occurred in 1935 when Larry Mac-Phail was the general manager.

A dynamic, blustery individual, MacPhail had worked turnstile magic with night baseball at Columbus of the American Association. In an early meeting with Crosley, MacPhail obtained the owner's consent to seek league approval to install arc lights at the old park.

MacPhail made his plea at a major league meeting. Fellow executives were horrified at a newcomer's suggestion that would shatter the game's daylight pattern.

But MacPhail persisted. Citing the club's financial problems and expressing the thought that night baseball would fatten the team's coffers, Larry eventually gained permission to play seven night games a season, one contest against each N.L. rival.

In Cincinnati, the momentous day was May 24, 1935. National attention was focused on the city

for this innovation that had been a lifesaver for so many minor league clubs during the Depression.

National League President Ford Frick was on hand along with 20,422 other curiosity seekers.

In Washington, President Franklin D. Roosevelt pushed a button in the White House, illuminating over 600 lamps in Crosley Field. The night was completely successful when Paul Derringer defeated the Phillies, 2-1.

By actual count, the 1935 night contest marked the third time a game was played under lights in Cincinnati. On June 8, 1909, George Cahill of Holyoke, Mass., erected five steel towers in the Palace of the Fans from which lights were strung for a game between teams representing Elks lodges of Cincinnati and Newport, Ky.

"Night baseball has come to stay," enthused Garry Herrmann. "It needs some further development, but proper lighting conditions will make the sport immensely popular."

A second demonstration of after-dark baseball was presented on September 12, 1931, several hours after the Reds had played the Brooklyn Dodgers in a day game.

With 1,000 fans on hand, the Reds played a team from Dayton, O., using portable equipment belonging to the touring House of David team, which had been barred from major league parks by Commissioner K.M. Landis.

Grover Cleveland Alexander, then 44, pitched three innings for Dayton, yielding five runs. The Reds, scheduled to play a doubleheader against the New York Giants the next afternoon, lost the game, 14-7.

After the first major league night game in 1935, the Reds played the Pirates, Cubs, Dodgers and Braves before taking on the Cardinals, de-

The white line and explanation (above) served as a center-field ground rule during the late 1940s at Crosley Field. Crosley all but disappeared from view (right) when Mill Creek overflowed in 1937.

She urged Paul Dean to deliver the ball and, after a few feints, the Cardinal righthander obliged. The gal, an entertainer by the name of Kitty Burke, swung and dribbled a ball to the right side, where it was fielded by Dean.

Behind the plate, umpire Bill Stewart saw no harm in the unscheduled episode and smiled charitably.

In addition to its pioneering role in professional baseball and night-time play, the Cincinnati club introduced radio broadcasts on a regular basis in 1929. Bob Burdette of WLW aired the Reds games from a booth on the rooftop, paving the way for Red Barber in the MacPhail era and Waite Hoyt in the years following World War II.

Johnny Vander Meer hurled the first of his two consecutive no-hit masterpieces at Crosley Field, blanking the Boston Bees, 3-0, on June 11, 1938. It was the sixth no-hitter by a Cincinnati pitcher and the first since Hod Eller's in 1919.

Crosley Field disappeared from view in January of 1937 when Mill Creek overflowed to a depth of 21 feet. The situation gave a wire service photographer an idea. As Cincinnati pitchers Gene Schott and Lee Grissom paddled a rowboat over the outfield fences, the photographer rowed nearby snapping the unlikeliest of pictures.

In the three decades that remained to the park, painted lines marked the height of the flood waters in 1937.

The Reds played their final game at Crosley Field on June 24, 1970 when 28,027 turned out for the final rites. The Reds sent them home with a pleasant memory in the form of a 5-4 victory over the San Francisco Giants. Consecutive eighth-inning home runs by Johnny Bench and Lee May supplied a rousing climax to the final drama in Crosley Field.

fending world champions, in a contest that produced unparalleled pandemonium at Crosley Field.

Hundreds of tickets had been sold to fans who arrived late by train from adjoining states. In the meantime, general admission spectators, noting the unoccupied reserved area, piled into that section. When the legitimate ticket holders arrived, chaos ensued. The crowd spilled onto the field. Nobody knew how many fans jammed into the park, but at the height of the bedlam, Larry MacPhail departed, turning matters over to his faithful secretary, Frances Levy.

Conditions grew so awkward that Judge Landis, trying to obtain a view of the game, was forced to stand on tiptoe, dodging and weaving behind a broad-shouldered burgher.

The spectators reached their peak of disorderliness in the eighth inning as ushers were trying to restrain fans behind outfield and baseline ropes. A female fan rushed out of the crowd, sprinted to home plate and grabbed a bat from unresisting Babe Herman.

Crosley Field (above) was nearing the end of its tenure by opening day of 1968. Note the incline of the playing field at the left-field wall and scoreboard.

Reds captain Pete Rose and Giants captain Willie Mays (above) joined the umpires for the final pregame lineup exchange at Crosley Field on June 24, 1970.

RIVERFRONT STADIUM

Cincinnati

Bowie Kuhn had made a special trip to Cincinnati to attend inaugural ceremonies at $48 million Riverfront Stadium, yet when he strolled into the circular arena on June 30, 1970, he was asked to leave.

The Commissioner had emerged from a cab in downtown Cincinnati, encountered Pete Rose and, after a 10-minute stroll, the pair entered the handsome structure on the banks of the Ohio River.

"You guys gotta get outta here!" shouted a construction foreman, ignorant of the identity of the pair who were sizing up the stadium. He was trying to clear out the stadium before the gates were opened at 6:05 p.m.

"I didn't expect to be recognized," Kuhn commented, "but I thought everyone recognized Pete Rose."

From that clumsy start, matters proceeded more smoothly. Two hours after the gates opened, 51,050 seats were occupied.

Before the Reds batted for the first time, however, the Atlanta Braves enjoyed a 3-0 lead. Hank Aaron, who had collected his 3,000th major league hit only a few weeks earlier at Crosley Field, blasted a two-run homer and Orlando Cepeda and Tony Gonzalez smacked back-to-back doubles.

The Braves won the game, 8-2, but when the '70 campaign ended it was the Reds who reigned as N.L. champions, with a club-record season attendance of 1,803,568.

By 1973, the Reds had scaled the two-million

mark and they turned the trick six more times during the 1970s.

In the same decade, the Reds captured four N.L. pennants and two world championships. In 1970 the Big Red Machine was beaten in the World Series by the Baltimore Orioles and in 1972 by the Oakland A's.

In 1975 the Reds disposed of the Boston Red Sox in a seven-game World Series, and in '76 they dispatched the New York Yankees in four games.

The 1970 and '75 classics produced king-size controversies stemming from umpires' decisions at home plate.

In the first Series, the first to be played on artificial turf, N.L. umpire Ken Burkhart was bowled over when Baltimore catcher Elrod Hendricks lunged for base-runner Bernie Carbo, trying to score on a tap in front of the plate.

Insisting that he saw Hendricks make the tag from his prone position, Burkhart called Carbo out. The Reds protested that Burkhart's vision was obscured by the tangled bodies. Television replays revealed that Hendricks tagged the runner with his mitt while clutching the baseball in his other hand.

Burkhart's decision loomed ever larger as the game progressed, with the A.L. champions eventually winning, 4-3.

Five years later, another home plate decision in the World Series involved the Reds.

In the 10th inning of the third game, the first at Riverfront, Cesar Geronimo was on first base with none out and pinch-hitter Ed Armbrister of

The only link between former Reds' home Crosley Field and new Riverfront Stadium was the home plate (above) that was moved from one park to the other.

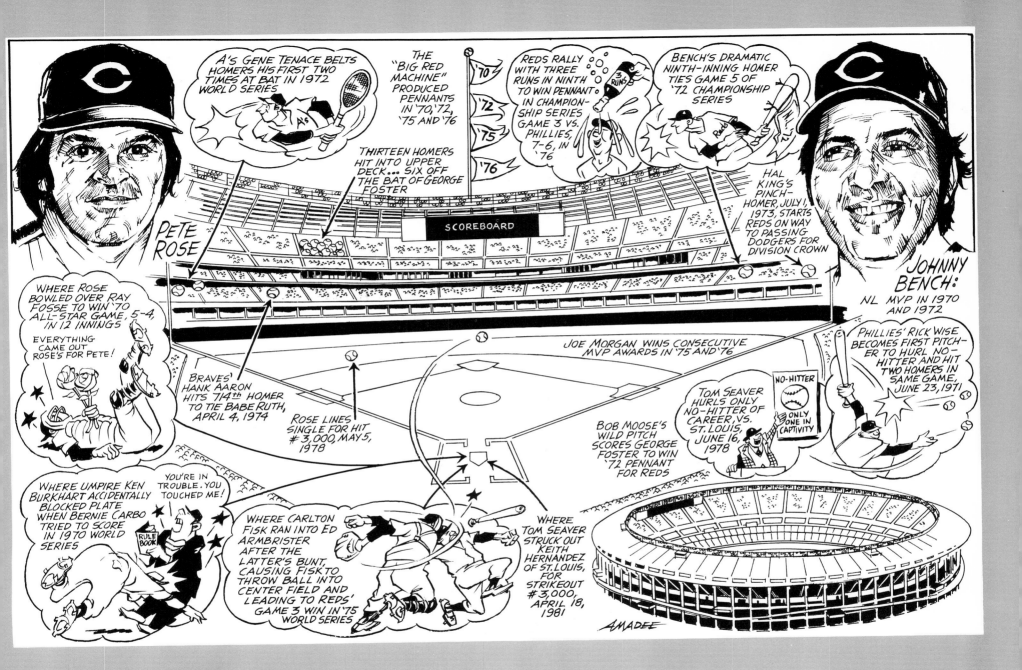

the Reds attempted to sacrifice. As Boston catcher Carlton Fisk leaped for the ball, he collided with the batter and threw erratically into center field, trying for a forceout on Geronimo.

The Red Sox howled that Armbrister had interfered with Fisk but Larry Barnett, the arbiter working the plate, refused to listen. The Reds went on to win, 6-5.

In addition to his baptismal home run on June 30, 1970, Hank Aaron hit another landmark round-tripper at Riverfront. On April 4, 1974 the Atlanta superstar swatted a first-inning home run off Jack Billingham. It was No. 714 for Aaron, matching the record career total of Babe Ruth.

Other momentous home runs on the banks of the Ohio were clouted by Rick Wise, a Phillies pitcher who, on June 23, 1971, became the first hurler to crack two homers while hurling a no-hitter and Oakland catcher Gene Tenace, who rapped two into the seats in the first game of the 1972 World Series.

Riverfront regulars remember, too, Bob Moose's wild pitch that permitted Foster to score the deciding run in the last game of the 1972 League Championship Series; Tom Seaver's no-hitter against the Cardinals, on June 16, 1978; Seaver's 3,000th major league strikeout on April 18, 1981, and Joe Rudi's game-saving catch in the second game of the 1972 World Series.

The most memorable baserunning incident was that of Pete Rose in the 1970 All-Star Game. After tying the score with three runs in the ninth inning, the N.L. pulled out a 5-4 victory in 12 innings when Rose, Billy Grabarkewitz of the Dodgers and Jim Hickman of the Cubs rapped consecutive singles. After Hickman's hit, Rose charged full speed into Ray Fosse, dislodging the ball from the Cleveland catcher's grasp and giving the N.L. its eighth consecutive All-Star victory.

The above 1968 photo shows circular Riverfront Stadium in the early stages of construction with the Ohio River in the background dividing the shores of Ohio and Kentucky.

Reds Johnny Bench and Gary Nolan watch ceremonies (above) before
Cincinnati's Riverfront Stadium inaugural against Atlanta on June 30,
1970.

LEAGUE PARK

Cleveland

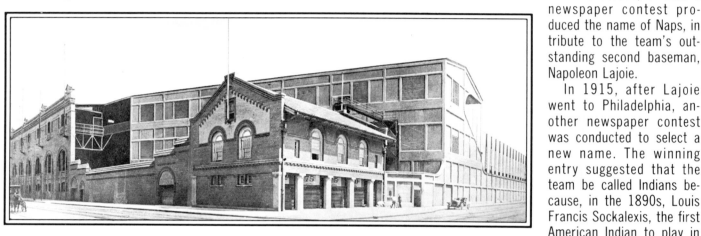

From June 2, 1869, when the Forest Citys engaged the peerless Cincinnati Red Stockings, until the present time, the professional baseball teams of Cleveland have performed at six separate locations under as many names, many of them long since forgotten.

The change in playing sites did not necessarily coincide with the change in names. In order, they were:

In 1869, the Forest Citys played at Case Commons, on East 38th Street between Central and Community College avenues.

In 1871, the team performed at East 55th and Garden streets.

The home park in 1879 was at East 46th Street and Cedar Avenue.

In 1889, the club played at East 39th Street and Payne Avenue.

Two years later, in 1891, new Owner Frank DeHaas Robison, holder of a street car franchise, constructed National League Park at Lexington Avenue and East 66th Street, a point served by two of his trolley lines.

League Park was rechristened Dunn Field in 1920 in honor of team Owner James Dunn. The name reverted to League Park following Dunn's death in 1927.

In 1932, the Indians played a limited number of games at Municipal Stadium, a huge lakefront facility, but did not move there permanently until 1947.

In the meantime, the club had undergone numerous name changes. In 1889, when the players reported to Cleveland, an executive took one look and exclaimed: "They look skinny and spindly, just like spiders."

White and dark blue uniforms only served to accentuate the players' lean appearance, prompting the same official to observe, "Might as well call them Spiders and be done with it."

The club retained that name until 1901 when, in their first year in the American League, they became the Blues, or sometimes the Bluebirds.

In 1902, the team was known as the Broncos, a name that endured for one season, or until a newspaper contest produced the name of Naps, in tribute to the team's outstanding second baseman, Napoleon Lajoie.

In 1915, after Lajoie went to Philadelphia, another newspaper contest was conducted to select a new name. The winning entry suggested that the team be called Indians because, in the 1890s, Louis Francis Sockalexis, the first American Indian to play in the major leagues, was a member of the Cleveland club.

As the club moved about the city, it also changed leagues. In 1871, it was in the National Association. From 1879 through 1884, the city had a franchise in the National League. In 1887-88, the city was represented in the American Association, a major league, and returned to the N.L. in 1889. When the American League emerged as a new major circuit in 1901, Cleveland was one of the eight charter members.

Opening day of the 1871 season—May 11—was a landmark date in Cleveland baseball history. In addition to a new park, there was another significant innovation. Whitey Lewis, writing in his "History of the Cleveland Indians," noted:

After the 1909 season, wooden League Park was dismantled and replaced by the steel and concrete structure (above) that served the Indians for 37 years.

League Park (above and right) was known through most of the 1920s as Dunn Field in honor of James Dunn, the team's owner. The park reverted back to its original name after Dunn's death in 1927.

In the early 1930s, League Park (the left-center field stands pictured above) began sharing with newer Municipal Stadium as home of the Indians.

"For the first time, a sale of season reserved seats, now accepted as an adjunct to operation of a big league franchise, was put into practice, and many fans flocked to the store of Rawson and Pratts on the Public Square to get choice locations.

"Purchasers were advised of two plans for the newfangled season tickets.

" 'If only for yourself, the cost will be six dollars for the season,' the store clerks informed the eager populace. 'But if you wish to bring a lady, there is a special deal available . . . only ten dollars for yourself, your lady and your carriage.'

"The carriage or rig could be pulled up to a specified location behind first or third base and there would be no necessity of stepping down on the turf at any time."

Twenty years later, on another opening day, May 1, 1891, a capacity crowd of 9,000 jammed new League Park to watch Cy Young beat Cincinnati, 12-3.

Because the owners of a saloon and two residences refused to sell their properties, League Park was constructed around these buildings and consequently assumed some unusual dimensions.

The left-field foul line was 375 feet, the right-field line 290 feet and the center-field wall 420 feet from home plate.

The stands, all of wood, consisted of a single deck behind the plate, a covered pavilion behind first base and a small bleacher section.

After the 1909 season, club President Ernest S. Barnard ordered the wooden park dismantled and replaced by a steel and concrete structure. That park would serve the Indians for 37 years.

To render right-field home runs more difficult, Barnard built a 40-foot-high wall in that sector. Among the sluggers who lined innumerable drives over the old wall was Sam Crawford.

When the Detroit outfielder caught his first glimpse of the new challenge, he snorted, "So that's Barney's dream! I'll show him."

Sam was as good as his promise. On an early turn at bat, he lined a drive over the high barrier.

One of baseball's most memorable games was played at League Park on October 2, 1908, when Addie Joss of Cleveland dueled Ed Walsh of Chicago. Big Ed allowed only four hits, but Joss permitted none, setting down 27 batters in order and winning, 1-0.

Three years later Joss was dead of tubercular meningitis, leaving a widow and a nine-year-old son. To aid the widow financially, an All-Star game was played at League Park on July 11, 1911.

A Cleveland newspaper described the American League stars as "the greatest array of players ever seen on one field." The team that opposed the Cleveland Naps included Eddie Collins, Ty Cobb, Sam Crawford, Frank (Home Run) Baker, Tris Speaker, Hal Chase, Gabby Street and Walter Johnson. Fans, paying 25 cents to one dollar, watched the All-Stars defeat the Naps, 5-3, and at the same time contributed to a $13,000 fund for the Joss family.

For spectacular, unprecedented events, no date in major league baseball can compare with October 10, 1920 in Cleveland. On that Sunday, 26,884 overflowed the stands, many of them standing behind ropes in front of the outfield wall, to watch the Indians and Brooklyn Dodgers in the fifth game of the World Series, which stood at two victories apiece. With the bases loaded in the first inning, Elmer Smith smacked a pitch from Burleigh Grimes over the right-field screen for the first grand-slam homer in Series history.

But there was more to come. In the fifth inning, with Pete Kilduff on second base and Otto Miller on first, Brooklyn pitcher Clarence Mitchell lined a Jim Bagby pitch to second baseman Bill Wambsganss, who leaped high to snare the ball, stepped on second base to double up Kilduff and then tagged Miller for the only unassisted World Series triple play.

The three-ply killing was not the first in League Park. On July 19, 1909, Cleveland shortstop Neal Ball pulled the trick against the Red Sox. On July 30, 1968, Washington shortstop Ron Hansen victimized the Indians with the same type of play at Municipal Stadium.

One of the most violent player-umpire brawls occurred at League Park following a Memorial Day doubleheader in 1932. Umpire George Moriarty's ball-and-strike decisions in the ninth inning of the second game had enraged the Chicago players, whose tempers soared even higher after Earl Averill tripled for a 12-11 Cleveland victory.

In the runway following the game, Moriarty challenged the entire Chicago team to fisticuffs. In the ensuing scuffle, Moriarty suffered bruises, spike wounds and a broken hand. Three White Sox players and Manager Lew Fonseca were fined a total of $1,350 by American League President Will Harridge. Pitcher Milt Gaston was suspended for 10 days, the others for shorter terms. Moriarty received a reprimand.

When construction started on Municipal Stadium in 1930, it presaged the demise of League Park. After 15 years (1932 through 1946) of dividing their schedule between the two parks, the Indians, in their first season under the presidency of Bill Veeck, switched all their games permanently to Municipal Stadium in 1947.

Unusual dimensions at League Park (above) included a left-field foul
pole 375 feet from home plate and a right-field distance of 290 feet
with a wall that rose 40 feet high.

MUNICIPAL STADIUM

Cleveland

Cleveland's Municipal Stadium, a huge lakefront park seating over 70,000 was completed on July 1, 1931 in an incredibly short period of 370 working days and at a cost of $2,844,000.

The Stadium's first sports event was not a baseball game, but a world heavyweight boxing match between Max Schmeling and Young Stribling on July 3, 1931.

The first baseball game was played two weeks later and involved two teams representing lodges at a national shrine convention in Cleveland. The winning pitcher was Bill Doak, a former major league hurler who designed a three-fingered glove that was marketed for many years.

The Indians played their first game at Municipal Stadium on July 31, 1932, a Sunday. To guarantee a sizable crowd, the Indians selected a date on which the Philadelphia Athletics, the defending A.L. champions, were in town.

The club was not disappointed. A paid crowd of 76,979 turned out and saw Lefty Grove pitch the A's to a 1-0 victory over Mel Harder.

The Indians played all of their home games at Municipal Stadium in 1933, then returned to League Park for all but Sunday and holiday dates in 1934 after the team's batting average in '33 dropped to seventh place in the eight-team league. The return to the smaller park also represented a substantial saving on operating costs in the depths of the Great Depression.

The first major league home run in the stadium was clouted by Johnny Burnett on August 7, 1932. The Indians shortstop clouted the homer

off Al Thomas of Washington.

Initially, the distances to the walls were 320 feet at the foul lines, 463 feet in the power alleys and 470 feet to center field. However, those measurements underwent changes through the years as owners attempted to tailor the park to the talents of the Cleveland players.

The third major league All-Star Game was played at Municipal Stadium on July 8, 1935 and 69,831 saw the American Leaguers, sparked by Jimmie Foxx's first-inning home run, win their

third straight mid-summer classic, 4-1.

Although Municipal Stadium was built with 250 floodlights of 1,000 watts apiece, the first night game was not played until June 27, 1939. Bob Feller was given inaugural honors and responded with a one-hit, 5-0 victory over the Detroit Tigers before 53,305.

In 1941, the attention of a nation was focused on Municipal Stadium as Joe DiMaggio attempted to extend his record hitting streak of 56 games. When the Yankees arrived in Cleveland, the Yankee Clipper had hit safely in 55 consecutive games. On July 16, at League Park, DiMaggio rapped three hits in four at-bats. The next game was played in Municipal Stadium so 67,468 could enjoy the drama.

On his first three trips to the plate against lefthander Al Smith, DiMag walked once and was retired twice on brilliant plays by third baseman Ken Keltner.

Facing righthander Jim Bagby, son of the Cleveland pitcher of many years earlier, in the eighth inning, DiMaggio grounded to shortstop Lou Boudreau, who converted it into a double play. The streak was over.

After 15 years of dividing their schedule between the two parks, the Indians, in their first season under the presidency of Bill Veeck, switched all their games permanently to Municipal Stadium in 1947.

Righthander Don Black hurled the first no-hitter in Municipal Stadium, blanking his former Philadelphia teammates, 3-0, on July 10, 1947. A year

A smiling Indian (above) at one of Municipal Stadium's entrances urges passing fans to purchase their 1959 season tickets early.

later, on September 13, after fouling off a pitch, Black collapsed from a cerebral hemorrhage. He was signed for a contract in 1949 but was unable to make a comeback.

The date May 7, 1957 was another dark day in Cleveland baseball annals. In the first inning of a game against the Yankees, Herb Score, a 20-9 pitcher the preceding year, was struck on the eye by a line drive off the bat of Gil McDougald.

The lefthander was incapacitated for the remainder of the season and attempted a comeback in 1958. But he failed to measure up to his former effectiveness and retired after the 1962 season.

With a winning team and an almost unlimited seating capacity, the 1948 Indians attracted 2,620,627 fans, a major league record until surpassed by the Los Angeles Dodgers in 1962. It was an American League record until eclipsed by the Yankees in 1980.

The 1948 Tribe tied for the A.L. pennant, then defeated the Red Sox in a one-game playoff at Boston. After splitting two World Series games against the Braves in Boston, the Indians captured two of the three contests at home. They then wrapped up the world championship back at Braves Field in the sixth game.

Game 5, at Cleveland, on Sunday, October 10, attracted 86,288, most of whom left the park disgruntled after an 11-5 Cleveland defeat.

The Indians captured their third flag in 1954. The club, which had set an American League record with 111 victories, then suffered the supreme ignominy by losing the World Series to the New York Giants in four games.

After hosting their first All-Star Game in 1935, the Indians repeated that role three times. On July 13, 1954, the A.L. triumphed, 11-9, in a game

that featured Red Schoendienst's unsuccessful attempt to steal home with the run that would have given the N.L. an eighth-inning lead. The winning pitcher was Dean Stone, a Washington lefthander who gained the victory without retiring a batter.

On July 9, 1963, the N.L. won, 5-3, before only 44,000 spectators. On August 9, 1981, the N.L. triumphed again, 5-4, as Gary Carter paced the attack with two homers. The game was witnessed by an All-Star record 72,086 fans who welcomed baseball back after a two-month strike.

Drama reigned supreme at Municipal Stadium

By 1948, the massive outfield distances at Municipal Stadium had been cut by a wire fence that permitted a standing-room view of on-field action.

Floyd Giebell, a righthander of limited experience, was given the starting assignment against Feller.

The game was played on Ladies Day and attracted more than 40,000 customers, most of them vociferous females and many of them armed with fruit and vegetables.

When Greenberg circled under a fly ball in the first inning, he found himself in the midst of a fruit and vegetable shower. Somehow he made the catch.

Later, an ice peddler, sitting in the upper deck over the Detroit bullpen, dropped a basket of empty bottles that glanced off Birdie Tebbetts, a bullpen occupant. The Tigers won the game, 2-0, on Rudy York's two-run homer off Feller. The victory was one of only three in Giebell's brief major league career.

In the Bill Veeck era of the 1940s and '50s, ball park promotions achieved their greatest success. Veeck held numerous promotions, giving away orchids, automobiles and even livestock at times. Late in the 1949 season, after the Indians were eliminated from the pennant race, Veeck held a ceremony in which the club buried its 1948 pennant behind the center-field fence.

On June 4, 1974, long after Veeck's departure, the Cleveland management booked a "Beer Night" that created some cause for concern before the night was over.

With beer selling at a discount, a crowd of 25,134 showed up. Many of them over-indulged and ran onto the field in the last of the ninth inning after the Indians had tied the score and had two runners on base.

Umpires and park attendants attempted unsuccessfully to shepherd the fans back into the stands. When all efforts failed, the umpires forfeited the game to the Texas Rangers.

in the final series of the 1940 season when the Tigers, needing one victory in three games to clinch the pennant, arrived in Cleveland to play the second-place Indians.

Detroit Manager Del Baker conferred with his veteran players on the eve of the series seeking their choice for starting pitcher in the opening game.

Hank Greenberg favored Hal Newhouser or Fred Hutchinson. But Baker, knowing Bob Feller would be tough to beat in the opener, decided to save his pitching aces for later in the series.

The center-field distance had been cut from 470 to 410 feet by 1948, the season in which the Indians defeated the Boston Braves in the World Series.

The right-field area in 1941 (above left) was more to the liking of home run hitters with a fence that curved toward the foul pole. By 1957, the standing-room area in center field had given way to a scenic garden (above right). The modern-day Municipal Stadium (left) has a symmetrical playing field.

Houston's Astrodome (above) was the first of the domed stadiums and was dubbed upon completion "the Eighth Wonder of the World."

Kansas City's Municipal Stadium (above) was home of the A's for 13 years and the expansion Royals for four before they moved into modern Royals Stadium, where the crown-shaped scoreboard and water display (right) provides scenic backdrops for major league baseball. The "One-Half Pennant Porch" and sheep grazing beyond the right-field wall (above) were Charlie Finley innovations during his 1960s ownership of the A's.

Tiger Stadium (above), also known at various times as Briggs Stadium and Navin Field, has defied time while serving as home of the American League Tigers since 1912.

When it comes to charm and ambiance, Chicago's Wrigley Field is right at the top of the list. Fans with connections can still get a good spot on the top of buildings (above) beyond the right-center field wall to view proceedings, but those willing to spring for the price of a ticket get a full view (right) of the National League's oldest park with its brick outfield walls, covered during the summer with ivy (left).

Cincinnati's circular Riverfront Stadium is shown (left) by a camera on the Kentucky side of the Ohio River. Dodger Stadium (right, during 1982 opening-day ceremonies, and above), features the most active turnstiles in baseball.

TIGER STADIUM

Detroit

Baseball habits in Detroit have remained virtually unchanged since the turn of the century.

Whether fans have traveled by carriage, motor car, public conveyance or on foot, whether they have gone to Bennett Park, Navin Field, Briggs Stadium or Tiger Stadium, their destination has always been the intersection of Michigan and Trumbull avenues, the home grounds of the city's professional baseball team.

Only the name of the park and the mode of transportation has changed.

When Mayor W.G. Thompson obtained a National League franchise in 1881, the team was known simply as the "Detroits."

Club headquarters were listed as "the Mayor's Office" and games were played at Recreation Park, near what is now the intersection of Brady and Brush streets.

The city retained its franchise for eight seasons, but woeful yearly attendance was a continual problem, despite the fact the club won a pennant in 1887 and defeated the St. Louis Browns, champions of the American Association, in a traveling World Series.

After a five-year absence from Organized Baseball, the city joined the Western League in 1894 after it was reorganized by Byron Bancroft John-

son, a 30-year-old Cincinnati sportswriter who later became the president of the American League.

The Detroit Western League club played in a small park at Helen Avenue and Lafayette Boulevard in what was then the eastern limits of the city.

George Tweedy Stallings, later the manager of the Miracle Boston Braves, was brought in to manage the team in 1895 and, in that role, was responsible for the nickname of Tigers, which has remained for nearly 90 years.

Stallings explained to Fred Lieb, veteran author, that "When I was first manager in Detroit, I changed a lot of things. I thought maybe a change of uniforms would change their luck. I put striped

stockings on them, black and a sort of yellowish brown. I didn't think of their resemblance to a tiger's stripes at the time, but some of our fans and our early writers noticed it and soon started calling our team the Tigers. And they have been Tigers ever since."

When the Western League graduated into the American League, in competition with the National as a major league, a new playing site was selected at Michigan and Trumbull, a centrally located area.

This was the site of the old Haymarket, where farmers of the late 19th century brought their hay for weight and sale under municipal supervision. The site had been paved with cobblestones. To convert it into a baseball park, a few inches of loam was scattered on the surface, a grandstand and fence were erected and the Tigers were ready for business.

Bennett Park contained 8,500 seats. In addition there were wildcat seats on the rooftops of homes on Cherry Street and National Avenue.

On Sundays, when games were not allowed within the city, the Tigers played at Burns Park, named for George D. Burns, a hotel man and sheriff of Wayne County who was an early president of the club. The park was located on Dix

Night baseball finally came to Detroit (above) on June 15, 1948, and the Tigers celebrated the occasion by defeating the Philadelphia Athletics, 4-1.

Avenue, just beyond the city's western boundary in Springwells Township close to the stockyards.

Bennett Park was named for Charley Bennett, an outstanding catcher with Detroit in its National League days.

The park, with its meager capacity, was the setting for the World Series of 1907, '08, and '09. The first renovation, in 1911, increased the capacity to 14,000.

The first game in the reconstructed park was played on April 20, 1912. George Mullin provided the heroics by singling in Donie Bush in the 11th inning to defeat Cleveland, 6-5. In the first inning of the contest, Ty Cobb and Sam Crawford pulled a pair of double-steals, including a theft of home by Cobb.

Two years later, in 1913, a single-decked, concrete stand with seats for 23,000 replaced the run-down park and was dedicated as Navin Field. Frank Navin, a former bookkeeper with a flair for cashing in sizable wagers at the race track, had invested $5,000 in the ball club some years earlier and now occupied the president's chair.

In 1924, the area from first to third base was doubled-decked, raising the capacity to 29,000.

At the same time an elaborate press box was installed on the roof, and the next year a press box elevator was constructed, the first in the major leagues.

In 1936, after the Tigers had won two consecutive pennants and a World Series, the owners invested their World Series money in another park enlargement. The right-field pavilion and bleachers were double-decked, raising the capacity to 36,000.

Navin died in a fall from a horse before the expanded facility was opened to the public, but his successor as owner-president, Walter O.

Briggs, instituted another expansion program in 1938.

The plant was converted into a bowl. Two-story stands were erected in left and center fields after the city council provided space by closing off a street that had formed the northern boundary of the park. The capacity was now 58,000.

A giant scoreboard also was erected in center field of what was now known as Briggs Stadium. Smaller scoreboards were installed in the grandstand on the first and third base sides.

The park was renamed Tiger Stadium on January 1, 1961, after it was acquired by radio-TV magnate John Fetzer. Renaming the park cost approximately $20,000. The cost would have been even greater if it had not been for the fact that only two letters, a "T" and an "E", were needed to change "Briggs" to "Tiger" on the neon sign identifying the park.

Concessionaires, however, were required to dispose of more than 4,000 scorecard pencils bearing the park's old name, more than 2,300

Bennett Park (above), named for an outstanding catcher in Detroit's N.L. days, held only 8,500 fans before being expanded but was the setting for World Series in 1907, 1908 and 1909.

Cobb repeated as batting champion in 1908 and the Tigers retained their league supremacy. In the five-game World Series against the Cubs, another Detroit defeat, Cobb batted .368. He rapped seven hits, all in the first three games, then went hitless in the last two games, at Bennett Park, when the Tigers were blanked by Brown, 3-0, and Orval Overall, 2-0.

The Tigers made it three pennants in a row in 1909 as well as three consecutive World Series losses, bowing this time to the Pittsburgh Pirates. However, the Bengals extended the Buccos to seven games before capitulating.

Cobb batted .231, collecting only four hits in 16 at-bats at home. The Series had been billed as a summit struggle between Honus Wagner, veteran shortstop of the Pirates, and Cobb, newly arrived superstar of the Tigers. It was scarcely a match. Wagner outhit his young rival by more than 100 points and, Cobb recalled years later, put his own stamp of superiority on the young Georgian.

"I was on first base early," Cobb remembered, "and, cupping my hands, I yelled to Wagner, 'Hey, Krauthead, I'm coming down to second on the next pitch.' He didn't say anything, but when I got to second he had the throw and was waiting for me with the ball. He snapped it on my mouth and cut it for three stitches."

One of baseball's wildest donnybrooks occurred at Navin Field on a Sunday afternoon late in the 1915 season, in which the Red Sox edged the Tigers for the pennant by one game.

Detroit third baseman George Moriarty, later Bengal manager and an American League umpire, attempted to steal home in the last of the ninth inning with the Red Sox leading, 3-2, and two out.

As the umpire waved Moriarty out, Bill Carri-

pennants and 4,500 souvenir buttons, all of which bore the Briggs Stadium label.

Briggs Stadium was the last American League park to install arc lights. On June 15, 1948, the Tigers defeated the Philadelphia A's, 4-1, on a field reportedly illuminated by the equivalent of 6,000 full moons. The eight light towers contained 1,458 lighting units that provided 2,750,000 watts of light.

When an 18-year-old outfielder joined the Tigers in August 1905, few people could envision the manner in which the youngster would dominate baseball during the next two decades.

Ty Cobb batted only .240 in the 41 games that remained in the 1905 season, but by the time the Tigers won the 1907 pennant, the Georgia Peach had already won his first batting championship.

In the World Series, however, Cobb batted only .200. In the two games at Bennett Park, including the 2-0 shutout by Mordecai Brown in the Cubs' clinching victory, Cobb collected two hits, one of them a triple.

The Detroit Tigers won their first World Series in 1935, beating the Chicago Cubs in six games and nailing down the title at Navin Field (above).

gan, Boston catcher-manager, spat a mouthful of tobacco juice in Moriarty's face and the rumble was on. Leaping to his feet, Moriarty ripped the mask from Carrigan's face and landed his Sunday punch flush on Carrigan's jaw.

In the few moments that it took for the crowd to realize what had happened, Carrigan ran to the Boston clubhouse. The crowd, large and menac-ing, surged around the door, brandishing clubs and rocks, even ropes, determined to deliver fron-tier justice when the villain emerged.

Owner Frank Navin pleaded with the infuriated mob, but to no avail. For hours the multitude maintained its vigil, awaiting Carrigan's exit.

Eventually, they discovered that Carrigan had made his escape. A kindly maintenance man had attired Carrigan in an old hat, rubber boots and shabby coat, smeared his face with mud and stuck a rake in his hand. Too late, the crowd discovered that the bedraggled figure that shuf-fled past them was Carrigan, who joined his teammates in time to catch the train out of town.

A quarter of a century elapsed between the Tigers' 1909 World Series appearance and their

Flag-raising ceremonies (above) were part of the pregame festivities for the 1946 American League opener at Briggs Stadium matching the Tigers against the St. Louis Browns.

return to the big show. In 1934, under the leadership of Mickey Cochrane, the Tigers engaged the St. Louis Cardinals in their fourth attempt to win a world championship.

Dizzy Dean, a 30-game winner for the Gashouse Gang, defeated Alvin Crowder, 8-3, in the opening game at Navin Field; but Schoolboy Rowe, who had equaled an American League rec-

ord by winning 16 consecutive games during the season, squared the Series at a game apiece by beating Bill Walker, 3-2, in the 12-inning second game.

Two victories in three games at St. Louis put the Tigers within one win of the long-awaited championship, but Paul Dean deadlocked the Series again with a 4-3 decision in the sixth contest.

Dizzy Dean then gamboled to an 11-0 triumph in the finale, which was marked by the famous ''Battle of Produce Row.''

The unscheduled episode resulted from a sixth-inning fracas between Joe Medwick of the Cardinals and Marv Owen of the Tigers. Medwick, sliding into third base with more gusto than Owen thought proper or necessary, engaged in a kicking

Detroit fans head for a 1951 game at Briggs Stadium (above). Ten years later, the ball park at Michigan and Trumbull avenues was renamed Tiger Stadium.

match with the infielder.

The incident blew over quickly and was all but forgotten when Medwick returned to his left-field position at the end of the Cardinals' two-run spurt that produced a 9-0 lead.

The frustrated bleacherites, however, did not forget the little flareup, nor did they let Medwick forget it. Overripe produce of all types and description showered down on Medwick. Field attendants cleaned up the debris, only to discover on turning their backs that another barrage had littered the field. Where the fans obtained the fruit and vegetables nobody was able to explain.

Convinced that the bleacherites were not about to cease firing as long as Medwick remained before them, Judge K.M. Landis summoned the two players, Managers Cochrane and Frank Frisch and umpire Bill Klem to his first-row box.

"Did Owen do anything to you as you slid into the base?" the shaggy-maned Commissioner asked Medwick.

"It was one of those things that is likely to happen anytime a player slides," answered Jersey Joe.

In the interest of Medwick's safety, Landis ordered him removed from the game.

The game was played to an orderly conclusion but Medwick fretted ever after. He already had 11 Series hits, one short of the record, when he was banished. He was certain to have one more at-bat, which went to his replacement, Chick Fullis, who collected the hit that Medwick might have gotten.

The Tigers repeated as pennant winners in 1935, again under Cochrane, and faced the Chicago Cubs, their opponents of 1907-08, in the World Series.

Although it was the National League's turn to open the Series at home, the Cubs waived their right. The Chicagoans won the N.L. flag with a 21-game winning streak that carried them almost to the eve of the Series. The Cubs were not prepared for the Series, the Tigers were, and both teams agreed to the switch.

Shut out in the 1934 Series finale, the Tigers also opened the '35 classic by losing a shutout as Lon Warneke outpitched Schoolboy Rowe, 3-0.

An 8-3 victory by Tommy Bridges evened the Series the next day, but it took a heavy toll. In the seventh inning, Hank Greenberg collided with Gabby Hartnett in a play at the plate and suffered two broken bones in his wrist. Hank missed the remainder of the Series.

Despite the absence of Greenberg, the Tigers won two one-run decisions in Chicago, then lost the third game there before returning to Navin Field for Game 6. Goose Goslin's ninth-inning single produced a 4-3 victory and the first World Series title in Detroit history.

A five-year lapse intervened before the Tigers regained championship heights. In 1940, they snapped the Yankees' four-year reign and faced the Cincinnati Reds in the World Series.

Of the three games at Briggs Stadium, Tommy Bridges won one, 7-4, and Bobo Newsom won another, 8-0, on a three-hitter. Bucky Walters and Paul Derringer captured the last two contests in Cincinnati, however, and the Tigers were saddled with their fifth Series setback in six tries.

After another five-year hiatus, the World Series returned to Detroit in 1945, chiefly through the efforts of Greenberg, one of the first major leaguers to return to civilian life after the conclusion of World War II.

The big slugger rejoined the Bengals in time to play 78 games and hit 13 home runs. His most telling blow came in the last game of the season when his grand slam at St. Louis produced the victory that enabled the Tigers to win the pennant from the Washington Senators. The Senators had concluded their season a week earlier so that Clark Griffith could rent his stadium to the Washington Redskins.

Because wartime travel restrictions still were in effect, the first three World Series games were played in Detroit; the final four were scheduled for Wrigley Field in Chicago.

Virgil Trucks' 4-1 victory in the second game was the Tigers' only triumph at home as Hank Borowy took the opener, 9-0, and Claude Passeau

Part of a turnout of 48,000 fans at Detroit's Briggs Stadium heads down the exit ramps (above) after watching another Tigers game.

118

at St. Louis, the Tigers dropped the first two contests in Detroit. Three-run homers by Tim Mc-Carver and Orlando Cepeda sparked the Cardinals to a 7-3 win in Game 3. The fourth game, delayed 33 minutes at the start and interrupted for 74 minutes in the third inning by rain, was won by Bob Gibson, 10-1, on a five-hitter. Gibson also distinguished himself with a home run, thereby becoming the first pitcher to hit two World Series homers.

The Tigers trailed, 3-2, and were only nine outs from extinction when they rallied for three runs in the seventh inning of the fifth game. Mickey Lolich ignited the explosion with a one-out single and after a single by McAuliffe and a walk to Mickey Stanley, Kaline singled in a pair of runs. Norm Cash singled in the final run to clinch a 5-3 victory. The triumph sent the Series back to St. Louis, where the Tigers won two games to annex the club's third world title.

Three All-Star Games have been played at Tiger Stadium. The most memorable, perhaps, was the 1941 game in which Boston's Ted Williams smacked a three-run ninth-inning homer to give the American League a 7-5 victory.

The 1951 All-Star Game, originally scheduled for Philadelphia, was switched to Detroit to be part of the city's 250th anniversary celebration. The occasion was tarnished by N.L. sluggers, who belted four home runs in an 8-3 victory before 52,075.

Six home runs, three by each team, were smacked in the 1971 All-Star Game at Tiger Stadium, when the A.L. won, 6-4. The N.L. gained an early 3-0 lead on homers by Johnny Bench and Hank Aaron, but Frank Robinson, Reggie Jackson and Harmon Killebrew responded for the A.L. before Roberto Clemente closed out the barrage.

earned a 3-0 triumph in which he allowed only one hit, a second-inning single by Rudy York.

Despite their unimpressive performance at Briggs Stadium, the Tigers took three of four games in Chicago to clinch their second world championship.

The World Series spotlight focused on Detroit again in 1968, by which time the ball park was known as Tiger Stadium. The brightest star over the Michigan and Trumbull site belonged to Denny McLain, the major leagues' first 30-game winner since Dizzy Dean scaled that peak for St. Louis in 1934.

McLain's momentous day occurred at Tiger Stadium on September 14.

Entering the last half of the ninth inning, the Tigers trailed the A's, 4-3, primarily because Reggie Jackson had belted two home runs. On the bench McLain watched soberly as Al Kaline pinch-hit for him and walked. Dick McAuliffe popped out, but Mickey Stanley singled, sending Kaline to third. When Jim Northrup bounced to Danny Cater, the first baseman threw to the plate, but the throw was off line, permitting Kaline to score the tying run.

With the Oakland outfield drawn in, Willie Horton singled over left-fielder Jim Gosger's head and Stanley romped home. McLain had his 30th victory.

After dividing the first two World Series games

A mid-1950s view of Briggs Stadium from the center-field stands (above) offers a panorama of the playing field and grandstand at the Tigers' ball park.

Tiger Stadium, with the skyline of Detroit as a backdrop (above), was the site of a press-box fire (below) in 1977. A 1971 photo (right) presents a field-level view of the park.

ASTRODOME
Houston

Branch Rickey took one bushy-browed look at baseball's first covered park and observed: "The day the doors on this park open, every other park in the world will be antiquated."

As usual, The Mahatma was correct.

A publicity release of late 1964 exclaimed: "The world's first air conditioned, domed all-purpose stadium, sitting like a precious jewel in southwest Houston, was constructed by the citizens of Harris County at a cost of $20.5 million, plus $3 million for the land on which the site is located at a total cost of $31.6 million for the entire project including access routes and parking.

"The stadium is leased for 40 years to the Houston Sports Association, which owns and operates Houston's National League baseball club. The HSA pays an annual lease of $750,000 plus all operating expenses."

Credit for this revolutionary concept in baseball parks was attributed to Judge Roy Hofheinz, president of the club and former mayor of the city.

"He wanted something to combat heat, cold, rain and mosquitos," said George Kirksey, vice president of the club and a prime mover in obtaining a major league franchise for the city.

Houston was granted a National League franchise in the circuit's first expansion in 1962. Previously, the city had been represented briefly in

the South Texas League, the Southern Association and the American Association, but chiefly in the Texas League from 1917 through 1958.

In the city's minor league era, the Houston Buffalos, named for Buffalo Bayou which bisects the city, played in the 4,000-seat, centrally located West End Park.

The team moved into 14,000-seat Buff Stadium, called "the finest minor league plant" when it was opened in April of 1928. The foul lines there were 344 feet from home plate and the distance to center field was 430 feet.

In the inaugural game that year, Ken Penner defeated Waco for his first of 20 victories that season.

Dizzy Dean was a 26-game winner as a member of the Buffs in 1931, Chick Hafey batted .360 in 1924 and Joe Medwick .354 in 1932, all while preparing for Hall of Fame careers with the parent St. Louis Cardinals.

Buff Stadium was the scene of a suicide on June 11, 1950. While a game was in progress, a 50-year-old unemployed laundry route manager

Buff Stadium (above), with its Spanish style of architecture, was home for the Texas League Houston Buffalos from 1928 through 1958.

took a seat in a television booth, drew a pistol from his shirt front and shot himself in the right temple.

After Houston entered the National League, a furniture store was constructed on the Buff Stadium site. The owner, Sammy Finger, determined where home plate had been located and erected the Houston Sports Hall of Fame on the spot.

Houston's first N.L. club, known as the Colt .45s, played in new Colt Stadium, a 32,601-seat park on South Main Street. The park was symmetrical in design with foul lines of 360 feet and a center-field fence 420 feet away.

The team retained the name of Colt .45s for three years under an agreement with the Colt Firearms Company. However, when the club started to market novelties under the same name, the Colt firm threatened a suit. The team name was changed to Astros because of the nearby Aero Space Center.

The Colts debuted in the National League on April 10, 1962 with Bobby Shantz posting an 11-2 victory over the Chicago Cubs.

Don Nottebart hurled the club's first no-hitter on May 17, 1963, defeating Philadelphia, 4-1. The majors' first Sunday night game was played on the same site on June 9, 1963, when the Colts beat the Giants, 3-0, in a game marked by Skinny Brown's 6⅓ innings of one-hit relief pitching.

Colt Stadium gained a permanent place in history as the spot where a major league pitcher first lost a complete-game no-hitter. It occurred on April 23, 1964, when Ken Johnson of the home team lost to Cincinnati, 1-0, as the result of errors by himself and Nellie Fox.

The curtain fell on Colt Stadium on September 27, 1964. A crowd of 6,246 saw Bob Bruce mark the occasion with a 12-inning, 1-0 win over Ron

Perranoski and the Dodgers.

Hailing the demise of Colt Stadium, a club publicist wrote: "Gone will be the gripes of the players on the bad lighting, gone will be the mosquito-spraying chores, gone will be the sweltering heat that sent over 100 fans to the first-aid room during a Sunday afternoon doubleheader, and gone will be the stiff wind blowing in from right field that frustrated so many lefthanded hitters."

The Astrodome, originally called the Harris County Domed Stadium and sometimes referred to as "The Eighth Wonder of the World," was the focus of the nation's attention during construction. Some hailed it as marking the dawn of a new era in major league baseball while others expressed skepticism that a game could be played satisfactorily under cover.

Before that landmark event, however, the public was inundated with facts and figures pertaining to the stadium.

There was, for example, the startling fact that the stadium contained enough plumbing for 40,000 persons to wash their hands simultaneously.

The stadium occupies nine and a half acres and the outside diameter measures 710 feet.

Low-pitched ramps and two escalators carry spectators to 45,000 seats. Overhead, the dome, rising 208 feet from the floor, measures 642 feet across and consists of 4,596 skylights, each approximately 7-by-3 feet.

The air conditioning system, it was reported, cost $4.5 million and has a 6,600-ton cooling capacity. Each minute the system circulates 2.5

Colt Stadium (above) was built as an interim home for the Houston major league franchise.

This 1964 view (above) of the Astrodome, still under construction,
shows its close proximity to Colt Stadium, its small predecessor.

Among the spectators were President and Mrs. Lyndon B. Johnson, who were en route to their Texas ranch when they decided to stop in Houston out of respect for Judge Hofheinz, a campaign manager for LBJ in the 1940s.

Several hours before the Johnsons' arrival, the White House ordered nine special telephone lines installed for the Chief Executive's use.

The presidential party arrived in the second inning and watched the Astros win a 12-inning, 2-1 decision, with pinch-hitter Nellie Fox driving in the deciding run.

Mickey Mantle had the honor of hitting the park's first home run to provide the only New York tally.

The first five games in the Dome, all exhibitions, attracted 188,762, including a whopping 48,172 for a Sunday afternoon doubleheader.

The series included a Friday night game against the Yankees and split doubleheaders against the Yankees and Baltimore Orioles the next two days.

The daylight games revealed a glaring fault in the stadium: The transparent dome made it virtually impossible for an outfielder to track a high fly ball on a sunny afternoon.

General Manager Paul Richards detected early the possibility of a game with the Orioles degenerating into a comedy of errors and sought the advice of Judge Hofheinz.

"We've had a billion dollars worth of publicity and can't jeopardize it now," said the Judge. "If the game turns into a farce, offer to refund the money of any dissatisfied fans."

To correct the visibility problem, the transparent dome was painted, eliminating sunlight but creating another problem—dying grass.

That was solved a year later when the Mon-

million cubic feet of air.

To prevent heat and humidity backup, the air conditioning system operates continuously.

For night games, floodlights consuming enough power to match that of a town of 9,000 people is used.

The grass, it was pointed out, was a special Bermuda strand, selected and tested to stand up under indoor play.

The gates of the Astrodome opened to the public for the first time on April 9, 1965, and 47,876 fans—far exceeding capacity—packed the stadium for an exhibition game between the Astros and the American League champion New York Yankees. Press credentials for the historic occasion, at which Governor John Connally of Texas threw out the first ball, were issued to 253 writers.

Early gimmicks included spacemen (above) who swept and vacuumed the artificial surface at the Astrodome.

The world's largest scoreboard, 474 feet long and weighing 300 tons, provided a raucous display for every Astro homer, such as Leon McFadden's (above) in April of 1965.

santo Chemical Co. produced a serviceable synthetic grass named AstroTurf.

The first regularly scheduled N.L. game in the Astrodome was played on April 12, 1965 and attracted 42,652, including Commissioner Ford Frick, league President Warren Giles and 24 of the nation's 26 astronauts who received lifetime passes to major league games in pregame ceremonies.

Chris Short dampened the crowd's enthusiasm by allowing only four hits and Richie Allen poled a third-inning home run to give the Phillies a 2-0 victory.

The first season was barely underway when another feature of the Astrodome created discontent—the scoreboard.

The world's largest board, 474 feet long, weighing 300 tons and costing $2 million, was presenting sights and sounds that visiting players, as well as umpires, found objectionable.

A pitcher, knocked out of the box, did not take kindly to an electronic portrayal on the message board of a figure in the shower.

Although there were no official protests, opposing players squawked privately when that figure was shown turning on the shower. As tears coursed down his cheeks, black water rose over his head so that only two eyeballs peered out of the blackness. The show, accompanied by funeral music, was ''bush,'' according to visiting players.

Bill Giles, an Astro vice-president in charge of promotions and commander-in-chief of the scoreboard, defended the oversized toy, declaring, ''The management of the Astros considers baseball an entertainment art form. It is the job of everyone in the organization to make every game as entertaining as possible. That's all we strive to do with the board.''

Opposing hurlers also did not appreciate a sign exhorting the fans to shout ''Charge'' when a hometown rally was needed. In one ''Charge'' episode, Chicago pitcher Bill Faul turned his back to the plate and waited for the noise to subside. He pitched only when ordered to do so by the umpire.

Giles did concede, however, that he exercised faulty judgment in flashing an uncomplimentary remark about umpire Bill Kibler.

When the arbiter, who had aroused the Astros' ire in an earlier game by calling a runner out in a close play at the plate, ejected third baseman Bob Aspromonte for protesting too strongly over a decision, the board announced, ''Kibler Did It Again.''

Crew chief Frank Secory contacted league President Warren Giles at once, asserting, ''This

With the Astrodome less than three weeks old, Lindsey Nelson and producer Joel Nixon broadcast a game from the gondola (above), suspended from the apex of the dome over second base.

landed in short center field for one of the longest singles on record.

The 1980 League Championship Series produced a number of remarkable events. In Game 3, an 11th-inning single by Denny Walling drove in Rafael Landestoy to break a scoreless deadlock with the Phillies.

In Game 4, Houston pitcher Vern Ruhle caught a soft line drive off his shoetop and tossed to first base for an apparent double play. The Phils protested that the ball was trapped. Plate umpire Doug Harvey, whose view of the play was blocked by batter Garry Maddox, conferred with fellow arbiters, during which time first baseman Art Howe trotted to second base and claimed a triple play.

Eventually, after consulting with N.L. President Chub Feeney, the double play was permitted to stand. The third out was disallowed because time had been called.

The Astros were within six outs of the pennant, but the Phillies scored five runs in the eighth inning and pulled out an 8-7 victory when Del Unser and Maddox doubled in the 10th inning of the fifth game.

When the Astrodome was dedicated, there was little doubt that all weather hazards had been eliminated. Never again would a Houston game be interrupted or postponed because of climatic conditions.

Rain forced the postponement of a game on June 15, 1976. Players were already in the Astrodome when a torrential rainstorm struck the city, flooding streets and highways. Umpires, stadium personnel and fans were prevented from reaching the stadium.

It was baseball's first postponement because of wet grounds outside the park.

is an attempt to incite the fans. That's about as low as you can get."

Bill Giles assured his father that the incident would not be repeated.

The Astrodome was less than three weeks old when historic events started to occur. On April 28, 1965, Lindsey Nelson, the voice of the New York Mets, broadcast a game from a gondola suspended from the apex of the dome, directly over second base.

Willie Mays of the San Francisco Giants socked his 500th career home run in the Astrodome on September 13, 1965. On July 9, 1968, Say Hey Willie scored the only run of the All-Star Game on a double play to give the N.L. an unexciting victory over the A.L.

On June 10, 1974, Mike Schmidt of the Phillies smashed a ball that caromed off a speaker and

A view from the right-field section of the Astrodome (above) shows the contours of the field and stands with the expansive dome protecting the stadium from outside influences.

ROYALS STADIUM

Kansas City

Early baseball history in Kansas City revolved around a number of one-year stands at long-forgotten sites.

Riverview Park was the scene of most of the games in the 1870s. One of these contests, between Kansas City and the Ottawa (Kan.) Red Stockings, was announced as follows:

"The Ottawa nine arrived last night and is quartered at the Hotel Barnum. The Kansas nine put in a good part of the day yesterday in industrious practice for today's game. Trouble will begin at 3:45 sharp."

Kansas City acquired its first Organized Baseball franchise in 1884 when it obtained the Altoona club of the Union Association after the Pennsylvania team won only six of 25 games before the end of May.

The first game at Athletic Park, Southwest Boulevard and Summit Street, attracted 1,500 persons. They saw the hometown club drop a 12-inning, 6-5 decision to Chicago.

Although the Union Association was classified as a major league, it was not always big-time in the eyes of a local sports editor. A dogfight be-

tween "Dan" and "Tiger" received top billing on a day the Unions lost to Baltimore, 17-5. The highlight of the game was a home run that was certified as "the longest in the park's history, the ball going fully one square over the center-field fence."

In 1886 the Kansas City Cowboys were members of the National League, playing their games in a park at Independence and Lydia. The Cowboys are remembered best for their feat of scoring a record 10 runs in the 11th inning of a 12-2 victory at Detroit on July 21.

In 1887, the city was represented in the Western League. When the team opened the 1888 campaign at League Park, it was known for the first time as the Blues, a name that was associated with Kansas City professional baseball clubs for more than 65 years.

One season in the American Association, a major league, was followed by a decade in the Western Association.

In 1901 the Blues were members of the Western League again. The next season they joined the American Association, a new minor organization. They remained there until the city acquired the Philadelphia American League franchise in November of 1954.

In their first game, on May 11, 1902, the Blues defeated Columbus, 5-4, before 3,000 at Exposition Park.

As baseball grew in popularity, 11,000-seat Association Park was constructed at 20th and

The Kansas City Blues, a farm club purchased by Yankee Owner Jacob Ruppert in the late 1930s, played in single-deck Ruppert Stadium (above), a predecessor to enlarged Municipal Stadium.

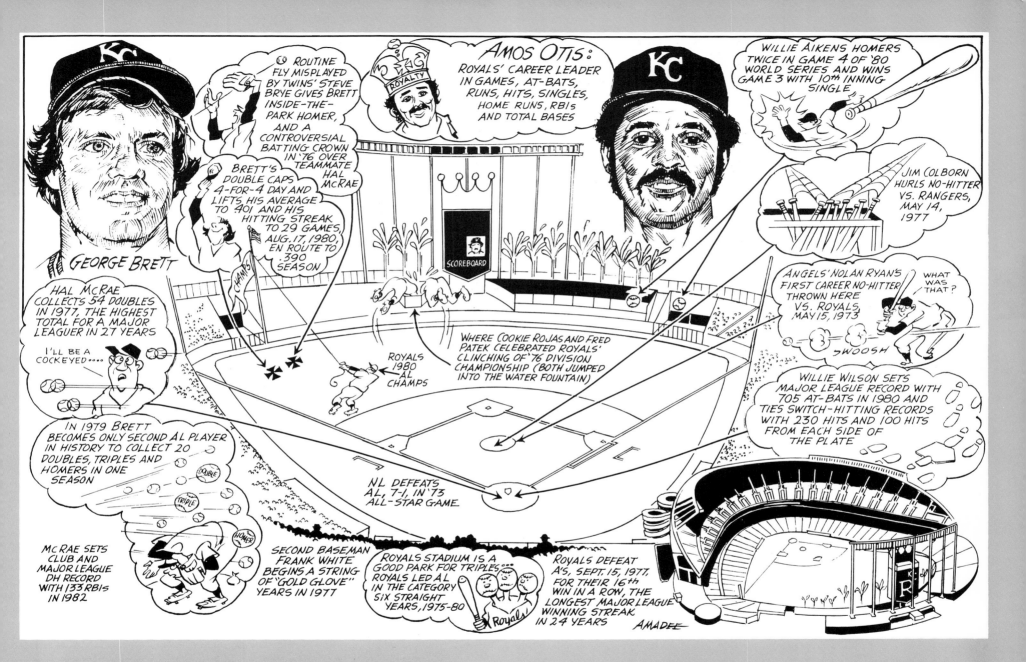

Prospect. But when the Federal League placed a franchise in Kansas City in 1914-15, that club played at 49th and Tracy.

When brewer George Muehlebach bought the Blues from the George Tebeau estate in the 1920s, he built a 17,500-seat stadium on what had been a frog pond and ash heap at 22nd Street and Brooklyn Avenue. In the first game at the $400,000 concrete park, Ferdie Schupp thrilled 14,000 with a 10-7 win over Milwaukee on July 3, 1923.

During Muehlebach's ownership, the park was known as Muehlebach Field. When the New York Yankees acquired the franchise and property for $230,000 in the late 1930s, the field was rechristened Ruppert Stadium for the Yanks' owner, Colonel Jacob Ruppert. Later it was named Blues Stadium and, in the city's early years in the American League, it was known as Municipal Stadium.

Shortly after Arnold Johnson and his associates purchased the Philadelphia A's, a survey of Blues Stadium showed that the underpilings of the stands were sufficiently strong to support a second deck.

However, when engineers discovered that the pilings were barely able to support one deck, the new owners faced the prospect of rebuilding the stadium approximately three months before opening day in 1955.

Under ordinary circumstances, at least six months would have been required for such a project.

"I don't know how in the world we'll get ready in time," said the Kansas City mayor.

"I don't know either," agreed the project foreman. "But we'll do it, you can bet on that."

In late January, when the first concrete was

poured for the new footings, huge trucks crowded the infield and dotted the outfield. And with superhuman effort work continued under almost impossible conditions.

There were raw, windy days when painters sprayed as much paint on themselves as on the structure; when carpenters, with the temperature 10 degrees below zero, tied themselves to the roof with ropes in order to continue their work.

Impossible situations were part of the daily routine, but long hours and determination invariably solved the problems. By opening day, 400 workmen viewed with pride the fruits of their labors.

Other stadiums were built for $120 to $150 a seat. Municipal Stadium, with its 30,611 seats, was constructed for $80 a seat.

Oldtimers were reminded that building miracles were not uncommon in Kansas City. In 1900, three months before the scheduled start of the Democratic National Convention, Municipal Auditorium was destroyed by fire. Yet the hall was rebuilt in time for each delegate to be seated before the opening gavel. What could be accomplished for politics could also be accomplished for baseball.

On April 12, 1955, Kansas City celebrated its return to the major leagues. A crowd of 32,844, the largest paid attendance in K.C. history, watched the A's beat Detroit, 6-2. The crowd

With grazing sheep and the Brooklyn Avenue wall providing a backdrop (above) at Municipal Stadium, Charlie Finley's "Pennant Porch" saw service for two 1964 exhibition games against St. Louis.

exceeded by nearly 10,000 the Tigers' total attendance for 11 games in Philadelphia the previous season.

Former President Harry S Truman threw out the first pitch. Connie Mack, legendary owner-manager of the A's, was among the spectators, as was his Hall of Fame slugger, Jimmie Foxx.

The new stadium's left-field foul line was 330 feet. The right-field line was 354 feet. The center-field fence was 422 feet from home plate.

To many, the scoreboard had a familiar appearance. It was the old board from Braves Field in Boston, purchased for $100,000 by Arnold Johnson. The city had paid Johnson $500,000 for Blues Stadium and the right to rename it Municipal Stadium.

Johnson died suddenly in March 1960 and for several months the future of the club appeared in doubt. However, before the end of the year, American League club owners approved the sale of controlling interest in the club to insurance tycoon Charles O. Finley for just under $2 million.

Finley's years in Kansas City were laden with squabbles—with managers, general managers and media people. There also was the matter of a lease on Municipal Stadium. In 1964 there were strong rumors that Finley risked expulsion from the league if he did not sign a lease for the following season. Eventually, he signed a four-year agreement.

Charlie missed no opportunity to keep turmoil at a fever pitch. His targets were abundant and included the American League establishment.

One of Charlie's major irritants was a "pennant porch," a right-field structure whereby he sought to duplicate the home run distance at Yankee Stadium. Telegrams from Commissioner Ford Frick and A.L. President Joe Cronin impressed upon Finley the likelihood of fines and forfeitures unless he removed the structure.

At another time, Charlie ordered a roof built over the bleachers in the right-field corner. But the roof did more than simply cover the bleachers; it extended over part of the field, again to match the Yankee Stadium home run range of

Finley attractions included a picnic area and zoo (above left) and "Harvey" the mechanical rabbit (above right), who provided balls for umpires and a few laughs for groundkeeper George Toma.

296 feet.

Cal Hubbard, A.L. supervisor of umpires, arrived in Kansas City three days before the start of the season to check on Finley's latest joust with authority.

"It must come down, it's illegal," snorted Hubbard, ignoring Charlie's thinly veiled protest that the roof was "protection for the spectators against the sun."

Finley reacted slowly. The roof stayed in place through a preseason weekend series with the Cardinals and through batting practice by the A's and Tigers on opening day. Finally, at 6:30 p.m., two trucks carrying workmen rolled through the center-field gate and toward the objectionable structure in right field. Spectators were removed from the area for their own safety—and in 30 minutes the roof was gone. Before leaving the field, the trucks, containing the workmen, cruised in front of the stands in mock salute to constituted authority.

The foreman of the work crew estimated that the roof had cost Finley $4,000 to erect, $700 to demolish.

"I still think I'm right," fumed Finley. "They better change the rules. I may put it up again next year. I'm tired of Yankee domination because of a 296-foot fence in right field." But the "pennant porch" never returned.

If Charlie was prohibited from reducing the home run distance for his own hitters, he could make it more difficult for opposing sluggers. So he erected a 40-foot high screen in right field, making it necessary for hitters to drive a ball anywhere from 338 feet to 392 feet—and 40 feet high— to clear the barrier.

An animal lover at heart, Charlie installed quadrapeds as part of the Kansas City scene. One of

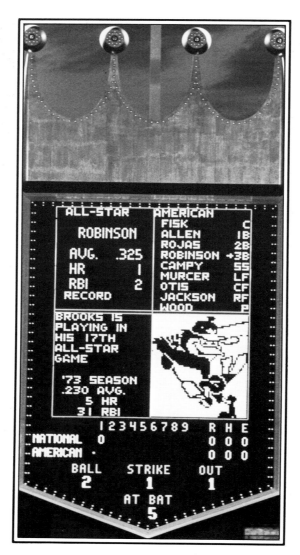

his creations was "Harvey," a mechanical rabbit who, at the press of an umpire's foot, would emerge from his subterranean hideout and deliver a supply of fresh baseballs.

There also were vari-colored sheep grazing under the watchful eye of a shepherd between the outfield fence and the stadium wall. The sheep helped cut down on lawn manicuring costs.

There also was "Charlie O.," the Missouri mule that served as team mascot and occupied a place of honor at Municipal Stadium, and a zoo for children in the picnic area behind bleacher seats down the left-field line.

In the summer of 1967, Jackson County voters approved a $43 million bond issue for a sports complex that would provide stadiums for the A's as well as the Kansas City Chiefs of the National Football League. But Charlie the owner couldn't wait. And at season's end the disaffection between magnate and citizens was complete. With his mule in tow, Finley trucked off to Oakland for the anticipated riches of California.

For one year Kansas City was without organized ball, but in 1969 the city returned with an expansion franchise under the ownership of Ewing Kauffman, owner of a pharmaceutical laboratory.

Completion of the sports complex was several years away, so the new club, christened the Royals by virtue of a fan contest, performed at Municipal Stadium.

One of the first moves by Executive Vice President Cedric Tallis and Manager Joe Gordon was to remove the right-field screen.

Five events of special significance occurred at Municipal Stadium during its 17 seasons. On July 11, 1960, a capacity crowd sat in 101-degree temperature to watch the National League All-Stars, behind home runs by Ernie Banks and Del Crandall, defeat the A.L., 5-3.

The following year, on June 16, 1961, a $125,000 bonus baby, 18-year-old righthander Lew Krausse Jr., attracted nationwide attention

The Royals Stadium scoreboard (above), 12 stories high in the shape of a crown, contains more than 16,000 light bulbs that flash at computerized commands.

The gigantic water spectacular, located in left and right-center fields
on each side of the scoreboard, was not operating when the Royals
hosted Texas (above) on opening night in 1973.

when he hurled a three-hit, 4-0 victory over the Los Angeles Angels, only nine days after graduating from high school in Chester, Pa.

On July 13, 1963, Early Wynn, in his 23rd major league campaign, annexed his 300th—and last—victory. The Cleveland righthander pitched the first five innings of a 7-4 win over the A's.

Two events in September 1965 focused the national spotlight on Municipal Stadium.

On September 8, Bert Campaneris, a shortstop by profession, established a modern major league mark by playing every position in a game against California. The A's lost the game, 5-3, and lost the services of Campaneris for five days because of neck and shoulder injuries suffered in a collision at home plate. Campy's well-advertised stunt attracted 21,576, considerably more than the 1,271 the A's drew for the other game of the series.

On September 25, Satchel Paige, at the age of 59, pitched the first three innings of a game against Boston. The redoubtable righthander allowed only one hit and struck out one batter in a scoreless performance.

The long-awaited dedication of the Harry S Truman Sports Complex arrived on April 10, 1973. Because of strikes and weather delays, the cost of the complex, set originally at $43 million, had escalated to $70 million by the time the Royals faced the Texas Rangers in the season inaugural.

A crowd of 39,464 braved 39-degree temperatures to watch the Royals triumph, 12-1, as John Mayberry contributed a single, home run and four runs batted in.

They also saw a colorful stadium of 40,635 seats, all facing second base and arranged in tiers of maroon, gold and orange. They saw, too, the league's first all-synthetic playing surface, foul lines of 330 feet, power alleys of 385 feet and a center-field wall 410 feet distant.

The outfield wall was a uniform 12 feet high.

In center field was a 120-foot high scoreboard built in the shape of the Royals' crest. The electronic marvel, operated by computer, contains more than 16,000 lights with which to flash statistics, messages and animations.

One delight denied opening night spectators was the water spectacular, which, because of weather delays, was not placed in operation for several months.

In this right-field display, stretching 322 feet horizontally, a 10-foot-high waterfall descends from an upper cascade pool which serves as a background for two water fountain pools, each 40 feet wide, and terminates in front with five 10-foot high horseshoe falls.

One jet of water responds to the cheers of the fans, rising as high as 70 feet as the volume increases.

The display uses 70,000 cubic feet of water which is circulated by 19 pumps averaging 40 horsepower. There are 670 lamps, each of 500 watts, which illuminate the water spectacular.

The $2.7 million scoreboard and the $750,000 water display were gifts to the stadium from Ewing Kauffman.

The water show was barely completed in time for the All-Star Game on July 24, 1973, when a throng of 40,849 saw the National League All-Stars, led by Bobby Bonds' home run and double, defeat the A.L., 7-1. The two managers employed a record total of 54 players.

The water fountain served as a baptismal pool in 1976 when shortstop Fred Patek and second baseman Cookie Rojas leaped into it to celebrate the Royals' divisional championship. The Royals also won A.L. West titles in 1977, '78 and '80, but reached the World Series only the last year.

In 1980, the Royals won the first two games of the League Championship Series at home, then eliminated the Yankees in Game 3 at New York.

In the World Series, the Royals lost the first two contests at Philadelphia, then won the third game at home on Willie Aikens' 10th-inning single. They also won Game 4 when Aikens socked two home runs. A defeat in Game 5 at Kansas City and another in Game 6 in Philadelphia shattered the Royals' dreams of a world title.

Except for two no-hit games—by Jim Colborn (6-0 vs. Texas on May 14, 1977) and Nolan Ryan of California (3-0 on May 15, 1973)—Royals Stadium is remembered best for hitting achievements.

On May 28, 1979, George Brett hit for the cycle, including a 16th-inning home run that defeated the Baltimore Orioles, 5-4.

Brett experienced another memorable day at home on the closing day of the 1976 season. Minnesota left fielder Steve Brye's misplay of a routine fly ball gave Brett an inside-the-park homer, the hit he needed to beat out teammate Hal McRae for the league batting championship.

The finest hitting performance, however, was a season-long show by Brett in 1980, when he flirted with a .400 average before tailing off in the final weeks to .390.

Gloom also has pervaded Royals Stadium, but never deeper than on the night of Sunday, October 9, 1977 when the Royals, only three outs away from the A.L. pennant, permitted the Yankees to score three ninth-inning runs and pull out a 5-3 victory in the fifth and decisive game of the League Championship Series.

The Harry S Truman Sports Complex, as seen above from Blue Ridge Cutoff just off Interstate 70, includes Royals Stadium and Arrowhead Stadium, home of the NFL Chiefs.

DODGER STADIUM
Los Angeles

Considering the extraordinary success of the Dodgers in the past 25 years, it is near inconceivable that there was a time when a Los Angeles franchise was returned to the league because of poverty.

It happened in 1906 as a direct consequence of the great earthquake that demolished San Francisco. The quake not only deprived the San Francisco team of a ball park, but also denied the Los Angeles club its customary hefty revenue from games in the City by the Bay.

Fortunately for Los Angeles, Pacific Coast League officials operated the club until a group of businessmen came to the rescue. The San Francisco club was invited to play its games in Oakland and the league succeeded in completing its schedule.

Los Angeles did not enter Organized Baseball until 1903, when its Coast League representative played at Chutes Park in one of the city's amusement centers.

The city did have an earlier professional team, however. It was a member of the California League, a circuit unassociated with Organized Baseball. The team gained national recognition on July 2, 1893 when it participated in a night game

against Stockton at Athletic Park.

Four poles were erected on the field, with 20 kerosene lamps suspended from wires between the poles. From the roof of the grandstand, a swiveled search light followed the course of the ball in play. Los Angeles, featuring a center fielder named Billy Sunday, later a famed evangelist, won the game, 5-2, before 9,000.

Ten years later the city gained a franchise in the Pacific Coast League. The team played its games at Chutes Park until 1911 when, feeling the need for larger quarters, it moved to nearby Washington Park, at Washington and Hill streets.

By this time the city boasted a second club in the PCL. In 1909, Sacramento sportsmen expressed an interest in fielding a PCL club. To maintain an even number of clubs, the established teams donated players to form a sixth organization that was placed in Vernon, a municipality on the outskirts of Los Angeles.

Henry Berry, owner of the L.A. club, agreed to the infringement of his territorial rights so that fans could enjoy baseball continually throughout the season.

The Vernon Tigers functioned from 1909 through 1912, playing in Maier Park, which was named for the club owner, Fred Maier. In 1913-14 the team carried the name of Venice, L.A.'s beach-front suburb. Except for Sunday morning and special holiday games, however, the Venice team played all its games in Washington Park. The franchise reverted to Vernon in 1915 where it remained until 1926, when it was moved to San Francisco and became the Missions.

During the period from 1909 to '15, the Vernon-Venice club was described as "perhaps the most colorful and aggressive in the history of the Pacific Coast League and for many years, until

A view from center field during a Giants-Dodgers game at Dodger Stadium (above), a little more than a month after the ball park opened in 1962.

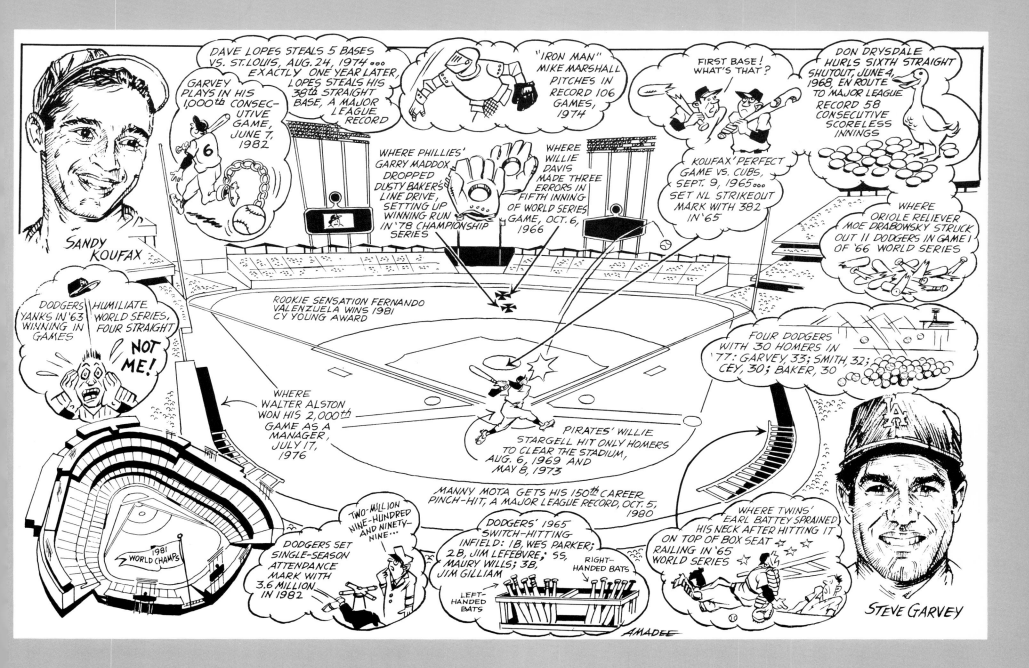

139

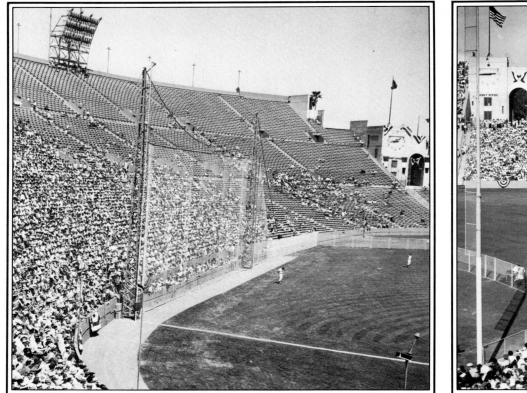

his death in 1915, was managed by a fiery but lovable character, Hap Hogan, whose real name was Wallace Bray."

One of the PCL's most dramatic pennant races involved the Los Angeles and Vernon teams in 1919. Entering the final week of the season, Los Angeles held a slight advantage and needed only two victories in the closing seven-game series against Vernon to wrap up the championship.

The Angels won only one game as the Tigers clinched the flag in a final-day doubleheader before an overflow crowd of 22,000 at Washington Park.

When the Vernon franchise was shifted to San Francisco after the 1925 season, a replacement was found quickly to fill the vacancy in Los Angeles. William H. (Hardrock Bill) Lane was happy to move his Salt Lake City team to L.A. In Los Angeles, as the Hollywood Stars, it shared the Angels' new park, Wrigley Field—named for gum magnate William Wrigley Jr., who had bought the club from Johnny Powers in 1921.

Wrigley was content to operate in Washington Park until city officials rejected his request to build underground parking facilities. At that point he started to draw up plans for a modern park at 42nd and Avalon.

The $1.1 million park, seating 22,000, was dedicated as a memorial to soldiers of World War I on September 27, 1925, with Commissioner Kenesaw M. Landis delivering the dedicatory speech. The Angels climaxed the gala occasion with a 10-8 victory over San Francisco.

The first night game at Wrigley Field was played on July 22, 1932, with the Angels defeating Seattle, 5-4, in 11 innings.

The left-field screen (above left) was an inviting home run target, but the right-field area (above right) was another story at the massive Los Angeles Coliseum (right).

The largest crowd in Wrigley Field's 35 years, 23,497, turned out on August 7, 1952 for a game with the Hollywood Stars.

This second edition of the Stars was created in 1935, after Bill Lane shifted the originals to San Diego. In their stead came the Missions franchise from San Francisco. Rechristened the Stars, they were owned by Victor Ford Collins and Bob Cobb and played at Gilmore Field. This 12,000-seat park at Beverly Boulevard and Fairfax was named for oilman Earl Gilmore and was located near Gilmore Stadium, the home field for the Loyola University football team.

For years L.A. citizens had maintained that a major league baseball club was a divine right in their burgeoning metropolis. Almost daily they read about enticements being offered to established franchises.

Don Barnes was about to transfer the St. Louis Browns to L.A. in 1942, but his plans were skewered by the Japanese attack on Pearl Harbor.

In 1953, American League directors approved the proposed sale of the Browns to Los Angeles interests and their transfer to the West Coast. That project floundered when the Los Angeles Coliseum Commission refused to open its doors to baseball. That team later ended up in Baltimore.

Frustration finally turned to jubilation in 1957 when Walter O'Malley announced that the Brooklyn Dodgers, who couldn't obtain municipal help in getting a larger stadium, would move to Los Angeles in 1958.

Three possible playing sites awaited O'Malley. The Dodgers could play in Wrigley Field, even smaller than the Dodgers' former park in Brooklyn; they could try the Rose Bowl in Pasadena, with a capacity of 100,000, or they could play in the L.A. Coliseum, where the governing body

looked more kindly on baseball than it had some years earlier.

To the surprise of nobody, O'Malley chose the Coliseum, not an ideal baseball facility certainly, but adequate until O'Malley could build his long-envisioned dream home.

But the Coliseum was not immediately suitable for baseball. Constructed for the 1932 Olympic Games, it had served in the meantime as the home of local college football teams. Renovations would be necessary.

For approximately $200,000, the Dodgers management added three new banks of lights at the west end to help brighten the infield. Sunken dugouts were built, as was a wire screen behind home plate, a press box and the Chinese Screen.

The Chinese Screen was a 40-foot high screen extending from the left-field foul line 140 feet toward center field. Fault finders were most vehement in ridiculing the left-field screen, 251 feet from home plate. Some suggested that home runs in the Coliseum be disallowed as a possible threat

Groundbreaking ceremonies were held at Chavez Ravine (above) in September of 1959, more than 2½ years before the Dodgers played their first game at Dodger Stadium.

142

Club publicist Red Patterson (above) took time in January of 1961 to check the progress of construction at Chavez Ravine, site of Dodger Stadium.

to Babe Ruth's existing record. Commissioner Ford Frick thought otherwise.

"I do not think Ruth's record is in particular danger," he said. "Foul lines are not especially important where home runs are concerned. The other distances in left-center and right-center determine the number of homers."

The left-field power alley was 320 feet, center field was 425 feet and the right-field power alley was 440 feet. After one season, an inside fence was constructed to reduce the center-field and right-field alley distances.

Wally Moon, a lefthanded-hitting outfielder of the Dodgers, took maximum advantage of the left-field screen, popping pitches off the screen regularly with his "inside-out" swing.

During the Dodgers' four-year occupancy of the Coliseum, it was the opposing clubs that profited most from such changes. In each of the four seasons, visitors collected more homers in the Coliseum than the Dodgers.

But nobody complained about attendance.

When an early 1958 series with the Giants drew more than 180,000, the visitors pocketed a check for $42,000. It was, said Eddie Brannick, the largest payoff in his many years as traveling secretary.

Despite a seventh-place finish, the 1958 Dodgers attracted 1,845,000 customers, a gain of more than 800,000 from their gate as a third-place club in Brooklyn the previous season.

In 1959, on their way to a world championship, the Dodgers scaled the two million attendance mark. And they set a virtually unbeatable record in the World Series by drawing three consecutive throngs of more than 90,000.

An all-time baseball record crowd of 93,103 jammed into the uncovered Coliseum on May 7, 1959, when the Los Angeles Herald Examiner sponsored a night for Roy Campanella, a former Brooklyn catcher confined to a wheelchair because of a crippling car accident.

The Dodgers closed out their four-year Coliseum era on September 20, 1961 when Sandy Koufax defeated the Chicago Cubs, 3-2 in 13 innings, before 12,000. In their Coliseum debut three years earlier, the Dodgers defeated the Giants, 6-5, but attracted more than 78,000.

As the Coliseum lights blinked out, a 56,000-seat facility was being constructed in an area known as Chavez Ravine, two miles from the center of the city.

Chavez Ravine, a hilly, depressed region, had been inhabited by squatters and goats. Through an intricate series of deals and agreements, O'Malley was to receive 166 acres of this land for his new ball park. When a referendum approved the transaction by a narrow 20,000-vote majority, O'Malley and city officials signed a contract in 1958.

But the matter did not rest there. A suit was filed charging the city lacked authority to sell property that the federal government originally had sold to the city with the stipulation that it be devoted to public use only.

The suit was rejected unanimously in the lower court and was appealed to the State Supreme Court, where it met the same fate. The United States Supreme Court refused to consider the case.

Construction on the Dodgers' new home commenced on September 17, 1959, with the expectation that all would be ready for occupancy by 1961. However, the lawsuits and landslides intervened. In the early weeks of 1962, laborers worked around the clock to get the park ready for the opening on April 10.

Despite the frenzied last-minute efforts, opening-day fans spotted one grievous flaw in the park's construction: There were no water fountains, an oversight that subsequently was corrected.

The stadium, budgeted originally at $12 million but costing nearly twice that amount, was the first park built by private capital since Yankee Stadium in 1923.

The six-level structure, dubbed the Taj Mahal of Baseball or simply Taj O'Malley, offered several new twists in park design. For one, there were "dugout boxes," located between the dugouts that afforded a ground-level view of the game.

Four scoreboard units kept all spectators informed. The power necessary to illuminate the boards, it was pointed out, was equal to that consumed by 200 homes. The power used in the entire complex, it was said, equaled that used by a city the size of Seattle.

Dimensions of the symmetrical playing area are 330 feet on the foul lines, 385 feet in the power alleys and 400 feet in center field.

Cincinnati outfielder Wally Post was the first to conquer the home run distance in the new park, smacking a three-run homer in the seventh inning to break a 2-2 tie and send the Reds on their way to a 6-3 victory before 52,564 in the first game, played April 10, 1962.

The next afternoon, with 35,000 on hand, the Dodgers returned the favor, defeating the Reds, 6-2, behind the four-hit hurling of Sandy Koufax.

Koufax enjoyed some of his most glittering moments in the huge horseshoe, including his perfect game against the Cubs on September 9, 1965. Later that same season, the southpaw established an N.L. record on the same mound by striking out batter No. 382.

Sandy's teammate, Don Drysdale, spun his sixth consecutive shutout in his home park on June 4, 1968, blanking the Pittsburgh Pirates, 5-0.

Davey Lopes drove the St. Louis Cardinals to distraction on the same field on August 24, 1974 by stealing five bases. Walter Alston celebrated his 2,000th victory as a major league manager when the Dodgers edged the Cubs, 5-4, on July 17, 1976.

The Dodgers won the 1978 pennant at home, beating the Phillies, 4-3, when Phillies outfielder Garry Maddox misplayed Dusty Baker's line drive to set up the winning run in the Championship Series.

In 1978, Dodger Stadium gained the distinction of being the first park to seat three million spectators in one season.

And in 1982, Dodger Stadium was the site where the all-time major league attendance record—3,608,881—was established.

In this park, too, was hatched one of the sweetest of Dodger memories, the conclusion of a four-game World Series sweep over the New York Yankees on October 6, 1963. The Dodgers were held to two hits by Whitey Ford and Hal Reniff. One was a 420-foot home run by Frank Howard, the first ball to be hit into the second deck of the two-year-old park. Howard also accounted for the Dodgers' other hit, a single, in the 2-1 win.

Dodger Stadium was the scene of six other World Series. The Dodgers outlasted Minnesota in a seven-game Series in 1965, but were humiliated in four straight games by Baltimore the following year. The Dodgers also won pennants in 1974, '77 and '78 but were conquered in the World Series all three years. They were not denied in 1981, however, as they beat Montreal in a thrilling Championship Series and then defeated New York in a six-game World Series.

Two of the darkest days in Chavez Ravine occurred on October 5-6, 1966. On the first date, reliever Moe Drabowsky fanned 11 Dodgers in pitching Baltimore to a 5-2 victory in the first game of the World Series. The next day, center fielder Willie Davis committed three fifth-inning errors as Jim Palmer whitewashed the Dodgers, 6-0.

Another Willie, Stargell of Pittsburgh, gained a singular distinction in Dodger Stadium on August 6, 1969 and May 8, 1973, when he drove the only two fair balls out of the stadium in its first 21 years. The Dodgers won both games.

Dodger Stadium was also where first baseman Steve Garvey, one of the most popular players in L.A. history, achieved a career milestone reached by few players. On June 7, 1982, the iron-man Garvey, an eight-time All-Star, played in his 1,000th consecutive game.

Large crowds are commonplace at baseball's Taj Mahal, Dodger Stadium (above), where major league attendance records have been shattered by the Los Angeles franchise.

COUNTY STADIUM

Milwaukee

Like a fickle lover, Milwaukee has showered its affections on the National League, then the American, back to the N.L. and lastly to the A.L.

The Milwaukee baseball story, which attained storybook flavor in the 1950s, began in 1836 when, historians reported, a contest was played at what became the intersection of East Wisconsin Avenue and North Milwaukee Street. The ball, consisting of a rubber core, yarn wrappings and a deerhide cover, was the property of a local museum a century later.

Credit for organizing the city's first professional team was accorded to Rufus King, a newspaper editor, superintendent of schools and later a Union Army general. In 1860, he formed a team that played on a lakefront site that became a Civil War campground.

By 1878, the game had achieved sufficient popularity so that promoters obtained a franchise in the National League. The Cream Citys, named for the color of Milwaukee-made bricks, survived one season and performed in a park bordered by North Tenth and Eleventh streets, West Michigan and West Clybourn.

In 1884, the city returned to Organized Base-

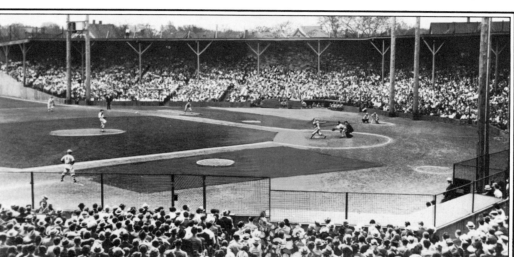

ball as a member of the Union Association. The U.A. collapsed after one year and the Milwaukee club caught on with the Western League. The team's luck was even worse in the W.L., which folded in mid-season.

The following year, 1886, Milwaukee had a club in the Northwestern League. The affiliation endured for one season. In 1887, the city turned its attention to the Western Association. The team played in a new park, at Eighth and Chambers, which became the location of Borchert Field, home of the Milwaukee Brewers when that club was a pillar of the American Association in

the twentieth century.

In 1888, the field was known as Athletic Park. On opening day, May 11, 6,000 were in the stands for the Creams' victory over St. Paul.

Gradually, the name of Creams disappeared and the team became known as the Brewers.

Many years after this period, when Clark Griffith was the octogenerian owner of the Washington Senators, he remembered the 1888-90 seasons when he pitched in Milwaukee.

"The Irish sat on the right-field side and the Germans on the left-field side," the Old Fox recalled. "It was a standing rule that the manager had to have an Irish first baseman and a German third baseman."

In 1894, brothers Harry and Matt Killilea, owners of the Brewers, rebelled over the lease terms at Athletic Park and built another structure, the Milwaukee Baseball Park, at North Sixteenth and West Lloyd streets.

The park contained a single deck, angled down the base lines from behind home plate, and also boasted a tower, reserved for newspapermen, behind the plate. The field was dedicated on May 2, 1895 when the Brewers lost to Minneapolis, 4-3,

Borchert Field (above), formerly called Milwaukee Athletic Park, was home of the American Association Brewers from 1902 through 1952.

147

before 5,000 spectators.

When Ban Johnson declared the American League a new major circuit in 1901, Milwaukee was one of the members. After one season under the management of Hugh Duffy, however, the club owners withdrew from the A.L. and cast their lot with the new American Association, a minor organization.

For two seasons, 1902-03, the city was represented in a second league, the Western. This club, reviving the old name of Creams, performed at Lloyd Street Park while the Brewers reclaimed Athletic Park.

In the early years of the A.A. Brewers, their home park was known as Brewer Field, but when Otto Borchert bought the club in 1919, the park was renamed Borchert Field.

Otto Borchert, who loved to conceal a philanthropic heart behind a gruff disposition, was accustomed to sunning himself in the outfield before Sunday and holiday games, when the park invariably was jammed. As game time approached, he strolled majestically toward his seat in the stands, swinging his walking stick and smiling broadly to the customers. They booed him goodnaturedly every step of the way.

Borchert suffered a fatal heart attack while speaking at an Elks Club dinner on the eve of the 1927 season. The park, however, retained his name until it was demolished to make way for a playground in the 1950s.

Borchert Field was not a classic piece of architecture. It was once described as "a lot of kindling wood called a grandstand."

From a seat in the grandstand it was impossible for a spectator to take in the entire field at a glance. Mike Kelley, a founder of the A.A. and owner of the Minneapolis club, once quipped:

"You have to pay two admissions to see one game at Borchert Field. The first day you see what happens in right field. The next day you come back to see what happens in left field."

When Borchert Field was not used for baseball, it was the site of high school football games and, in winter, was used as an ice skating rink. A dressing room for skaters adjoined the left-field foul pole. When Borchert purchased the Brewers, he converted the dressing room into a chicken coop, where he raised White Rocks for many years.

The Brewers may have been the only team in Organized Ball that boasted a goat as a mascot. The animal was adopted by Ralph Cutting, a pitcher, and grazed in the infield and outfield when a game was not in progress. At night, it retired to the roof, where it deposited an odor that rendered the coop unfit for human occupancy.

After Cutting retired, the reporters issued an ultimatum: Either the goat goes or we do. The goat went.

Before the Volstead Act outlawed alcoholic beverages, a bar was installed behind home plate.

With Warren Spahn warming up in the foreground (above), the Braves and Cardinals line up for County Stadium opening-day ceremonies on April 14, 1953.

toward the major leagues. Big league officials had spoken favorably of the city as a potential site. Nothing resulted, but Milwaukee, just to be prepared, broke ground for a $5 million park in 1950.

The first ball park built with public money, County Stadium had a left-field foul line of 320 feet, a 315-foot right-field line and a center-field wall 402 feet away.

Originally, the capacity was 35,911. Through the years the capacity was increased to 53,192 while the distances to the fences remained unchanged.

The park was nearing completion when, on March 18, 1953, word was received that the Boston Braves, having lost $1 million in three years, would be transferred to the Wisconsin metropolis. While it shattered the 50-year-old major league alignment, the move was a relatively simple matter. The Braves already owned the Milwaukee franchise in the American Association and a new park was awaiting a tenant.

The marriage of the Braves and Brewtown was a golden success from the start. On opening day, April 14, 1953, a crowd of 34,357 welcomed the team and the Braves responded with a 10-inning, 3-2 victory over the Cardinals. The manner in which the win was achieved enhanced the fairy-tale drama that was about to unfold.

With one out in the first extra inning, Bill Bruton hit a drive to right field where Enos Slaughter attempted a leaping catch. The ball caromed off his glove and over the low wall. Initially, umpire Lon Warneke ruled it a ground rule double. After a few moments, however, he decided it was a legitimate home run. It was the rookie's only home run of the season.

At season's end the Braves had attracted a

Here thirsty burghers could occupy two rows of seats and quench their thirsts without missing a single pitch.

Tragedy struck the 10,000-seat park on June 15, 1944 when a violent windstorm invaded the area during the seventh inning of a game against Columbus. The roof over the first-base stands was ripped off and for a while reporters in the area behind the plate were certain that they would be the next to go. The lights went out and panic-stricken spectators raced onto the field. Fortunately, only 35 persons were injured.

On the advice of the building inspector, the roof on the first-base grandstand was never replaced.

Bill Veeck and Charley Grimm combined their light-hearted talents during banner seasons at Borchert Field in the early 1940s. It was here that Veeck built his early reputation as a promoter, luring fans into the park with countless, usually zany, stunts, like presenting Grimm a huge birthday cake from which leaped Julio Acosta, a just-acquired lefthanded pitcher.

For years Milwaukee had cast covetous eyes

On May 15, 1968, the Chicago White Sox lined up for ceremonies marking their first of 20 "home games" at County Stadium. The Braves had transferred to Atlanta after the '65 season.

No. 3, 450 Ft.

No. 4, 430 Ft.

No. 2, 400 Ft.

No. 1, 420 Ft.

After splitting two World Series games in New York, the Braves took two of three decisions at home.

Games 4 and 5 were etched indelibly on the memories of the more than 45,000 fans who shoehorned into County Stadium on October 6 and 7.

Eddie Mathews' 10th-inning homer netted a 7-5 victory in the first contest, but his heroics may have been impossible had it not been for a reversed decision by an umpire.

The Braves were trailing, 5-4, when Nippy Jones, batting for pitcher Warren Spahn, was struck on the foot by a pitch from Tommy Byrne. Home plate arbiter Augie Donatelli refused to award Jones first base until Jones retrieved the baseball and showed Donatelli a black smudge, a telltale indication of shoe polish. Johnny Logan's double tied the score and Mathews followed with his home run off Bob Grim.

The next day Lew Burdette won his second of three games, beating the Yankees, 1-0. Singles by Mathews, Aaron and Joe Adcock with two outs in the sixth inning and a spectacular catch by Wes Covington against the left-field fence, depriving Gil McDougald of a home run, pinned the defeat on Whitey Ford.

For 19,194 customers, no pitching performance in County Stadium could match that of May 26, 1959. The Braves won the game, 1-0, in 13 innings, but the cheers—and sympathies— went to a visiting pitcher, Pittsburgh lefthander Harvey Haddix.

For 12 innings, Haddix retired the Braves as quickly as they came to the plate. However, the Buccos, despite 12 hits off Burdette, were unable to score, either. Haddix's mastery was broken in the 13th inning when third baseman Don Hoak

league record 1,826,397 into County Stadium. In their final season in Boston, the Braves had played to only 281,278.

Before the 1954 campaign, an expansion project raised the seating capacity to over 43,000 for the Braves' second season. The Braves responded by drawing 2,131,388.

County Stadium served as home of the Braves for 13 seasons, during which the club scaled world championship heights. They topped the two million attendance figure in four consecutive seasons (1954-57), in which they won one world title (1957) and a second National League pennant (1958).

Disenchantment, born perhaps of success gained at too early a stage, took root in 1958. By 1965, the gate had dropped below 600,000 and the Braves were bound for Atlanta.

While the frenzy lasted, however, County Stadium was the hub of the baseball universe. While fans showered the athletes with gifts of every description, the players responded with mutual admiration. The 1957 World Series served as a case in point.

The Braves clinched the N.L. pennant on September 23, when Hank Aaron's 11th-inning home run off Billy Muffett produced a 4-2 victory over the Cardinals.

County Stadium (above) was the site of a four-homer barrage that San Francisco's Willie Mays rained on the Braves April 30, 1961.

In September of 1958, Braves fans (above left) lined up to buy tickets for a World Series. In April of 1970, Brewers fans (above right) lined up to buy opening-day tickets.

threw low to first base after fielding Felix Mantilla's grounder.

A sacrifice and intentional walk to Aaron preceded Adcock's long drive to right-center field. Bill Virdon made a frantic attempt to catch the ball, but it dropped over the fence.

Aaron, thinking the ball had bounced over the fence for a ground rule double, touched second base and headed for the dugout as the tie-breaking run crossed the plate. Adcock, meanwhile, ran with his head down and was ruled out for passing Aaron on the baseline. He received credit for only a double instead of the home run to which he was entitled.

Stan Musial left his imprint on County Stadium in the All-Star Game of July 12, 1955, when The Man crashed a 12th-inning home run to give the N.L. a 6-5 triumph.

The clout made a winner of hometown favorite Gene Conley who, moments earlier, received a standing ovation from the 45,000 spectators by fanning Al Kaline, Mickey Vernon and Al Rosen in succession.

County Stadium exerted a therapeutic effect on Willie Mays' hitting. Hitless in seven consecutive at-bats, the Giants outfielder belted four home runs on April 30, 1961 to highlight an eight-homer San Francisco barrage in a 14-4 triumph. Willie became the ninth player to perform that feat.

The stadium, on South 46th Street off Bluemound Road, also was the spot where the Phillies halted a record losing streak in 1961. Beaten in 23 consecutive contests, the Phils defeated the Braves, 7-4, behind John Buzhardt, who raised his record to 4-13, on August 20, 1961.

After the departure of the Braves in 1966, County Stadium remained dark for two seasons, then reopened on a limited basis in 1968 and '69

on the earlier date, the N.L. posted another victory, this time by the score of 6-3. Bill Madlock's bases-loaded single in the ninth inning decided the issue.

Milwaukee's long quest for another title was realized on the next-to-last day of the 1981 season when a 2-1 victory over the Detroit Tigers clinched the second-half crown of a strike-torn campaign.

The jubilation did not last long, however. The Yankees, first-half winners, defeated the Brewers, 5-3 and 3-0, at County Stadium en route to a five-game mini-series victory that decided the A.L. East title.

But what happened in '81 was only a pretext for what was to happen the following year. Led by shortstop Robin Yount, who was the American League MVP, and pitcher Pete Vuckovich, who won the league's Cy Young Award, the Brewers won 95 games, tops in the majors, and beat the Orioles in Baltimore, 10-2, on the final day of the season to capture the A.L. East Division crown.

In the A.L. Championship Series, County Stadium really proved to be "Home Sweet Home" for Milwaukee. After losing the first two games to the California Angels in Anaheim, the Brewers did what had never been done before in Championship Series play—they won the next three games at home to reach the World Series for the first time in club history.

But the Brewers' dream season ended on a sour note with a 6-3 loss to the St. Louis Cardinals in the seventh game of the World Series. Although they won two of the three games played at County Stadium, the Brewers lost three of four in St. Louis, including the finale. The Brewers' best season ever wasn't quite as sweet as it could have been.

when the Chicago White Sox transferred a total of 20 games to Milwaukee. Attendance, while not spectacular, was encouraging, and when the Seattle Pilots floundered financially, the franchise was shifted to Milwaukee for the 1970 season. Fans started to resume their old baseball habits. But while the turnstiles did not whirl as dizzily as in the 1950s, the team, renamed the Brewers, drew 933,690 the first season. By 1973, the club had topped the one million attendance mark.

Hank Aaron, who had been a dominant figure during the Braves' heyday in Milwaukee, closed out his career with the Brewers. On July 20,

1976, he socked the 755th, and last, home run of his record-setting career against California Angels pitcher Dick Drago.

Don Money distinguished himself afield and at bat during County Stadium's second term as a major league playing site. On July 7, 1974, Money established a record for third basemen by playing in his 78th consecutive errorless game. On April 12, 1980, he combined with teammate Cecil Cooper in clouting grand-slam home runs in the same inning.

Twenty years after its first visit, the All-Star Game returned to Milwaukee on July 15, 1975. As

The panoramic view (above left) and the overview (above) show the current design of County Stadium and the surrounding area.

METROPOLITAN STADIUM

Minneapolis-St. Paul

Until the arrival of major league baseball in 1961, the Twin Cities of Minneapolis and St. Paul waged athletic warfare from opposite banks of the Mississippi River. It lasted for more than six decades, first in the Western League and then in the American Association.

St. Paul's professional baseball history predates even the Western League of the 1890s. In 1884, the Saints played briefly in the Union Association, a self-styled major circuit. Replacing Pittsburgh late in the season, St. Paul won two games and lost six, after which the club folded. As a result, the city gained the distinction of holding a major league franchise for a shorter period than any other city.

The Twin Cities were represented in the American Association in 1902; the Millers operated out of Nicollet Park on Nicollet Avenue and the Saints out of Lexington Park on Lexington Parkway.

That initial season in the A.A. was climaxed with tripleheaders for both clubs. Entering the final day, Indianapolis led Louisville by two games with three to play. Indianapolis had scheduled three games at Minneapolis and Louisville three games at St. Paul.

Indianapolis won two contests to clinch the pennant while Louisville swept three games at St.

Paul, 2-1, 3-2 and 11-6. The Louisville and St. Paul clubs did not dally long on getaway day, completing their games in 1:10, 1:12 and 0:50. The third game was a seven-inning affair.

The 1902 Saints were managed by Mike Kelley, who produced pennants in 1903 and '04. In the mid-1920s, after winning three more flags with the Saints, Kelley bought the Minneapolis franchise, which he operated until 1948, when he sold it to the New York Giants.

Nicollet Park was the scene of two ugly incidents in mid-season of 1906 when the Millers played two games against the Columbus Senators. At the time the Millers were in first place, one game ahead of the visitors.

The umpire for the games was Clarence (Brick) Owens, later a prominent American League arbiter, but at this stage a youngster just signed out of a semipro league in Michigan.

In the opening contest, Owens made several unpopular decisions. At game's end, 9,000 spectators poured onto the field threatening to dismember Owens, who was spirited away by police.

The stands were packed again for the second game. As Owens prepared to announce the batteries, he was bombarded by eggs, fruit and vegetables. Immediately, he forfeited the game to Columbus and once more the mob set upon him, bursting through a police cordon in its determination to maul the umpire.

At the last possible second, two brawny arms encircled Owens and a commanding voice ordered the multitude to stand back.

"Friends," shouted the peacemaker, "you are about to do something that will forever disgrace the good name of Minneapolis, an act you will always regret. I am going to escort this man to his hotel and any man who harms him will have to answer to me."

As the mob melted away, Owens strolled to a patrol wagon, accompanied by Walter (Pudge) Heffelfinger, a four-time All-America guard at Yale and a public idol in the Upper Midwest.

Old Lexington Park in St. Paul (above) saw its last service on September 5, 1956, when future major leaguer Stan Williams shut out arch-rival Minneapolis, 4-0.

The Millers manager at the time was Mike Kelley, who had been lured away from St. Paul. For "inciting a riot and failing to provide adequate police protection," Kelley was suspended for the remainder of the season by League President Joseph O'Brien. It was said O'Brien acted at the urging of a league director hostile to Kelley.

Four key Minneapolis players also were suspended for shorter periods. Because of it, the Millers slipped out of contention and crowds, which had been in the 5,000-6,000 range, dwindled to a few hundred a game.

O'Brien's harsh penalty did not remove Kelley from command, however. By drilling a hole in the wall behind the dugout, Kelley was able to watch the game and issue orders as usual.

The right-field foul line at Nicollet Park was only 280 feet, and the right-center power alley only 328 feet. The field was built for a lefthanded power hitter such as Joe Hauser. In 1933, Hauser clouted 69 home runs, an Organized Baseball record for that era.

He hit 50 homers at Nicollet, including three in one game against Toledo.

At the time of Hauser's feat, the right-field fence consisted of a single tier of signs topped by a screen. In 1935, a second tier of signs was installed, plus a 16-foot screen extending from the foul line to the major league scoreboard. Any ball hit into the screen—erected to protect windows across the street—was a home run.

Despite the chummy right-field barrier, the foremost batting accomplishments at Nicollet were by righthanded batters. On June 14, 1935, Kansas City first baseman Dale Alexander poled four homers in the Millers' park. On July 4, 1940, Minneapolis outfielder Ab Wright whacked four homers and a triple, all against righthanded pitch-

ers. His first-inning clout was said to be one of the longest drives in Nicollet history, clearing the center-field wall between the flagpole and scoreboard.

Wright's fireworks featured a 17-5 victory in which the Millers rapped eight homers and accumulated 50 total bases. Wright also homered in the morning segment of the holiday twin bill, won by the Saints, 3-2.

While the Millers were setting American Association records at Nicollet, the St. Paul Saints were flying nine pennants from the Lexington Park flagpole. No championship was relished more than that of 1920, when the Saints won 115 games and finished 28½ games ahead of second-place Louisville. In the first Junior World Series that followed, the Saints won only one of six games from Baltimore in the International League.

The Millers sang Auld Lang Syne to Nicollet on September 28, 1955, closing out the historic stadium in high style. Before 9,927, the largest home crowd of the year, the Millers defeated Rochester, 9-4, in the finale of the Junior World Series. The Millers cracked four home runs—by Bob Lennon (who also had five runs batted in), Carl Sawatski, Monte Irvin and Don Bollweg.

On April 24, 1956, the Millers inaugurated Metropolitan Stadium, a $4.5 million structure in suburban Bloomington. A crowd of 18,366 jammed the 18,200-seat facility, which was only partially completed because of an explosion and two fires during the previous winter. Among the spectators at Wichita's 5-3 win was Horace

When the St. Paul Saints moved into Midway Stadium (above) in 1957, many hoped the new facility might bring overtures from a major league franchise.

In St. Paul, Midway Stadium was doomed for destruction. An industrial office complex now occupies the site.

For the next 20 years, the team, now known as the Twins, performed in the Bloomington park. The Met was expanded to accommodate more than 45,000 fans.

From the outset there was near unanimous agreement that Metropolitan Stadium was a hitters' park. No home run record was safe in a park that showed 330-foot foul lines and where the ball carried exceptionally well.

The fears did not materialize, however, and the left-field foul line later was lengthened to 343 feet.

There were some remarkable hitting achievements at The Met. On June 9, 1966, the Twins socked five home runs in one inning against the A's. And on July 18, 1962, Harmon Killebrew and Bob Allison became the first teammates to wallop grand slams in the same inning, turning the trick in a 14-3 victory over Cleveland.

It was at The Met, too, where Killebrew belted his 500th home run on August 10, 1971 and socked the second of his three All-Star Game homers in 1965.

Two Baltimore players enjoyed memorable hitting days at The Met. On May 9, 1961, Jim Gentile rapped grand slams in consecutive innings of a 13-5 triumph. On October 3, 1970, pitcher Mike Cuellar stroked a long right-field fly that, aided by a strong cross wind, drifted from foul territory to

Stoneham. The owner of the New York Giants, the parent club of the Millers, asserted that The Met "is the finest minor league park in the country, and there are not over two in the majors that are better."

The curtain fell on Lexington Park on September 5, 1956. The old structure that survived fires in 1906 and 1914, and a wind storm that destroyed a large portion of the right-field fence in 1951, bowed out in memorable fashion. Stan Williams hurled a six-hit, 4-0 victory over arch-rival Minneapolis before 2,227 mourners. A shopping center now occupies the old Lexington Park site; a bank stands where Nicollet Park once stood.

The Saints moved into Midway Stadium, a new $2 million park at 1000 North Snelling Avenue, on April 25, 1957. The Saints scheduled a day-night

doubleheader for the occasion and attracted a total of 16,109 into the 10,000-seat stadium. Wichita ruined the day by winning both games.

Midway Stadium had foul lines of 321 feet. The distance to the 16-foot high fence in center field was 410 feet.

By the summer of 1957, the city fathers of the two communities agreed to coordinate their efforts in a bid to attract a major league franchise. As a result, Metropolitan Stadium, equidistant between the midtowns of each city, was enlarged to 21,000. Exhibitions between major league clubs drew well. On August 5, 1957, the Detroit Tigers and Cincinnati Reds attracted 21,689. Major league executives took notice.

By 1961 The Met capacity exceeded 30,000. Calvin Griffith, the majority stockholder of the

Nicollet Park (above) served the Minneapolis community well until 1956, when the Millers inaugurated new Metropolitan Stadium, future home of the Twins.

fair and turned into a grand-slam homer in a 10-6 victory in the first game of the League Championship Series.

Four World Series games were played at the Met, all in 1965. The Twins captured three of the contests. Unfortunately for Minnesotans, the Twins encountered Sandy Koufax in the seventh game. The Los Angeles lefthander was at his best, scattering three hits in a 2-0 Dodger win.

The Series also was marked by a spectacular fielding play by Bob Allison. In the second game, the left fielder sprinted far in pursuit of a curving ball off the bat of Jim Lefebvre. Allison caught the ball as it was about to hit the turf, then skidded 15 feet in what veteran observers termed one of the finest catches in Series annals.

Perhaps the most curious mark of all at The Met was credited to Eddie Stanky. Named manager of the Texas Rangers on June 21, 1977, Stanky piloted the club to a 10-8 triumph over the Twins

the next day and then resigned, "because I felt my place was with my family" in Mobile, Ala.

There was growing agitation in the Twin Cities for a domed stadium that would allay fears over a possible departure of the Twins and football Vikings. By the close of the 1981 season, The Met had run its course as a major league ball park. The Twins bade farewell on September 30, bowing to the Kansas City Royals, 5-2, before 15,900.

The result was not unlike that of the Twins' 1961 debut at The Met. They lost that game to the expansion Washington team, 5-3. The only difference was that 24,606 were in the stands 20 years earlier.

When the 1982 season opened, the Twins were housed in the Hubert H. Humphrey Metrodome, a structure covering nearly 10 acres just east of downtown Minneapolis.

Perhaps the most remarkable aspect of the Dome was that it was constructed for approxi-

mately $2 million under budget. Downtown businessmen donated the land in exchange for area development rights. Construction capital was raised by the sale of $55 million in bonds. Another $25 million was realized from the sale of 100 acres of the old ball park property in Bloomington.

Builders made no effort to produce a luxury stadium. "The idea is to get the fans in, let 'em see a game and then let 'em go home. That's all we want from a stadium," explained a spokesman for the Dome.

Playing field dimensions in the 54,711-seat stadium on Chicago Avenue South are 343 feet to left field, 408 feet to center and 327 to right. The Dome, at its peak, is 186 feet from the SporTurf floor, compared to 208 feet in Houston's Astrodome and 250 feet in Seattle's Kingdome.

Like other recently built domes, the Minneapolis structure features an air-supported fiberglass,

By 1961, Metropolitan Stadium (above left and right) seated more than 30,000 and featured the big bats of such stars as Harmon Killebrew and Bob Allison.

fabric roof. The 340-ton cover is held in place by steel cables and air pressure generated by 20 90-horsepower fans. Composed of a double layer of fabric, the roof is dark enough to permit outfielders to track a fly ball, yet translucent enough so that the shadow of a passing cloud can be traced on the field.

The roof is equipped with snow-melting ducts to prevent a collapse due to excess weight, but even if it should deflate, the roof would settle 100 feet above the floor—well above the heads of spectators.

An exhibition game between the Twins and Philadelphia Phillies opened the Dome "unofficially" on April 3, 1982. The dedication took place on April 6, when 52,279, including Mrs. Muriel Humphrey Brown, widow of the former senator and vice president for whom the Dome was named, watched the Twins bow to the Seattle Mariners, 11-7. Fulfilling predictions that the park would favor hitters, five home runs sailed into the seats. Two of the bombs were fused by Minnesota

rookie Gary Gaetti. Jim Maler had three hits and five RBIs for Seattle.

One bomb that failed to reach the seats was a cherry bomb tossed by a thoughtless fan, who was ushered to the nearest police station.

Other than that, and sloppy corridors resulting from malfunctioning toilets, opening night went smoothly. After all, the air-conditioning system worked efficiently, providing delightful 70-degree temperature indoors while the city shivered in 28 degrees.

The Hubert H. Humphrey Metrodome (above), which opened in 1982, features an air-supported fiberglass, fabric roof that weighs 340 tons.

OLYMPIC STADIUM

Montreal

Probably no city suffered sharper birth pangs of Organized Baseball than Montreal.

In 1890, the metropolis acquired an International League franchise when the Buffalo club folded. After six games, one at Hamilton, Ont., two at London, Ont., and three at Atwater Park in Montreal, the franchise was transferred to Grand Rapids, Mich., on June 11.

Atwater Park did not remain unoccupied for long, however. The Hamilton franchise was shifted to Montreal in late June, but the second time around was no sweeter than the first. After games of July 5, the league collapsed and Montreal disappeared from professional baseball for seven years.

It resurfaced in 1897, again as a result of disaster elsewhere. When fire destroyed the park of the Rochester club in the Eastern League, forerunner of the modern International League, the team moved to Montreal and played its games at Atwater Park.

The team won the pennant in 1898, but by 1902 fan support had dwindled to such a degree that the club was shifted to Worcester, Mass. Public enthusiasm there was equally poor, however, so on August 3 the team was returned to Montreal. It remained there until the close of the 1917 season, when it folded due to a manpower shortage created by World War I.

Montreal returned to Organized Ball in 1922 as a member of the Class B Eastern Canada League and transferred to the Quebec-Ontario-Vermont League in 1924. It then rejoined the International

League in 1928, when the franchise was managed by George Stallings, the skipper of the Miracle Boston Braves of 1914.

Construction of a new park that was known at various times as Delorimier Downs, Montreal Stadium and Hector Racine Stadium, commenced on January 1, 1928. The $1.15 million project on the east side of town was completed in time for the May 5 inaugural against Reading. Park capacity was announced as 17,757, but opening day attendance included that many paying customers,

plus 2,500 non-paying guests that included Commissioner Kenesaw M. Landis. Bob Shawkey, a onetime mainstay of the New York Yankees staff, rewarded the huge throng by pitching the Royals to a 7-4 victory.

Park dimensions strongly favored lefthanded batters, with a right-field foul line measuring only 295 feet. The distance to left field was 340 feet and to center 440 feet.

The only lefthanded hitter to drill a home run over the left-field barrier was Charlie Keller, a Newark Bears slugger who accomplished the feat in 1938.

The steel and concrete park, with bleachers in left and right field, housed its largest crowd in 1941 when 24,458 overflowed the premises for a playoff game between the Royals and Bears.

International League pennants flew from the stadium flagpole in 1935, and in 1945, '46, '48, '51, '52, '55 and '58, when the Royals were a farm club of the Dodgers.

A crowd of 15,745 welcomed Jackie Robinson to the stadium on May 1, 1946. The first Negro in modern Organized Baseball, Robinson, who had rapped a home run and three singles in his debut at Jersey City two weeks earlier, rapped a single and started two double plays in his first Montreal appearance, a 12-9 victory over Jersey City.

In 1948, the Royals, featuring such stars as Don Newcombe, Duke Snider, Sam Jethroe and Bobby Morgan, attracted more than 600,000 to Delorimier. They swept every conceivable honor that season, winning the International League

Known at various times as Delorimier Downs, Montreal Stadium and Hector Racine Stadium, Montreal's foremost minor league park (above) housed eight pennant winners.

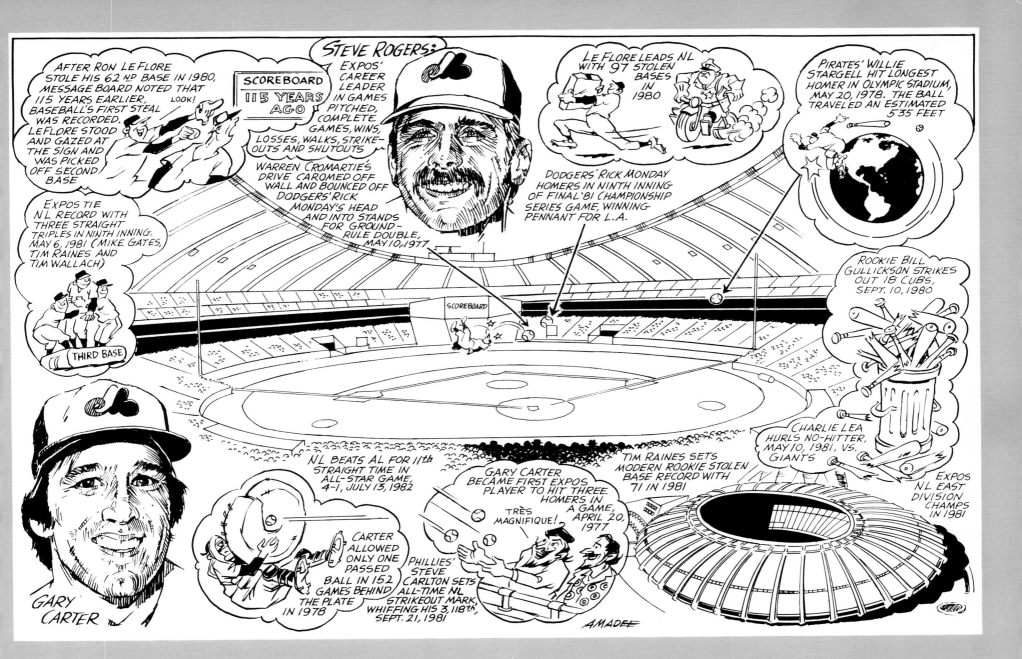

161

pennant and playoffs before capturing the Junior World Series from St. Paul, another Brooklyn farm in the American Association.

The Dodgers sold the stadium in 1956 for an estimated $1.25 million to a development corporation, but retained a lease on the property through 1960. At the expiration of the lease, the franchise was returned to the league and the city was without Organized Ball representation for eight years.

In the summer of 1968, the city was awarded an expansion franchise in the National League provided that a suitable playing site would be available for the 1969 season.

Originally, the 25,000-seat Autostade, located on the site of the 1967 World's Fair, was selected as a park, but when city officials rebelled at the $7 million cost for a roof and 12,000 additional seats, Mayor Jean Drapeau was forced to scurry for an alternate site.

After N.L. President Warren Giles and the city fathers failed to agree on a satisfactory park location on August 7, the odds of Montreal seeing major league baseball in 1969 were virtually nonexistent. Only Drapeau failed to surrender.

Accompanied by Giles, the mayor visited Jarry Park, a recreational area in the northeast section of the city that contained 3,000 seats.

Drapeau emphasized several advantages to the location: It was only a five-minute walk from the nearest subway station. It was less than a mile from the nearest expressway. It was less than 200 yards from a railway that handled commuter traffic. Within a few months, Drapeau promised, the park capacity could be increased to 30,000. Parking facilities would be provided for 5,000 vehicles, the mayor said, and Giles was convinced that the park could serve as a satisfactory stop-gap.

The Expos, named for the 1967 Exposition, made their Jarry Park debut on April 14, 1969, when 29,184 saw the 8-7 victory over the St. Louis Cardinals.

Jarry Park was a single-deck structure with seats extending to the corners in left and right fields and a bleacher section in left field. The front rows of the bleachers contained reserved seats; those in the rear were not reserved.

A wire fence around the outfield created foul lines of 340 feet and a center field 420 feet deep.

Although the Expos' home attendance topped the 1.2 million mark the first season and continued over the million mark for the next four seasons, Jarry Park was proving less satisfactory with each passing year.

On the club's fifth anniversary in 1974, President John McHale complained: "We were told that we would have a covered stadium for the 1972 season. That's what the mayor promised us when we were given the franchise. That's what we promised the league when we applied for the franchise.

"We get a reprieve each year when the matter comes up at league meetings. The league has the right to revoke the franchise. However, I'm quite sure they wouldn't think about that with a team that's drawing better than 1.2 million.

"Our toughest decision throughout the season is when to call a game. We know there is absolutely no protection for the fans. On the other hand, they show up and want to see us play.

"These are tough decisions and only will become easier or be eliminated entirely when we move into a domed stadium."

Much to McHale's consternation, the Expos were required to make do in Jarry Park for eight seasons. When they eventually bade it adieu, it wasn't to move into a covered stadium, but into Olympic Stadium in 1977.

The $770 million Olympic Stadium, with a capacity of over 58,000, was erected for the 1976 Olympics and originally was to include a retractable roof. However, construction strikes and soaring costs quashed such plans.

When Mayor Drapeau was unable to raise funds for the roof, the matter was tossed into the lap of the provincial government of Quebec. The cost-conscious officials pigeon-holed the matter. Visions of a 550-foot tower, and an umbrella-type cover that would be opened and closed according to the weather conditions, disappeared.

A suggestion that a permanent roof be constructed was dismissed when it was revealed that the stadium was not strong enough to hold a winter's snow load on a fixed roof.

But, with or without a cover, Olympic Stadium offered benefits that the Expos could not ignore, and they moved into the huge saucer in 1977. In their new home, the Expos found a playing field with 325-foot foul lines and a center-field fence 404 feet away.

A crowd of 57,592 welcomed the team into Olympic Stadium on April 15, 1977. Ellis Valentine provided a measure of excitement for the huge gathering with two runs batted in on a home run and infield out. His efforts were matched, however, by Jay Johnstone and Greg Luzinski, who also drove in two runs apiece to lead the Phillies to a 7-2 victory.

The fifth-place Expos attracted 1.4 million paying customers in 1977 and duplicated that gate total in '78, when they climbed to fourth place.

Second-place finishes the next two seasons produced attendances in excess of two million.

Much to the consternation of Expos President John McHale, makeshift Jarry Park (above) served as Montreal's home field for eight National League seasons.

The club very likely would have topped that mark again in 1981 except for a two-month players strike.

In the Expos' sixth game at Olympic Stadium on April 20, 1977, catcher Gary Carter clouted three home runs against Pittsburgh, the first Montreal player to accomplish that feat. The achievement failed to avert a loss, however, as the Pirates triumphed, 8-6.

A year and a month after Carter's outburst, Willie Stargell of the Pirates set a target for other N.L. sluggers by belting a 535-foot home run on May 20, 1978. The homer, the longest in the Stadium's first six seasons, was one of two hammered by the first baseman, who drove in five runs in a 6-0 triumph.

Ron LeFlore was a popular gate attraction in 1980 when he stole a league-leading total of 97 bases. He also was the source of frustration and object of censure on the day he swiped his 62nd base. As the message board noted that 115 years earlier baseball's first steal was recorded, LeFlore stood transfixed—off second base—and was tagged out.

Rookie righthander Bill Gullickson caught the public's fancy on September 10, 1980 by striking out 18 Chicago batters, a Montreal record.

Two notable events occurred within a five-day period at Olympic Stadium in '81. On May 6, the Expos tied a league record when Mike Gates, Tim Raines and Tim Wallach smacked consecutive ninth-inning triples in a 13-5 loss to San Diego. On May 10, Charlie Lea hurled the first no-hitter in Olympic Stadium, beating San Francisco, 4-0. During the Expos' early years, Bill Stoneman pitched a pair of hitless games, one at Jarry Park and one at Philadelphia.

The Expos came within a hair's breadth of N.L.

East Division championships in 1979 and '80, but defeats in season-ending series at home against Philadelphia knocked them out of contention.

In 1981, the Expos experienced their first title thrill, winning the second-half championship in the strike-torn campaign. They eliminated the Phillies, the first-half kings, and then engaged the Los Angeles Dodgers for the National League pennant.

The teams split two games on the West Coast. When the series moved to Olympic Stadium on October 16, Steve Rogers hurled the Expos to a 4-1 victory before more than 54,000.

The Expos were now within one game of bringing a World Series to Canada for the first time. They were tied, 1-1, after seven innings in the fourth game. But the Dodgers exploded and registered a 7-1 win to even the series.

The Expos were only five innings away from the pennant in the deciding game, on October 19, leading 1-0 after four innings. Rick Monday's single led to the tying run for the Dodgers in the fifth inning, however, and his ninth-inning homer off Steve Rogers crushed Montreal's hopes with a 2-1 Expo defeat.

But Olympic Stadium was the scene of happier times for Expos fans less than a year later.

Montreal was the host city of the 1982 All-Star Game, the first such event played outside the United States. Behind starting and winning pitcher Rogers, the National League won the game, 4-1, for its 11th straight triumph. Expos first baseman Al Oliver contributed a double, single and scored a run for the winners.

The appearance of former players from around the world added to the international flavor of the 1982 All-Star Game, played at Montreal's Olympic Stadium (above).

Construction strikes and soaring costs quashed plans for a retractable
roof, but Olympic Stadium (above) nevertheless proved a boon to the
Montreal Expos.

POLO GROUNDS

New York

Few major league baseball parks could match the Polo Grounds, starting with that misleading name. Few, if any, could compare with its unique design or the memorable moments that occurred within its horseshoe contours between 1891 and 1963.

A polo match was never played in the Polo Grounds, but the historic arena came by its unusual name in a perfectly logical manner.

When John B. Day shifted the Troy National League franchise to New York in 1883, he arranged to play games on the polo field of James Gordon Bennett, publisher of the New York Herald, at 110th Street and Fifth Avenue.

When the city fathers voted to cut a street through the property, just north of Central Park, Day went in search of another playing site. The team, now called the Giants—because Manager Jim Mutrie was heard to exclaim, "My big boys, my giants"—played some games at St. George on Staten Island and some in Jersey City before moving to Manhattan Field at the corner of Eighth Avenue and 155th Street in 1890.

In a larger stadium a few hundred feet north, the New York team of the Players League offered rugged competition to Day's club, stripped of many first-line players by the rival organization. But after one season the Players League collapsed and Day transferred the Giants into the rival club's park, christening it the New Polo Grounds.

When John T. Brush, an Indianapolis clothing tycoon, owned the club in the early years of the

20th century, efforts were made to change the park's name to Brush Stadium. The baseball public, however, would not accept the sacrilege and it remained the Polo Grounds thereafter.

The Polo Grounds was located in Coogan's Hollow, the last vestige of a farm granted by the King of England in the 17th century to John Lion Gardiner. The property became the Coogan estate when a Gardiner descendant married James J. Coogan, an upholsterer who was elected the first borough president in 1890.

The stadium of 1891 accommodated 16,000, with 5,500 seats in the grandstand.

Prior to the opening game in 1891, those Giants players who had jumped to the Players League the preceding year lined up with Buck Ewing along the left-field line. The loyal players, plus the rookies, lined up with pitcher Amos Rusie along the right-field line. On signal the two groups rushed together in a symbol of fraternalism.

Twenty years after that historic day, the 1911 Giants were out of town when a watchman at a tower of the elevated railroad that passed nearby noticed flames shooting skyward from the grandstands. He sounded the alarm, but it was too late to save anything but the bleachers.

Owner Brush, a victim of locomotor ataxia, surveyed the estimated $100,000 damage from his wheelchair the next morning. According to Joseph Durso in "The Days of Mr. McGraw," the

club owner "turned to his wife, a former actress, and said, 'Elsie, I want to build a concrete stadium, the finest that can be constructed. It will mean economy for a time. Are you willing to stand by me?'"

Elsie was agreeable and work commenced on the third steel and concrete stadium in the major leagues, following those in Philadelphia and Pittsburgh.

During construction, the Giants played their home games at Hilltop Park, home of the American League Highlanders, at the invitation of their owner, Frank Farrell.

By the latter part of June, 16,000 seats in the Polo Grounds were in position, but only 6,000 attended the first game. By World Series time, when the Giants met the Philadelphia Athletics, 34,000 seats were available, including 16,000 in the bleachers.

One of the new park's distinctive features was a series of coats of arms representing all the National League clubs on the summit of the grandstand. The cost of painting the ornaments was extremely high and they were removed during the Stoneham ownership in the 1920s.

With the disappearance of the carriage trade, there no longer was a need for an open outfield area where local swells and their ladies could park their vehicles to watch games, so the park was enclosed in 1923. Only the small bleachers in center field remained uncovered. The capacity now was 55,000.

The Polo Grounds gained undying fame as the

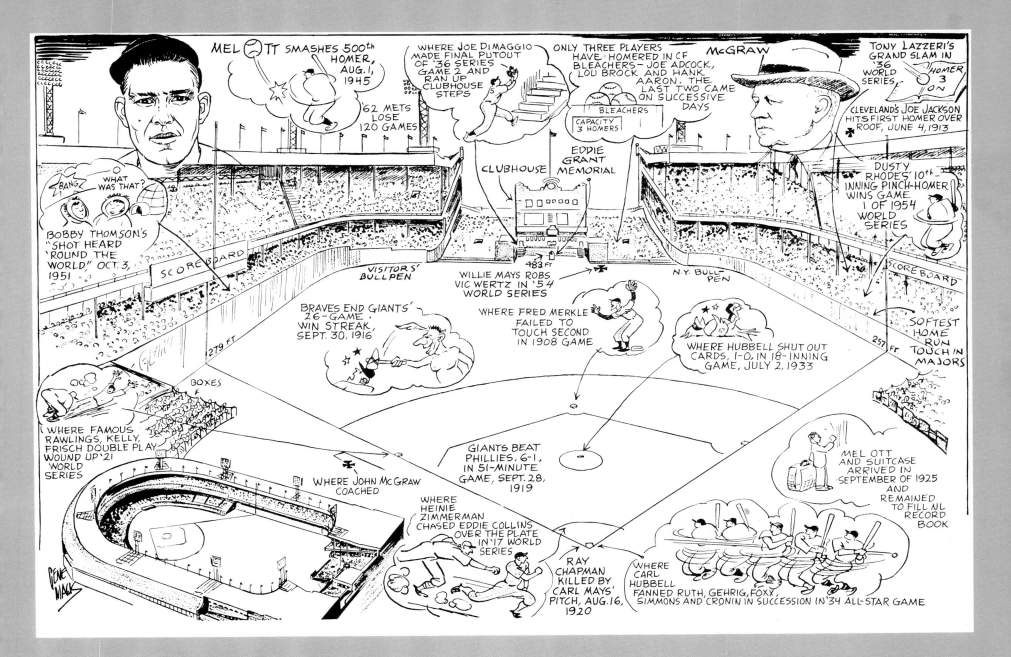

scene of one of baseball's most tumultuous incidents on September 23, 1908. The Giants and Cubs, running neck and neck in the pennant race, were tied, 1-1, in the last of the ninth inning with Harry McCormick running at third base and Fred Merkle at first.

When Al Bridwell singled to center field, McCormick crossed the plate and Merkle, after running part way to second base, swerved toward the Giants clubhouse in center field. Instantly, the crowd swarmed onto the field and writers started composing stories of the Giants' 2-1 victory.

Suddenly a commotion developed at second base. Johnny Evers was calling for a baseball. He got one, stepped on second base and appealed to umpire Hank O'Day to call Merkle out on a force play.

Evers maintained stoutly that the ball in his hand when he stepped on the base was the same one hit by Bridwell.

Another version was that Floyd Kroh, a Chicago benchwarmer, had thrown a ball to Evers.

According to the Giants, pitcher Joe McGinnity, sniffing mischief in Evers' gestures, intercepted the return throw from the outfield and heaved the ball to a fan who disappeared in the multitude.

In any event, the Cubs tossed the controversy to O'Day, a former pitcher and highly respected arbiter.

The issue remained unresolved until 10 o'clock that night when O'Day announced that Merkle was out and the game stood as a 1-1 tie.

John McGraw, short-fused manager of the Giants, was furious. "If Merkle was out," he bellowed, "the game was a tie. O'Day should have cleared the field and the game resumed. But he wasn't out and we won the game and they can't take it away from us."

But take it away they did. O'Day stood firm and league President Harry Pulliam upheld the umpire. When the teams finished the race in a first-place deadlock, it was necessary to play off the tie game. A coin was tossed to determine the site of the game. The Giants won.

The game was played on October 8 under conditions seldom witnessed in a major league ball park. Fans stormed the park, bursting through a section of the outfield wall. They threatened to overrun the field until brought under control by a powerful stream of water from a fire hose.

Inside, the Polo Grounds spectators bombarded Chicago players with cushions and bottles, hisses and catcalls.

When McGinnity walked to the plate to hit grounders to New York infielders, he was accosted by Frank Chance. The Chicago manager maintained that the Cubs had not had their allotted time for fielding practice.

The two exchanged punches, whereupon a fan ran from the stands and cuffed Chance on the back of his neck with a bottle.

Umpires for the crucial game were Jim Johnstone and Bill Klem, already highly regarded although still in the early years of his distinguished career.

Although Christy Mathewson reported that his

The turn-of-the-century Polo Grounds (pages 168-169) attracted a horse-and-buggy crowd. After a fire swept the grandstand in 1911, the ball park was rebuilt and became a steel and concrete structure.

Giants and Phillies players inspect the rubble from the Polo Grounds fire of 1911 (above). From the ashes came a new Polo Grounds (right), whose horseshoe shape was familiar to big leaguers as recently as 1963.

arm was virtually lifeless, McGraw had no choice but to start his 37-game winner. Chance nominated Jack (The Giant Killer) Pfiester, who had opposed Matty in the Merkle game.

Pfiester lasted only one-third of an inning, during which he hit a batter, issued two bases on balls and yielded a double to Mike Donlin. From that combination the Giants scored only one run, due principally to untidy baserunning.

Pfiester was replaced by Mordecai (Three Finger) Brown. The righthander allowed only four hits and one run the remainder of the game. A four-run outburst in the third inning was sufficient to give the Cubs a 4-2 victory and the pennant.

The mood of the crowd on October 8, 1908, contrasted dramatically with that of the 34,000 fans who dotted the Polo Grounds stands on October 3, 1951.

In the last six weeks of the regular season, the Giants had rushed from nowhere to overhaul the Brooklyn Dodgers and tie for the pennant. On this date the teams were in the last half of the ninth inning with the Dodgers leading, 4-1, and only three outs removed from the championship they had considered already won in mid-August.

But Alvin Dark ignited the last-gasp effort of the Giants with an infield single. Don Mueller singled to right field, sending Dark to third. Monte Irvin popped up in foul territory, and some of the wind gushed out of the Giants' sails.

But Whitey Lockman, the next batter, doubled into the left-field corner, scoring Dark and sending Mueller to third. Mueller sprained his ankle sliding into third base and was replaced by Clint Hartung.

Bobby Thomson was up next, but just as he was about to step into the box, Dodger Manager

Charley Dressen removed pitcher Don Newcombe and brought in Ralph Branca.

Branca's first pitch was a called strike. On the second pitch, Thomson belted the ball into the lower deck of the left-field stands to win the game and the pennant for the Giants, 5-4.

From 1913 through 1922, the Yankees shared the Polo Grounds with the Giants.

Fourteen World Series played the Polo Grounds stage, but there would have been a 15th if Giants management had willed it.

In 1904, one year after the Boston Red Sox defeated the Pittsburgh Pirates in the first modern World Series, the Giants won the National League pennant. The public clamored for a post-season series, but Owner Brush, still peeved that the American League had placed a franchise in

the city and noting that there was nothing in the National League constitution that said an N.L. club had to face the American League in postseason play, decided his club would not face the A.L. champion Red Sox.

In 1905, however, Brush took a more charitable view of the World Series. In fact, he wrote the rules regulating the inter-league championships.

The Giants, repeat winners in the N.L., opposed the Philadelphia Athletics in a Series that established a standard for pitching excellence that, in all probability, never will be equaled. Every game was a shutout.

Christy Mathewson won the opener at Philadelphia and Chief Bender returned the compliment at the Polo Grounds. Matty won again in Philadelphia, Joe McGinnity in New York and Mathewson, with only two days of rest, clinched the title at Columbia Park with a 2-0 victory.

The teams met again in 1911 and Brush, seeking to recreate the atmosphere of 1905, attired the Giants in black uniforms with white trim.

For one game, at least, Brush's gimmick appeared effective as Mathewson defeated Bender, 2-1, at the Polo Grounds. But the A's won at Shibe Park, 3-1, and then defeated Matty, 3-2 in 11 innings, at the Polo Grounds.

The teams were scheduled to meet in Philadelphia on October 18, but met only rain. It rained the next day and the day after that. Rain fell for six straight days as the players grew ever more restless.

At last the elements relented and, after burning gasoline on the water-soaked field, the teams resumed action on October 24. Matty drew the Giants' starting assignment, but Big Six was unequal to Bender, who muzzled the Giants, 4-2.

One loss from extinction, the Giants engi-

Bobby Thomson (above) of the New York Giants receives a hero's welcome in 1951 after hitting a pennant-winning home run against the Brooklyn Dodgers in the N.L. playoffs.

Gil McDougald connects for a grand slam (above) off the Giants'
Larry Jansen in Game 5 of the 1951 World Series. The drive into the
left-field stands helped the Yankees to a 13-1 victory.

neered a minor miracle in Game 5 by scoring two runs in the ninth and one in the 10th to win, 4-3. The Giants' victory was only a reprieve because Bender allowed only four hits the next day as the A's waltzed to a 13-2 title-clinching victory at Philadelphia.

The Giants repeated as N.L. champions in 1912 and this time they met Boston in the World Series.

The Giants lost the opener to 34-game winner Joe Wood, 4-3, then played a 6-6 tie halted by darkness after 11 innings in Boston.

Rube Marquard deadlocked the Series at one victory apiece by winning the third game, 2-1, after which the clubs alternated at winning two straight games each. The eighth contest, at Boston, was won by the Red Sox, 3-2, in 10 innings, aided by Fred Snodgrass' muff of a fly ball and a botched play by Chief Meyers and Fred Merkle, who permitted a pop foul to drop untouched.

The Giants made it again in 1913, but this time the A's brushed them off in five games.

McGraw produced his fourth pennant winner in seven years in 1917, but bitter defeat again awaited him in the World Series. The Giants lost the first two games against the White Sox in Chicago, then won the next two games in the Polo Grounds as Rube Benton and Schupp hurled shutouts.

The White Sox won the fifth game in Chicago before laying the Giants to rest in New York in a game remembered for Heinie Zimmerman's pursuit of Eddie Collins across home plate. Collins was trapped off third base on a tap to the mound, but broke past catcher Bill Rariden and outraced third baseman Zimmerman as neither the pitcher nor first baseman covered the plate. The final score was 4-2.

As the home park for the Giants and Yankees, the Polo Grounds was the setting for the first Subway Series in 1921. For 15 years McGraw had thirsted for a world championship and was thoroughly crushed when the Giants were shut out in the first two games by Carl Mays and Waite Hoyt. McGraw's misery was compounded by the knowledge that no team, after losing the first two games, had bounced back to win a Series.

But the Giants wrecked tradition in this, the last of the nine-game Series.

They won 13-5 and 4-2, then lost 3-1 to Hoyt before running off three victories.

The finale concluded in a most dramatic fashion. With Aaron Ward on first base as the result of a walk, Frank Baker drove an apparent single toward right field. But second baseman Johnny Rawlings dived for the ball, smothered it and, from a kneeling position, threw out Baker. Ward, hoping to catch the Giants napping, attempted to go to third base but was cut down on George Kelly's throw to Frank Frisch.

The 1922 Series was perhaps even more gratifying to McGraw as the Giants again defeated the Yankees, this time in five games, including a tie.

The Giants had informed the Yankees that their lease on the Polo Grounds would not be renewed after the 1922 season, so when both teams repeated as league champions in 1923, only three games were played at the Polo Grounds. The other three were contested in handsome Yankee Stadium, which Colonels Jacob Ruppert and Til Huston, the A.L. club's owners, had built across the Harlem River in the Bronx.

The Giants won the opener in Yankee Stadium, before 55,000. The deciding run in the 5-4 victory was an inside-the-park home run by Casey Stengel, who flopped across the plate before Yankee outfielders could retrieve his drive to left-center field.

Herb Pennock deadlocked the Series at the Polo Grounds, 4-2, but Art Nehf put the Giants in front again with a 1-0 triumph, made even sweeter by another Stengel homer.

But that was the end of the Giants' fun. The Yankees won the next three games and McGraw tasted the dregs of World Series defeat for the fifth time in eight tries.

A fourth consecutive pennant matched the Giants and the Washington Senators in the 1924 Series. Although the Giants won two of three encounters at the Polo Grounds, they lost three of four in Griffith Stadium.

Brooklyn Dodger players (above) file down the stairs from the clubhouse in dead center field at the Polo Grounds prior to a game against their arch rivals, the New York Giants.

With the 483-foot marker and clubhouse area nearby, Willie Mays hauls in Vic Wertz's long smash (above) in Game 1 of the 1954 World Series and prepares to wheel around and throw.

John McGraw had retired, succeeded by Bill Terry, when the Series returned to the Polo Grounds in 1933. After winning two games at home behind Carl Hubbell and Hal Schumacher, the Giants finished off the Senators in three games in the nation's capital to gain a measure of revenge for the setback of nine years earlier.

The Giants tried their luck against the Yankees again in 1936 and '37, but came away empty-handed both times.

A 14-year pennant drouth ended for the Giants in 1951 on the strength of Bobby Thomson's historic homer, but the scenario thereafter followed a familiar plot.

A split at Yankee Stadium was followed by Jim Hearn's 6-2 victory at the Polo Grounds. The Bronx Bombers swept the next three contests to annex their 14th world title.

The Polo Grounds was host for its final World Series in 1954, and even the most rabid fan could not have anticipated a more appropriate farewell. Their invited guests were the Cleveland Indians, winners of 111 American League games and boasting a pitching staff that included two 20-game winners, Bob Lemon and Early Wynn, and a 19-game winner, Mike Garcia.

Impressive credentials mattered not to the Giants. A three-run, 10th-inning homer by Dusty Rhodes produced a 5-2 first-game victory at the Polo Grounds, but equally as noteworthy as Rhodes' blow was a spectacular catch by Willie Mays. In the eighth inning, with two runners on base and no outs, Say Hey Willie raced to the center-field wall for an over-the-shoulder catch of Vic Wertz' 450-foot blast.

The second game also was a Dusty Rhodes special. Pinch-hitting for Monte Irvin in the fifth inning, Dusty singled to drive in one run. Two

innings later, he clouted his second homer of the Series off the facade in deep right field for the final run in a 3-1 victory.

The Giants concluded the Series in Cleveland, 6-2 and 7-4.

Three years after attaining world championship heights for the last time, the Giants bade farewell to New York. On September 29, 1957, they lost to the Pittsburgh Pirates, 9-1. As the last out was registered, the players raced for the clubhouse, turning the property over to the souvenir hunters and vandals.

In 1962, however, with National League base-ball returned to New York in the form of the Mets, the Polo Grounds enjoyed a baseball rebirth. A $250,000 rehabilitation restored the ancient park to playable condition until Shea Stadium could be readied in 1964.

For two seasons, Casey Stengel's "Amazin' Mets" fumbled and stumbled where the Giants of McGraw and Terry had performed with near flawlessness.

When the Mets also turned their back on the onetime home of heroes, the city's Board of Estimates voted to level the old sports palace to make way for 1,700 low-cost housing units.

The "headache ball" takes a swipe at the Polo Grounds (above) in April of 1964. Longtime home of the New York Giants, the ball park also was a home park for the Yankees and Mets.

After the 1973 season, Yankee Stadium was closed and given a $100 million facelift. The result (above left and right) was a more modern look. One change that startled fans was the relocation of the Babe Ruth, Lou Gehrig and Miller Huggins monuments, part of the center-field playing area for years, beyond the left-center field fence.

This panoramic view (above) of remodeled Yankee Stadium shows the park as the players and umpires might view it during the course of a game.

The Metrodome (above) in Minneapolis is the newest of the domed stadiums featuring an air-supported, fabric covering. Montreal's Olympic Stadium (below) was supposed to have a dome before the construction budget went out of control.

180

New York's Shea Stadium (above), home of the Yankees for two seasons during a Yankee Stadium renovation, has played host to two World Series in the 19-year tenancy of the Mets.

The Oakland Coliseum (above) played host to three straight World Series during the A's glory years in the early 1970s. Milwaukee's County Stadium (right) was scene of the 1982 Series, its first since the 1958 Milwaukee Braves won a pennant. A feature at County Stadium is Bernie Brewer (right, inset), who slides into the beer mug for every Milwaukee home run or victory.

SHEA STADIUM

New York

Officially, it is the William A. Shea Municipal Stadium. In its early years, it was known commonly as Shea Stadium. But in the stripped-down, hurry-up style of the 1970s, it became simply "Shea," the home of the New York Mets.

The 55,300-seat structure, adjacent to the World's Fair site of 1939-40 and 1964-65 in Flushing Meadow, was born in the civic humiliation of the late 1950s when the Giants and Dodgers abandoned New York for the promise of a bonanza in California.

While most baseball officials dismissed New York as a viable National League city, a position endorsed by many non-New Yorkers, Mayor Robert Wagner espoused a contrary viewpoint: New York should and must have National League baseball.

To achieve this end, Wagner appointed a five-man committee chaired by corporation lawyer William Alfred Shea to acquire an N.L. franchise for the city.

Shea directed his initial efforts toward attracting an established club, but was rejected by the Reds, Pirates and Phillies. Next, he organized in-

fluential groups in eight cities, including New York, and announced late in 1958 the formation of a third major baseball circuit, the Continental League, with elder statesman Branch Rickey as its president.

The threat of antitrust suits, together with the danger of player raids against established clubs, convinced the major leagues that perhaps New York did deserve a National League franchise after all. In 1960 N.L. owners met in Chicago to

discuss expansion and Bill Shea was there. On the eve of the meeting, Shea was beset by ugly rumors. The magnates, he heard, would not look favorably upon New York's candidacy unless there was official assurance that a new stadium would be constructed to house the new club. It was midnight in New York, but Shea dialed the Mayor's home and implored the awakened Wagner: "You've got to send a telegram to each owner promising that the city will build a new ball park."

On the strength of the Mayor's wire, the owners awarded a franchise to New York and to Houston, with play to start in 1962.

Ground for the new park, originally called Flushing Meadow Park, was broken on October 28, 1961. Of circular design, the new facility was located on Grand Central Parkway and situated in the middle of a parking area accommodating 10,000 cars.

Late in 1962 a movement took root in New York to name the stadium in honor of Bill Shea. Conceived by the owner of a chain of Army and Navy stores, the suggestion gained quick support. One of the most energetic backers was merchant

Casey Stengel was forced to quit as manager of the Mets after being hurt in a car accident in July of 1965. Later that season he waved goodbye to Shea Stadium (above).

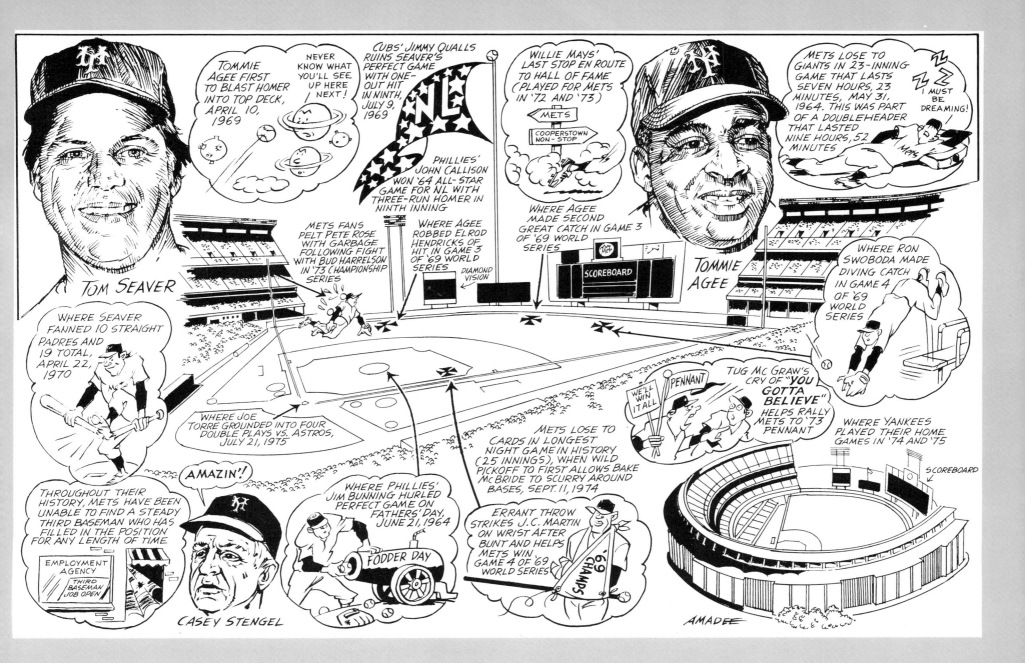

prince Bernard Gimbel, a member of the Mayor's original five-man committee, who said, "Without Bill Shea, whose enthusiasm was responsible for the support of newspapers, sportswriters and fans, there would have been no new Met Stadium. It would seem that his efforts should be recognized in this entirely fitting manner."

In this fashion, a corporation lawyer, a native of the Washington Heights section of Manhattan, and a graduate of the Georgetown University Law School gave his name to a sports stadium.

By the spring of 1964, New York was ready for its first glimpse of the new structure. So were the Mets, who for two years had bumbled their way to a composite 91 victories and 231 defeats while making their home at the antiquated Polo Grounds, discarded home of the Giants.

According to Parks Commissioner Newbold Morris, Shea Stadium was "the first of its size to have such an extensive escalator system carrying patrons to every seating level. It is the first capable of being converted from a football gridiron to a baseball diamond and back by means of two motor-operated stands, movable by underground tracks. It is the first in which every seat in the permanently fixed stands is directed at the center of the field, and not a single column obstructs the spectator's view."

Moreover, the park contained a 1,500-seat restaurant, 20 snack bars and 54 public rest rooms, plus an electronic scoreboard 86 feet high and 175 feet long.

The playing field dimensions were 341 feet on the foul lines and 410 feet to center field.

Opening day for the $28.5 million park was April 17, 1964. It was a memorable day, not so much for the fact the Mets bowed to the Pirates, 4-3, as it was for the monumental traffic snarl resulting from 3,000 commuter automobiles being parked on the stadium lot early in the day. Roads leading to the park were congested. Disgruntled motorists parked their cars where they could and found their way to the stadium by the best means available. When they returned to their cars, they found $15 traffic violation tickets affixed to their windshields.

Those who arrived in the five-tier stadium in time for pregame ceremonies cheered old-time favorites Bill Terry, Frank Frisch, Zack Wheat and Max Carey and the most recent Hall of Fame inductees Red Faber, Heinie Manush, Burleigh

After the Mets won the 1969 World Series, fans frolicked amid the players (above left). Later, Tom Seaver (41) and Gary Gentry (39) surveyed the damage (above right) of the wild celebration.

a walk to Willie Mays, a stolen base and Orlando Cepeda's single tied the score. And a few minutes later, Johnny Callison of the Phillies crashed a three-run homer off Dick Radatz to give the N.L. a 7-4 victory and even the midsummer series at 17 wins apiece, with one tie.

Sudol had a third memorable caper at Shea in that inaugural season. On May 31, after the Giants defeated the Mets in the first game of a doubleheader, Sudol started calling balls and strikes in the nightcap. For seven hours and 23 minutes, he called 'em until, after the Giants' 23-inning, 8-6 victory, he shuffled wearily to the dressing room.

At the start of the nine-hour and 52-minute marathon, 57,037 spectators were jammed into the park. When the last out was registered at 11:25 p.m., only about 5,000 remained.

But those diehards had plenty to remember. They saw Willie Mays play shortstop for three innings and Mets shortstop Roy McMillan start a triple play.

On September 11, 1974, Sudol was behind the plate once more when Lou Brock stepped into the batter's box to lead off a Cardinals-Mets night game. Sudol did not remove his chest protector until 3:12 a.m., after a 25-inning, 4-3 St. Louis victory.

An infield single by Bake McBride, an errant pickoff throw by Hank Webb and an error by catcher Ron Hodges on first baseman John Milner's throw to the plate permitted the Cardinal speedster to score the deciding run.

Two of Tom Seaver's more notable pitching performances were registered at Shea within a nine-month period across two seasons.

On July 9, 1969, the Mets righthander retired 25 consecutive Chicago batters until Jimmy

Grimes and Luke Appling.

Because of a dispute between telephone and electrical workers, reporters covering the game operated in a vacuum. Press copy was transported by runners to the World's Fair press center for transmission.

When the 1964 Mets drew more than 1,700,000 customers, plans were announced to add 15,000 seats and to cover the stadium with a $6 million dome.

"Shea Stadium is now booked approximately 100 days a year," reported Ben Finney, city sports commissioner. "Covered, there is no reason not to expect that Shea can triple its bookings. New York has long needed a convention auditorium."

Among the voices in opposition to a permanent dome was that of Bill Shea. "I think New York fans are entitled to fresh air, certainly on Saturday and Sunday afternoons and nice nights," declared Shea.

The entire project came to naught when a feasibility study determined that stadium pilings were inadequate for the added weight of a dome.

Jim Bunning accounted for the first landmark event in Shea Stadium. On Fathers Day, June 21, 1964, the Philadelphia righthander, a sire of six children, pitched a perfect game against the Mets, winning 6-0.

Ed Sudol was the plate umpire for Bunning's masterpiece, and he was at the same spot less than three weeks later at the start of the 35th All-Star Game. In that contest, the N.L. trailed, 4-3, entering the last half of the ninth inning. But

In a scene not unfamiliar at Shea Stadium, jubilant fans stormed the field (above) after the Mets had defeated the Cincinnati Reds and won the 1973 National League pennant.

Qualls, a .250 hitter, singled with one out in the ninth inning.

On April 22, 1970, Seaver was even more impressive as he tied Steve Carlton's record of 19 strikeouts in a game and established a major league mark by fanning 10 successive San Diego batters.

Seaver started the record streak by whiffing Al Ferrara for the final out of the sixth inning. Nate Colbert, Dave Campbell and Jerry Morales fanned in the seventh inning, Bob Barton, Ramon Webster and Ivan Murrell in the eighth and Van Kelly, Clarence Gaston and Ferrara in the ninth.

Seaver's achievement threw 14,000 spectators into ecstasy, but it was hardly equal to that which prevailed in October of 1969. The Mets, who had beaten the Atlanta Braves in the first League Championship Series, three games to

none, entered the World Series as a decided underdog against the Baltimore Orioles. The A.L. champions, battle-tested in the 1966 Series sweep over the Dodgers, won the opening game at Baltimore, 4-1, behind Mike Cuellar. They then lost the second contest, 2-1, to Jerry Koosman.

Then it happened!

Leading off the home half of the first inning in Game 3 at Shea Stadium, Tommy Agee homered over the center-field fence against Jim Palmer.

In the fourth inning, with two Baltimore runners on base, Agee raced from right-center field to the 396-foot mark in center field to make a fingertip catch of Elrod Hendricks' long drive.

In the seventh inning, Agee made a diving catch of Paul Blair's liner to right-center. With his home run and his dazzling defense, Agee made a difference of six runs in the Mets' 5-0 victory.

The fourth game belonged to Seaver, Ron Swoboda and controversy.

In the third inning, Earl Weaver of the Orioles was ejected for disputing ball-and-strike decisions. He thereby joined Frank Chance of the 1910 Cubs and Charley Grimm of the 1935 Cubs as the only managers ever to be banished from a World Series game.

Seaver blanked the Birds on three hits until the ninth inning, when Frank Robinson and Boog Powell singled. Brooks Robinson's screamer to right-center field appeared certain to fall in safely, but Swoboda, neither a gazelle nor a defensive giant, made a diving catch of the ball.

With the score deadlocked, 1-1, in the last of the 10th inning, controversy took over. Runners were on first and second base when pinch-hitter J.C. Martin bunted down the first-base line. Pitcher Pete Richert's throw toward first struck Martin on the left wrist. As the ball rolled free, the winning run crossed the plate.

The Orioles protested that Martin had run out of the baseline and was guilty of interference. N.L. umpire Shag Crawford disagreed, explaining, "As I saw it, Martin had one foot (presumably the right one) on the baseline when he was struck by the ball."

The Mets had a few more tricks remaining for the fifth game, including the shoe polish strategy that the Milwaukee Braves had employed so successfully in the 1957 Series.

In the sixth inning, Cleon Jones, who had only two hits up to that time, leaped from the path of a low pitch. Umpire Lou DiMuro turned a deaf ear to Jones' squawk that he had been struck on the foot. Then, Mets Manager Gil Hodges retrieved the baseball and displayed a black shoe polish smudge. Jones was awarded first base and scored

When there's a full house at New York's Shea Stadium, inventive fans have been known to stand atop buses (above) parked beyond the left-field bullpen.

188

when Donn Clendenon smacked his third Series homer, cutting the Baltimore lead to 3-2.

In the seventh inning, Al Weis, a light-hitting second baseman who would bat .455 in this classic, belted a game-tying, 371-foot home run. The round-tripper was Weis' first in his five years at Shea Stadium.

Doubles by Jones and Swoboda and a pair of errors on Jerry Grote's grounder produced two more runs in the eighth and a 5-3 Mets win.

The Mets repeated as kingpins of the National League East in 1973 and participated in one of the most bizarre episodes in the League Championship Series against Cincinnati.

In the third game, Pete Rose slid hard into second base trying to break up a double play. Shortstop Bud Harrelson made his throw to first base, then wrestled with Rose on the ground as both benches emptied. After the combatants were pulled apart, Rose trotted to his position in left field, where he was greeted by a shower of over-ripe produce.

Pleas from the public address announcer failed to halt the barrage. It wasn't until Mets Manager Yogi Berra, Tom Seaver, Willie Mays, Rusty Staub and Cleon Jones, at the request of League President Chub Feeney, strolled to the outfield and made personal entreaties, that the mischief ceased.

The Mets captured two of the three World Series games at Shea Stadium and led the A's, three games to two, when the tournament switched back to Oakland for the final two contests.

However, pitcher Tug McGraw's popular battle cry of "You gotta believe," lost its magic in the Oakland Alameda County Coliseum. The A's triumphed, 3-1 and 5-2, to repeat as world champions.

Shea Stadium (above), whose parking area can accommodate 10,000 cars, became the Mets' home in 1964 after the N.L. club played its first two seasons at the Polo Grounds.

YANKEE STADIUM
New York

Babe Ruth hit his 60th home run here and Roger Maris broke that record here with his 61st.

Lou Gehrig played the first of his 2,130 consecutive games in the South Bronx arena in 1925 and, terminally ill, bade an affectionate farewell to 61,808 misty-eyed spectators on July 4, 1939.

Don Larsen pitched the first and only perfect game in World Series history here in 1956, and Joe DiMaggio launched his record 56-game hitting streak here in 1941.

Ninety-one World Series games have been contested on this plot between 157th and 161st streets on River Avenue.

More prose has been inspired by what happened here, more spirits crushed and more emotions stirred than at any other major league ball park.

This is Yankee Stadium, The House That Ruth Built, The Home of Champions—33 in the American League and 22 in all of baseball.

Yankee Stadium was dedicated in 1923, in the club's 21st season.

American League baseball arrived in New York in 1903 when a couple of bartenders, Frank Far-

rell and Big Bill Devery, purchased the Baltimore franchise for $18,000. They established the team at Hilltop Park, a hastily constructed wooden park seating about 15,000 on Broadway between 165th and 168th streets.

Because the park was situated on high ground, it was christened Hilltop Park. The team was known as the Highlanders, partly because of the location of the playing field and partly because the name of club president Joseph W. Gordon

reminded some folks of a famed unit of the British Army, the Gordon Highlanders.

With a band playing patriotic songs, the Highlanders made their Hilltop debut on May 1, 1903, defeating Washington, 6-2. Jack Chesbro took the pitching honors and Willie Keeler contributed two doubles, two walks and three runs and nearly tumbled to the ground while chasing a fly ball.

The Highlanders barely missed a pennant in 1904. Entering the final day of the season, the New Yorkers trailed Boston by one game and needed a doubleheader sweep over the New Englanders to clinch the flag.

The spectators overflowed the stands and stood 12 deep in the outfield. Some reports listed the throng as 20,000, whose high anticipations turned to gloom in the ninth inning of the first game when Chesbro, a 41-game winner, uncorked a wild pitch that permitted the deciding run to cross the plate in a 3-2 Boston victory.

Walter Johnson's most spectacular pitching performance took place at Hilltop Park.

The fireballing Washington righthander, in his

Hilltop Park, pictured (above) in 1912 with Detroit's Ty Cobb at bat, was the hastily constructed home of the New York Highlanders from 1903 to 1913.

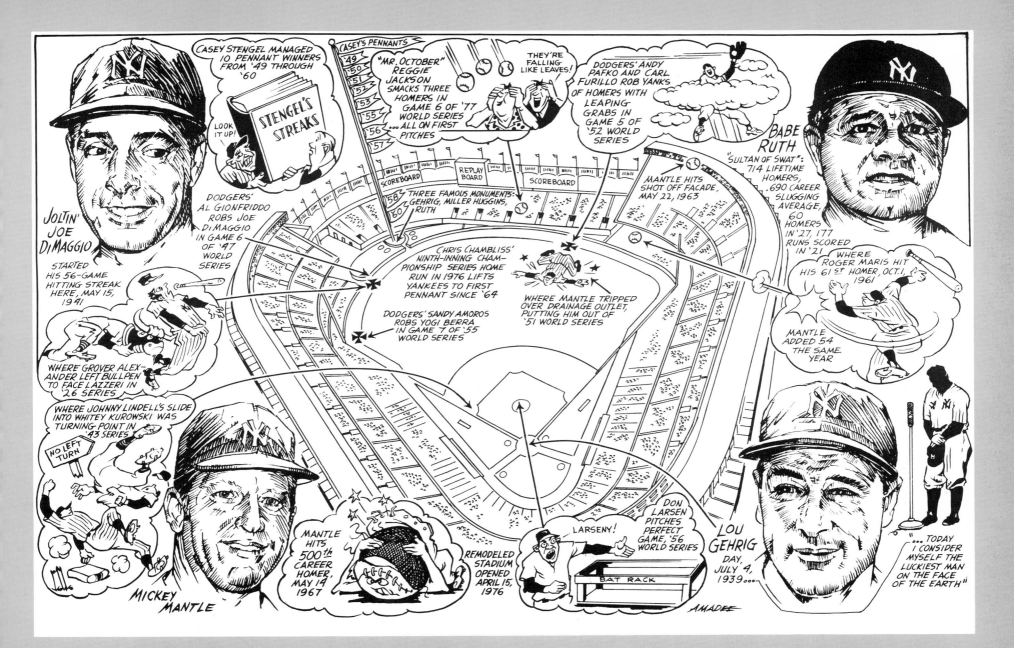

second major league season, shut out the High-landers, 3-0, with a five-hitter on September 4, 1908. The next day, a Saturday, the 20-year-old farm boy blanked the home club, 6-0, on a three-hitter.

Johnson rested on Sunday in obedience to the city's blue law. A reporter for the Washington Post wrote: "It seems that some of the players are talking about pitching feats and that no pitcher can win three shutouts in a row. Others said Walter Johnson could do it. They asked Johnson

and he said in the quiet way characteristic of him, 'I think I could do it.' "

On Monday, September 7, Washington was scheduled to play a holiday doubleheader in New York. Johnson was playing catch with battery-mate Gabby Street when he noticed that he was the only pitcher warming up.

A glance toward Manager Joe Cantillon drew an assenting nod and the Big Train accepted the challenge. Again he improved upon his previous performance, hurling a two-hit, 4-0 victory, his

third shutout in the space of four days.

The most serious black mark on Ty Cobb's illustrious career occurred at Hilltop Park on May 15, 1912. Heckled for several innings by a leather-lunged press agent, the Detroit outfielder leaped the fence and attacked his tormentor. Cobb was suspended indefinitely by A.L. President Ban Johnson.

The next day, a Thursday, was an open date and on Friday, May 17, the Tigers defeated the Athletics in Philadelphia, 6-3.

When the Yankees received notice of eviction from the Polo Grounds in 1921, they settled on a location at River Avenue between 157th and 161st streets for their new park, pictured in the above drawing.

In the meantime, however, the Detroit players had voted to strike on Saturday unless Cobb was reinstated. Faced with the option of fielding a team—any team—or paying a $5,000 forfeit fee, Detroit management recruited a team of Philadelphia semipro players which lost to the A's, 24-2, on May 18. The Detroit players yielded to Johnson's threats of extreme penalties a few days later and Cobb returned after a 10-day suspension and a $50 fine. The striking Tigers were fined $100 apiece.

In 1913, Farrell and Devery accepted an invitation from the Giants to share the Polo Grounds as their home park. By this time, the Highlanders had a new name as well. Sports editors, weary of attempts to fit "Highlanders" into headlines, had started to call the team the Yankees. Yankees they were to remain for many distinguished decades.

The Yankees remained in the big Harlem horseshoe for 10 years. The first indications of discontent between the Giants and Yankees surfaced in

1921. With Babe Ruth socking home runs ever more frequently, the Yankees set a major league record in 1920 by drawing 1,289,422 into the Polo Grounds, 350,000 more than the landlord Giants attracted.

Irritated at being relegated to a subordinate role, Giants Manager John McGraw told Owner Charles Stoneham, "The Yankees will have to build a park in Queens or some other out of the way place and wither on the vine."

The eviction notice was delivered that same

By 1925, methods of transportation had improved and the Yankees were attracting large crowds to their relatively new stadium, thanks largely to the exploits of such stars as Babe Ruth and Lou Gehrig.

year to Colonels Jacob Ruppert and Tillinghast Huston, who had bought the Yankees on January 11, 1915, from Farrell and Devery for $460,000. Ruppert and Huston started to search for a suitable ball park location. They settled on a 10-acre plot across the Harlem River, less than a mile from the Polo Grounds, which they purchased from William Waldorf Astor for $600,000.

In his book "Yankee Stadium," Joseph Durso recounts the role of the White Construction Company, taken from the corporate archives, in the building of Yankee Stadium:

"This is the story—briefly told—of the construction of the largest baseball stadium in America.

"It is about the building in twelve months of a three-deck, reinforced-concrete and structural steel grandstand and over 40,000 square feet of wooden bleachers for the American League Base Ball Club of New York, Inc., more familiarly known as the Yankees."

In 185 working days the structure was completed. When the gates were opened for the inaugural contest at noon on April 18, 1923, only 500 persons awaited entrance. But two hours later, the park was packed. The gates were closed as an estimated 20,000 swarmed about outside crying for admittance.

John Philip Sousa and the Seventh Regiment Band led the procession to the center-field flagpole for the raising of the 1922 pennant. Ruppert, Huston and the players of the New York and Boston clubs walked awkwardly behind. Governor Al Smith tossed the ceremonial first ball to Wally Schang, the Yankee catcher, who threw it to Bob Shawkey on the pitching mound. First baseman George Burns of the Red Sox rapped the first hit in the new park, a second-inning single, and Babe

Ruth clouted the first home run with customary flair in the third inning.

The Bambino, who had been held in check in the 1922 World Series by Giant pitchers throwing slow curves, slammed the same type of pitch from Howard Ehmke 10 rows deep into the right-field bleachers to feature a 4-1 Yankee victory.

The crowd, a record for the time, was announced as 74,000, although the Yankees subsequently confessed that the figure was inflated. It was closer to 60,000.

Originally, the foul line measurements in the $2 million stadium were 296 feet to right field and 301 to left. The deepest point of the park

from home plate was in left-center field, 461 feet away.

When the Stadium was rebuilt in 1974-75, during which period the Yankees played their home games at Shea Stadium, the distances were changed to 310 feet to right, 312 to left and 430 to left-center.

While Babe Ruth swatted the first home run in Yankee Stadium, another round-tripper by another outfielder who would leave his imprint on the club's history drew perhaps as much attention near the close of the 1923 campaign.

In the ninth inning of the first World Series game, Casey Stengel of the Giants sliced a drive

One of many unforgettable moments in Yankee Stadium history occurred on July 4, 1939, when terminally ill Lou Gehrig bade an affectionate farewell (above) to 61,808 misty-eyed fans.

between center fielder Whitey Witt and left fielder Bob Meusel. Describing Casey's tour of the bases, Damon Runyon wrote in the New York American:

"His arms flying back and forth like those of a man swimming with a crawl stroke.

"His flanks heaving, his breath whistling, his head far back. Yankee infielders (who were) passed by old Casey Stengel as he was running his home run home say Casey was muttering to himself, adjuring himself to greater speed as a jockey mutters to his horse, saying, 'Go on, Casey, go on.'

"The warped old legs, twisted and bent by many a year of baseball campaigning, just barely held out under Casey until he reached the plate, running his home run home.

"Then they collapsed."

The home run by Casey, 34 at the time, produced a 5-4 Giants victory, but the Yankees won the world championship, their first, in six games.

The Yankees first baseman for that historic event, as he had been for a number of years, was Wally Pipp. On June 2, 1925, Manager Miller Huggins suggested that Pipp take the day off so that an ex-Columbia University slugger up from Hartford of the Eastern League could get in some playing time. The solidly built 21-year-old was Lou Gehrig, who had pinch-hit the day before. Gehrig

remained the Yankees' first baseman for 14 years. Amyotrophic lateral sclerosis ended his streak abruptly in May 1939, but the Iron Horse remained in uniform as the non-playing captain through the season. On July 4, 1939, in one of baseball's most emotional and unforgettable moments, Gehrig assured 61,808 fans that, "Today I consider myself the luckiest man on the face of the earth." Two years later he was dead.

On June 13, 1948, a day designated as "Babe Ruth Day" the erstwhile Sultan of Swat, emaciated by the ravages of cancer, waved his farewell to 49,641 fans.

A few weeks before Gehrig's death a new Yankee hero, Joe DiMaggio, rapped a single against southpaw Eddie Smith of Chicago. It was the meager beginning of the longest consecutive-game hitting streak by a major leaguer. DiMag was not stopped until the Yankees played in Cleveland 56 games later.

Tom Zachary, a Washington lefthander, and Tracy Stallard, a Boston righthander, earned undying notoriety among trivia devotees 34 years apart for yielding record-shattering home runs in the South Bronx park.

On September 30, 1927, Babe Ruth smashed a Zachary pitch into the right-field seats for his 60th home run of the season, breaking his own record set in 1921.

On October 1, 1961, Roger Maris rang down the curtain on the season, as well as on Ruth's one-season record, by blasting a Stallard pitch for his 61st home run into the right-field stands.

Other Stadium homers of more than passing note were Mickey Mantle's 500th on May 14, 1967; Chris Chambliss' smash that won the League Championship Series over Kansas City in 1976, and Reggie Jackson's record-tying three cir-

Babe Ruth, emaciated by the ravages of cancer, makes his farewell address (above) to 49,641 loyal fans on June 13, 1948, at a Yankee Stadium tribute designated as "Babe Ruth Day."

cuit clouts that sparked the Yankees' 8-4 victory in the sixth and final game of the 1977 World Series against the Dodgers.

While no baseball ever has been driven out of Yankee Stadium, there was one wallop that came closer than any other to gaining that distinction.

On May 22, 1963, Mickey Mantle propelled a pitch thrown by Bill Fischer of Kansas City against the third deck facade in right field. The ball struck at a point 109 feet above the playing field and 374 feet from home plate. It had, an engineer estimated, the potential of a 620-foot clout.

In 11 World Series against the Dodgers, the Yankees have lost only three times (1955, 1963 and 1981). But extraordinary plays by the Dodgers are sprinkled throughout the contests.

Al Gionfriddo raced to the left-field exit gate to deprive Joe DiMaggio of an extra-base hit in the sixth game of the 1947 Series. Andy Pafko and Carl Furillo made leaping, home run-saving grabs in 1952, but none of these catches materially affected the outcome of the Series like that of Sandy Amoros in the sixth inning of the deciding game of the '55 classic.

Amoros sprinted from his spot in left-center field to overhaul a drive by Yogi Berra just inside the left-field foul line. He then threw accurately to Pee Wee Reese, who relayed to Gil Hodges to double up Gil McDougald at first base. Had it not been for that play, the Yankees would have scored two runs. As it was, Johnny Podres blanked the Yankees, 2-0, to give the Dodgers their first world championship.

Pitching achievements have attained dramatic dimensions at Yankee Stadium. One of the most emotional episodes was enacted on Sunday, October 10, 1926.

Grover Cleveland Alexander, a 39-year-old winner of the second and sixth World Series games, shuffled in from the St. Louis bullpen with two outs in the seventh inning and the bases full of Yankees.

Clearly showing the effects of a late-hour celebration the night before, Old Alex faced Tony Lazzeri, tied for second behind only Babe Ruth in the American League RBI department. The rookie slugger took one pitch, high and outside. He looked at a called strike, and then smashed a vicious liner to left field, foul by only a few feet. With the crowd watching in hushed anticipation, Lazzeri struck out on the fourth pitch.

Alexander pitched 2⅓ hitless innings and walked only one batter, Babe Ruth, with two outs in the ninth inning. Babe was cut down trying to steal in what was generally regarded as the only imprudent maneuver in his illustrious career.

In the third game of the 1927 World Series, Herb Pennock retired the first 22 Pittsburgh batters before Pie Traynor rapped a single. The Pirates reached the lefthander for a total of three hits, but he breezed to an 8-1 triumph.

Lazzeri was at bat again with the bases loaded and two outs in the ninth inning of the fourth game of the 1927 Series with the score tied, 3-3. Lou Gehrig and Bob Meusel had just been struck out by Johnny Miljus. Lazzeri did not strike out this time. He watched a wild pitch skip by catcher Johnny Gooch as Earle Combs pranced home with the Series-winning run.

Of the more than 450 World Series games ever played, none electrified the nation like that of Monday, October 8, 1956. The Yankees and Dodgers were knotted at two wins apiece in another autumn classic when Don Larsen pitched a flawless game, retiring 27 consecutive batters in

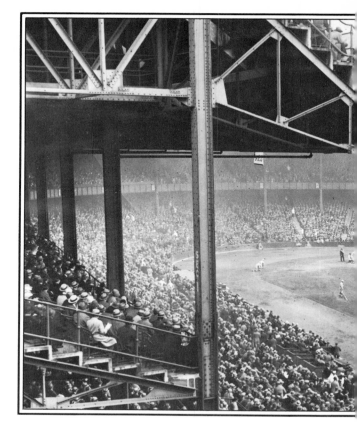

posting a 2-0 win.

Brooklyn righthander Sal Maglie allowed only five hits, but one was a fourth-inning homer by Mickey Mantle. Larsen pitched three balls to only one batter, Pee Wee Reese in the first inning, fanned seven and was aided by a spectacular catch by Mantle, who raced far into left-center field to make a backhand catch of a Gil Hodges liner in the fifth inning.

After 96 pitches, Larsen had two strikes on pinch-hitter Dale Mitchell with two outs in the ninth inning. The pitcher seemed to take an unu-

A view from the right-field bleachers at Yankee Stadium (above) shows the Yankees and Cardinals during action in the 1926 World Series. The overview (right) shows a closeup of Yankee Stadium in the 1940s with the Polo Grounds in the background, just across the Harlem River.

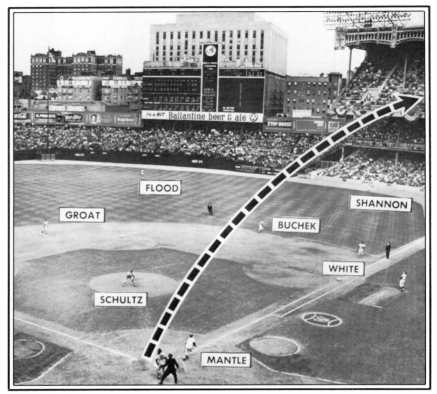

sually long time before delivering the next pitch, and later conceded that he would have preferred not to throw the ball, ever.

Eventually, of course, he did. The pitch seemed wide of the strike zone, and Mitchell watched it go by. But umpire Babe Pinelli's arm shot outward. It was strike three, Mitchell was out and Pinelli was off and running for the umpires' dressing room. It was the last pitch Pinelli ever called. He retired at the end of the Series.

The House That Ruth Built underwent a $600,000 renovation before the 1946 season. Among the improvements were arc lights that, it

was said, would provide illumination to equal that of 5,000 full moons.

After the 1973 season, the city of New York undertook a mammoth $100 million facelift on the 50-year-old park and surrounding area. While the Yankees played their home games at Shea Stadium for two seasons, their home park was dissected. Escalators and elevators eliminated coronary-inducing climbs to the third level, pillars were removed, wider seats were installed and roads leading to the Stadium were improved.

As a result of the wider seats, the Stadium capacity, once as high as 80,000, stood at

57,545.

The Yankees rededicated the park on April 15, 1976, by whipping the Minnesota Twins, 11-4, before 52,613. Bob Shawkey, who hurled the first game in the Stadium 53 years earlier, was the principal guest of honor on the historic event.

The Yankees won the pennant in 1976, their first in 12 years. However, they bowed to the Cincinnati Reds in four straight games in the World Series.

Four American League pennants followed in the next six seasons and two world championships, over the Dodgers in 1977 and '78.

The Yankee Stadium scoreboard told the story (above left) as Don Larsen reached perfection in the 1956 World Series. Mickey Mantle's third-deck homer (above right) ended Game 3 of the '64 Series.

A modernized Yankee Stadium was the scene (above) as fans celebrated after New York had defeated Milwaukee in the strike-forced
1981 East Division playoff series.

OAKLAND COLISEUM

A major league ball park that opened without a comprehensive scoreboard, a park in which a mule often attracted more attention than high-salaried athletes, and where controversy frequently created bolder headlines than victories and defeats could only be the Oakland-Alameda County Coliseum.

For years during the Charles O. Finley "reign of terror," the Oakland Coliseum ruled supreme as a journalist's delight, from which flowed a ready supply of bizarre events.

But Oakland's relatively late emergence as a baseball center may have been nothing more than compensation for the obscurity in which the city existed as the poor relation of colorful, vibrant, storied San Francisco across the bay.

Oakland boasted a franchise in the outlaw California League before the turn of the century. And it was a member of the new Pacific Coast League in 1903, organized by legendary J. Cal Ewing, a dynamic force in the PCL for a quarter of a century.

Three years later, when San Francisco was

wiped out by an earthquake and fire, the Oakland club invited its neighbor to share its ball park, thereby saving the San Francisco Seals as well as the league.

For years after the San Francisco park was rebuilt, the Oakland Oaks played most of their games in that stadium, performing on their own field only on Thursday afternoons and Sunday mornings.

In that era both the Seals and Oaks were controlled by Ewing, who continued in the dual role until the advent of Commissioner Kenesaw M. Landis. Ewing then divested himself of his San Francisco holdings.

In 1912, while sharing the San Francisco park, the Oaks won their first pennant, edging out Vernon by four percentage points.

To capitalize on the enthusiasm generated by the championship, Ewing built a new park in Emeryville, a small municipality between Oakland and Berkeley, in 1913. The park was built on a seven-acre plot leased from Key System, the area's public transportation company. In the prosperous days of the 1920s, Ewing purchased the land from Key System and the Oaks started to play all their home games at Emeryville.

The park was the scene of a unique occurrence on July 21, 1923, when the first and last pitches of a game resulted in home runs. Red Murphy hit

The forerunner of the major league Oakland Coliseum was Oaks Park (above), also known as Emeryville Park. By 1956, the former home of the PCL Oaks (below) was nearing its date with the wrecking crew.

201

Ray Kremer's first delivery for a round-tripper and in the ninth inning, Kremer, later a mainstay of the Pittsburgh staff, homered for a 4-3 Oakland victory over Vernon.

The Oaks won their first pennant as a fully based Oakland club in 1927. The following year Ewing sold the club to Victor (Cookie) Devincenzi and Robert Miller, former owners of a cab company, for $75,000.

In 1932, although nearly 20 years old, Emeryville Park was still rated by Bill Lane as the finest in the Pacific Coast League.

Although other parks were more modern, the Hollywood club owner maintained that the Oaks' park was designed for the fans. With outfield stands and bleachers curved toward the field, Lane said, there wasn't a bad seat in the park.

In the depths of the Depression, Miller sold his holdings to Devincenzi, declaring, "All the meat is gone from the bone." But his old partner, aided by the installation of arc lights, survived the hard times until, in 1943, he sold the Oaks to Brick Laws and Joe Blumenfield.

At the conclusion of World War II, Laws and Blumenfield launched a $250,000 renovation program. Among the improvements were: a new entrance, new office, new lighting system, new stands in right field and along the third-base foul line, new bleachers in center field and four new locker rooms, including two for semi-pro teams who used the facilities when the Oaks were on the road. The bleachers were elevated 10 feet so that batters would not be required to look into a white shirt background.

There also was a washing machine in the clubhouse. "If you want players to look neat on the field, you have to start from inside out," said trainer Red Adams in welcoming the revolutionary addition.

Adams lodged only one complaint against the changes: The knothole that "provided me with the best seat in the house," had been eliminated by modernization.

Emeryville Park enjoyed its finest season in 1948 when 550,000 filed through the turnstiles to watch the "Nine Old Men" win the PCL championship under Casey Stengel.

The team, averaging 34 years of age, consisted of first baseman Nick Etten, second baseman Dario Lodigiani, shortstop Merrill Combs, third baseman Cookie Lavagetto, left fielder Brooks Holder, center fielder George Metkovich, right fielder Les Scarsella, catcher Ernie Lombardi and pitcher Jim Tobin.

By this time the park was in its 36th season, and starting to deteriorate. Lombardi once remembered that, "every time a ball hit the left-field fence, the boards fell down."

Despite its rundown condition, the park's hominess, "made it intimate, with fans as nice as you'd want to see," according to another player.

The Oaks won their last pennant in 1950, and by 1955 the park was in such a bad state of disrepair that the cost of renovation was prohibitive. Moreover, attendance had fallen to 141,397. When Vancouver officials offered the use of a modern stadium, Brick Laws moved the club to British Columbia, where it became the Mounties.

A watchman was hired to guard Emeryville Park in 1956, and the field was plowed under before the grass became a fire hazard. In the spring of 1957, the old field at San Pablo and Park Avenue fell before the wrecking crew. The site is now occupied by a soft drink bottling company.

For 11 years Oakland fans were required to travel to San Francisco to watch professional baseball. They first saw the San Francisco Seals of the PCL and then, starting in 1958, the National League Giants who had been transferred from New York.

Oakland's personalized brand of baseball returned in 1968 when Charles O. Finley shifted the Kansas City A's to the Oakland-Alameda County Coliseum, touching off an era unmatched in baseball.

The new stadium, 15 miles from Emeryville, was two years old when the A's arrived. Located at Nimitz Freeway and Hegenberger Road in the southern section of Oakland, the Coliseum seats 50,219. The foul lines measure 330 feet, the power alleys 375 feet and the center-field fence 400 feet. An eight-foot high wall encloses the outfield.

After winning three of their first five games on the road, the A's made their Oakland debut on April 17, 1968. In the throng of 50,164 was Governor Ronald Reagan. The future president threw out the first ball and, just two days after the income tax deadline, drew a round of boos when he told the spectators, "One thing I'm sure of is that a lot of you paid your taxes." When the roar subsided, he added, "Up to a few moments ago, I was happy to be here."

Charlie O., the A's mule mascot, made a grand entrance in his luxury van, after which he walked around the diamond, stopping at each base to deliver what passed for a bow.

Tennessee Ernie Ford and the University of California marching band were scheduled to combine on the National Anthem, but the spectators were treated to a recording instead. Finley had failed to negotiate an agreement with the musicians' union, which was demanding more live

music in the stadium.

Four home runs sailed out of the park on opening night, but only one was credited to the A's, a sixth-inning smash by Rick Monday. Boog Powell, Mark Belanger and Brooks Robinson connected for the Baltimore Orioles, who won the game, 4-1, behind the two-hit pitching of Dave McNally.

Several stadium imperfections surfaced during the inaugural. The pitchers mound was constructed on a steel shell which could be removed easily for games by Oakland's professional soccer team. The mound underwent extensive work between innings. It was replaced later by a permanent mound.

The dirt in the batters box and around the bases also was too soft, providing uncertain footing. The condition was corrected before the second game by the addition of more clay.

Coliseum customers were required to get along without a comprehensive scoreboard for the first two months of the campaign. Finley's $1 million exploding board was installed in right field.

An elaborate message board, a computer-operated extravagance in left field, was introduced the second season. This board, called the Finley Fun Board, is 24 feet high and 126 feet long. It is located high above the left-field stands and, with the statistical board, requires one million watts of power to operate.

The A's finished sixth in their first season in Oakland, but produced one noteworthy event on May 8 when Jim (Catfish) Hunter hurled a perfect game against the Minnesota Twins.

When the American League split into two divisions for the 1969 season, the A's finished second in the Western Division. They repeated in 1970, then topped the division in 1971 when they

were eliminated in the League Championship Series by Baltimore in three straight games.

By 1972, when Dick Williams was at the helm, the A's were prepared to go all the way. They defeated the Detroit Tigers in the LCS and the Cincinnati Reds in the World Series.

In the playoffs, the A's were required to get along without the services of shortstop Campy Campaneris for the last three games. In the second contest at Oakland, a 5-0 victory for the A's, Campaneris collected three singles, scored twice and stole two bases. In the seventh inning, however, after being hit on the ankle by a pitched ball, Campy threw his bat at Detroit pitcher Lerrin LaGrow. Campy was fined $500 and suspended for the remainder of the LCS by A.L. President Joe Cronin. He was allowed to play in the World Series.

Division winners again in 1973, the A's defeat-

The picture (above left) shows the Oakland Coliseum (background) and the Coliseum Arena under construction in 1965. In 1968 (above right), major league baseball made its debut in Oakland.

ed the Baltimore Orioles in a five-game playoff, then captured the world championship from the New York Mets in a seven-game Series.

Because Mike Andrews committed two 12th-inning errors that led to an Oakland defeat in the second game, Owner Finley sought to have the second baseman disqualified from the Series on the grounds that he was injured. The A's players reacted vehemently to what they considered unfair treatment of a teammate. Commissioner Bowie Kuhn denied Finley's request and Andrews remained on the active roster, although he played no more second base.

The A's trailed, three games to two, after the New York segment of the Series, but pulled out the championship with 3-1 and 5-2 victories at home.

Williams resigned as manager of the A's at the close of the 1973 Series. Alvin Dark piloted the club to its fourth consecutive division title in 1974, followed by a four-game playoff conquest of the Baltimore Orioles and a five-game World Series triumph over the Los Angeles Dodgers.

One last gasp remained for the "Mustache Gang," so-named for Finley's bonus offer to all players who cultivated lip whiskers. They closed out the 1975 season in unique fashion, defeating the California Angels, 5-0, on the combined no-hit pitching of Vida Blue, Glenn Abbott, Paul Lindblad and Rollie Fingers.

A three-game playoff loss to the Boston Red Sox signaled the end of the Oakland dynasty.

In 1979, the once-proud A's lost 108 games. As defeats mounted, attendance plunged. One contest drew only 653 spectators.

By 1980, however, the A's were on their way back, winning with an exciting style of play known as BillyBall, as designed by Manager Billy Martin.

Emphasizing speed and daring, Martin turned his players into roadrunners, with Rickey Henderson stealing an American League record total of 100 bases for the season.

Only two seasons after becoming the first American Leaguer to hit the century mark in stolen bases, Henderson destroyed Lou Brock's modern major league single-season record of 118 in 1982. Henderson broke Brock's mark on August 27, a full month before season's end, and wound up the year with a total of 130—with 63 steals coming at home.

For only the third time in their 14 years in Oakland, the A's topped the million gate mark in 51 dates during the strike-torn 1981 season. They occupied first place throughout the first half of the campaign and finished second in the second "season." They then swept three games from Kansas City in the division series before bowing to the New York Yankees in three straight contests in the League Championship Series.

In 1982 the A's set a club mark by drawing over 1.7 million fans to the Coliseum. However, the team fell to fifth place in the standings.

A Charlie Finley innovation, the world's first computer-activated stadium scoreboard system (above), displays cartoons and almost any other graphic desired.

All was well in Oakland (above left) after the A's had clinched their second straight division title in 1972, but things had changed by 1979 (above right), when the A's attracted only 653 fans for a game.

SHIBE PARK
Philadelphia

Professional baseball in Philadelphia followed a long and tortuous course before arriving at Veterans Stadium in 1971, one century after the Athletics won the pennant in the National Association, baseball's first professional league.

The Athletics clinched the flag on October 30, 1871, defeating Chicago at the Union Grounds in Brooklyn, where the game had been transferred following the destruction of the Chicago park by Mrs. O'Leary's fire.

In 1873, Philadelphia was represented by a second club in the N.A. Officially, the team was the Philadelphia club, but quickly became known as the Quakers and eventually the Phillies. It played its games on the Jefferson Street Grounds when the Athletics were not using the facility.

The Quakers made a rapid getaway in their first season and were leading the league by a comfortable margin when their owners, flush with success, took the players to Cape May, N.J., for a vacation.

When the players resumed the baseball schedule, however, they discovered that the surf and sand, the night life and allied pleasures had taken

a heavy toll of their skills. Rusty and out of shape, they lost the flag to Boston.

When the National League was organized in 1876, the Athletics were awarded a franchise while the Phillies were excluded. As the initial season drew to a close, the A's and Mutuals of New York refused to make a western swing and were thrown out of the league.

After a five-year absence, Philadelphia returned to professional baseball in 1882 with the admission of the Athletics to the American Association, a new rival for the National League.

The following year, 1883, Alfred J. Reach, a successful sporting goods manufacturer and retailer, acquired the Worcester, Mass., franchise in the National League and transferred it to Philadelphia.

A new playing field, christened Recreation Park, was built on an irregularly shaped plot of ground bordered by Columbia Avenue and Ridge Avenue, 24th and 25th streets. The ground was leveled hastily, a small grandstand erected and Reach was ready for the season opener on May 1. The Quakers, or Phillies, launched their long affiliation with the National League by dropping a 4-3 decision to Charles (Old Hoss) Radbourn and the Providence Grays.

After the 1885 season, in which the Phillies finished third and outdrew the rival Athletics by a considerable margin, Reach determined that the route to greater profits was a new, more commodious ball park.

On April 30, 1887, Reach and his partner, Colonel John I. Rogers, introduced their new park to the public. Pregame ceremonies, in which Manager Harry Wright raised the flag on the center-field flagpole and a military band entertained, con-

By 1938, the condition of Baker Bowl (above) had deteriorated and the Phillies were forced to accept the invitation of the cross-town A's to join them at Shibe Park.

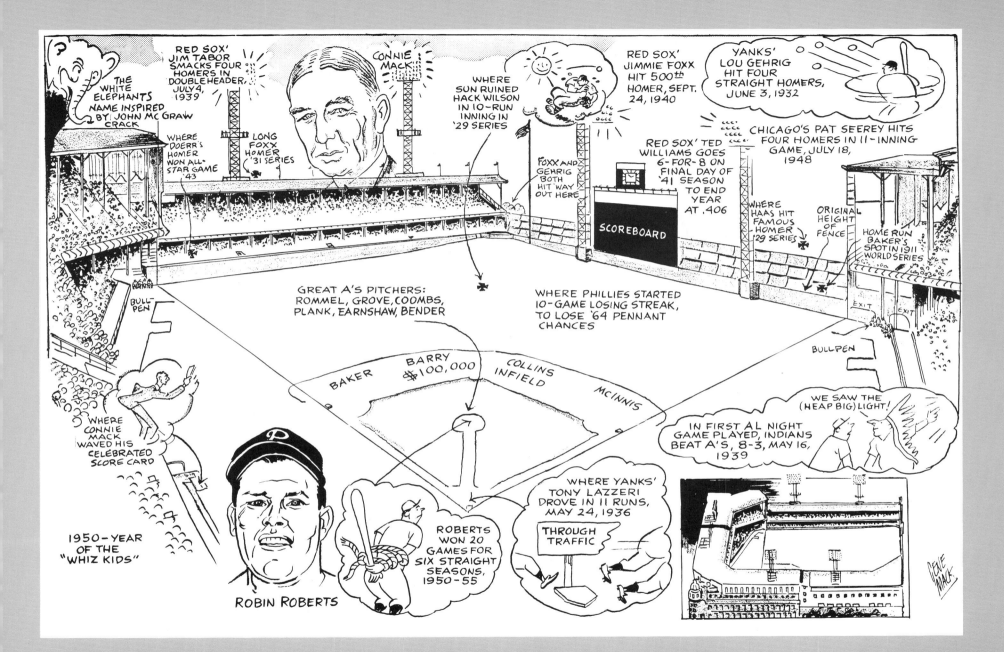

sumed more time than had been anticipated and the start of the game was delayed until 4 p.m.

But the capacity crowd of 20,000 quickly concluded that the wait was worthwhile. The first nine Phillies hit safely and all scored against the New York ace, Tim Keefe. The home club won the game, 19-10.

Park distances were 335 feet to left field, 408 to center and 272 to right. Club offices, the clubhouse and a swimming pool for players were located in the center-field sector at the corner of Broad Street and Lehigh Avenue. A bicycle track 15 feet wide and banked, rimmed the outfield so that flychasers were required to sprint up inclines when tracking long fly balls.

Disaster struck "The Huntington Grounds" on August 6, 1894, when a spark from a plumber's torch set off a fire that destroyed one grandstand, causing damage estimated at $80,000. Reconstruction, plus a $40,000 improvement in 1896, left the seating capacity at 16,000, plus space for 4,000 standees.

Another, more tragic mishap occurred on August 6, 1903, when a left-field balcony collapsed under the concentrated weight of 500 spectators who rushed to a back railing to watch a fight on 15th Street.

Rotted joists collapsed, catapulting the fans to the sidewalk. Twelve were killed and about 200 injured.

On May 14, 1927, while the Phillies were playing the St. Louis Cardinals, 10 rows in the right-field section of the park, now known as Baker Bowl because of Owner William F. Baker, collapsed and hurled 200 spectators onto Huntington Street. One man was trampled to death in the stampede and 41 people were hospitalized with injuries.

Three World Series games were played at Baker Bowl. Grover Cleveland Alexander defeated the Boston Red Sox, 3-1, on October 8, 1915, and Erskine Mayer lost, 2-1, on October 9 before a capacity crowd of 20,306 that included President Woodrow Wilson and his future bride, Mrs. Edith Galt.

When the scene shifted to Boston, the Red Sox peeled off consecutive victories behind Dutch Leonard and Ernie Shore. The Series returned to Philadelphia on October 13 and George Foster clinched the championship for Boston with a 5-4 triumph in Game 5.

As the Phillies' fortunes sagged in the 1920s and '30s, so did the condition of Alfred Reach's once elegant ball park. Funds for improvements and talent were in short supply.

On their last opening day at Baker Bowl in 1938, the Phils shared in an historic occasion with the Brooklyn Dodgers. After outfielder Ernie Koy homered in his first major league at-bat in the first inning for Brooklyn, second baseman Emmett Mueller of the Phils smacked a home run, also in the first inning and on his first major league trip to the plate.

It was Baker Bowl's last contribution to the record book.

By June the decision had been made to forsake the Broad Street park and accept the most recent of several invitations by the A's to share Shibe Park.

Baker Bowl was sold to a realty company and

Umpire Bill Klem (above, holding a face mask) officiates the traditional pregame meeting at home plate before a 1915 World Series game between the Phillies and Red Sox at Baker Bowl.

Opening day was scheduled for April 24, 1901, but a two-day rain delayed the inaugural to Friday, April 26, at which time municipal dignitaries extended congratulations to the new organization.

By pirating stars from the Phillies, including Larry Lajoie and Chick Fraser, and Lave Cross, who played for the St. Louis Cardinals and Brooklyn Dodgers in 1900, Mack fielded a competitive team when the A's opened to a full-house crowd that overflowed the stands onto the soggy turf. The A's lost their inaugural to Washington, 5-1, but Lajoie collected three hits, presaging the .422 average he posted in the first A.L. campaign.

Columbia Park was home to the Athletics for eight years. They hosted pennants there in 1902 and 1905, and played two World Series games there the latter year.

When the Series opened on October 9, Columbia Park overflowed with nearly 18,000 spectators, more than 6,000 above capacity. But there was no joy in Brewerytown that day as Christy Mathewson held the A's to four hits in winning, 3-0.

Chief Bender duplicated Matty's performance with a four-hit, 3-0 triumph in the second game, at New York.

For the third game, back at Columbia Park, only 10,991 turned out and suffered through another Matty shutout, 9-0, on four hits.

Back in New York, Joe McGinnity and Mathewson completed the whitewash pattern, 1-0 and 2-0.

The Athletics moved into Shibe Park on April 12, 1909, the Monday after Easter.

Shibe Park was the first steel and concrete plant. Located at 21st and Lehigh, it contained 30,000 seats, but exceeded that capacity on opening day.

bit by bit it yielded to the ravages of decay and destruction.

In the early years of the twentieth century, when the Phils were attempting to strengthen their position as a major league enterprise, there appeared on the horizon a cloud even more menacing than the perils of paucity.

It was the American League which, in 1901, swept out of the West, proclaiming itself a new major league under the aggressive leadership of Byron Bancroft Johnson.

Ban spotted one franchise in Philadelphia. The club was to be managed by Connie Mack, who had piloted Milwaukee in the Western League before Johnson converted that circuit into the A.L.

Controlling interest in the new franchise was offered to Ben Shibe, a minor stockholder in the Athletics of the nineteenth century. A close friend of A.J. Reach, Shibe was now a successful manufacturer of baseballs. If Shibe invested in the club, he was told, the American League would use his baseballs exclusively. Ben was a shrewd businessman. He accepted the proposition.

For a ball park, the novice clubowners leased property at 29th Street and Columbia Avenue in the section of the city known as Brewerytown. The aroma of yeast, hops and freshly brewed beer bathed Columbia Park and those who tarried there in the early years of the Athletics.

The park seated about 9,500 fans, most of them in the bleachers, where the club featured 25-cent admission.

Prior to Game 2 of the 1915 World Series at Baker Bowl President Woodrow Wilson (above with future bride Edith Galt) became the first president to throw out the first ball at a World Series game.

The A's finished third in 1912 behind Boston and Washington. They played a remarkable game on May 18, after Detroit players refused to take the field in a sympathy strike with teammate Ty Cobb. The outfielder had attacked a heckler in the stands at Hilltop Park, New York, on May 15, and was suspended by A.L. President Ban Johnson. In order to avoid a $1,000 forfeiture fine, the Tigers management recruited Philadelphia sandlotters to oppose the Athletics.

Against Aloysius Travers, later a Jesuit priest, the A's pounded out 26 hits—but no homers—in romping to a 24-2 verdict.

The A's regained A.L. supremacy in 1913 and disposed of the Giants in even more convincing fashion than in 1911. The A's won in five games, their only setback a 3-0, 10-inning loss to Christy Mathewson in the second game. They won the fourth game, 6-5, at Shibe Park behind Bender and three games at the Polo Grounds.

But it was a totally different and sadder story in 1914, as the A's lost two Series games at Shibe Park to the Miracle Braves, 7-1 and 1-0, before dropping the next two contests in Boston.

Dissolution of the four-time winners was followed by 15 years of heartache and rebuilding before the A's scaled the peak again in 1929. But just as he had done in 1910, Connie Mack watched his new champions defeat the Cubs in the five-game World Series.

The most memorable segment of the Series was the seventh inning of the fourth game at Shibe Park. Leading two games to one but trailing 8-0 on the scoreboard, the A's exploded for 10 runs, the most ever scored in a Series inning, and won the game, 10-8.

The A's clinched the championship in the fifth game when Rube Walberg decisioned Pat Malone,

Original dimensions of the playing field were 360 feet down the foul lines, 393 in the power alleys and 420 to center field.

Shibe Park underwent its first major renovation in 1913 when the uncovered stands were roofed over, and a left-field stand was added, extending to the center-field flagpole.

In 1925, a second deck was constructed from behind first base to the right-field corner, and from behind third base to left field and on to dead center field. A mezzanine section of 2,500 seats was added in 1929 and 3,000 more seats in 1930.

For 25 years, the right-field wall was only 12 feet high. The situation invited competition from 20th Street property owners who built bleachers on their rooftops and sold tickets at bargain rates. In 1935, however, the A's raised the wall to 50 feet, putting the wildcat operators out of business.

With his "$100,000 Infield" of Stuffy McInnis, Eddie Collins, Jack Barry and Frank (Home Run) Baker, Connie Mack produced four pennant winners and three world championships in Shibe Park's first six years.

In 1910, Chief Bender and Jack Coombs pitched the A's to 4-1 and 9-3 victories at Shibe Park before the World Series moved to Chicago, where the A's won two of three games from the Cubs.

The next year, gaining a measure of revenge for their 1905 humiliation, the A's defeated the Giants three times in Philadelphia. In a six-game set that alternated between the two cities, Eddie Plank won the second game, 3-1, Chief Bender the fourth, 4-2, and Bender the sixth, 13-2. The fourth game, scheduled for October 18, was postponed until October 24 because of rain.

Horses and buggies and derby hats were the order of the day (right) when fans crowded into Shibe Park for its first game in 1909. A 90-year-old Connie Mack (above) recalls his glory days at Shibe.

3-2.

Bench jockeys on both sides fired their choicest epithets during the first four games until Judge K.M. Landis summoned Managers Connie Mack and Joe McCarthy to his headquarters and announced: "If these vulgarities continue, I'll fine the culprits a full Series share."

Mack passed the word along to his players, then winced when he heard his fiery catcher Mickey Cochrane shout to the Cubs, "After the game we'll serve tea in the clubhouse."

If the Commissioner heard it, Mack reasoned, Cochrane could be in for a severe reprimand and possibly a fine.

When Landis entered the Athletics' clubhouse after the game, however, he shook Cochrane's hand and inquired: "Now, where's the tea?"

Repeating as league champions in 1930, the A's engaged the St. Louis Cardinals for the world championship. Lefty Grove and George Earnshaw gave the A's a two-game lead at Shibe Park with 5-2 and 6-1 wins as Cochrane homered in each game. The A's lost two of three in St. Louis before returning to Philadelphia where Earnshaw posted a 7-1 victory.

For the third consecutive year, an American League pennant flew over Shibe Park in 1931, but the A's, losing two of three games at home, bowed in the World Series to St. Louis in seven games.

World Series bunting decorated the park again in 1950, but this time the champions were the Phillies, who bowed twice to the Yankees at home, Jim Konstanty losing to Vic Raschi, 1-0, and Robin Roberts to Allie Reynolds, 2-1, in 10 innings.

Lou Gehrig enjoyed his finest day at Shibe Park on June 3, 1932, when he clouted four consecutive home runs. His achievement was forced to share the day's headlines with John McGraw's resignation as manager of the Giants after a 30-year tenure.

Shibe Park introduced night baseball to the American League on May 16, 1939, when the A's lost to Cleveland, 8-3. According to lighting engineers, "the infield is better lighted than the average well-lighted office. It is several hundred times brighter than Times Square on New Year's Eve."

Although the A's finished last in 1941, their park occupied the national spotlight on the closing day of the season when the A's met the Red Sox in a doubleheader. The center of attention was Ted Williams, who was hitting .39955 and was bidding to become the first major leaguer to bat .400 since Bill Terry of the Giants in 1930.

After collecting four hits in five at-bats in the opener, Williams went 2-for-3 in the second game to finish at .406. No major leaguer has hit .400 since.

Two All-Star Games were played at Shibe Park. On July 13, 1943, in the first midsummer classic played at night, the A.L. won, 5-3, sparked by Bobby Doerr's home run.

On July 8, 1952, in a game shortened to five innings by rain, the N.L. won 3-2. The winners collected only three hits, but two were homers by Jackie Robinson and Hank Sauer.

For years Connie Mack had resisted suggestions that the park be renamed in his honor. The Grand Old Man insisted that the historic structure continue to bear the name of his benefactor and long-time friend. However, in 1952, while Mack was in Florida, the board of directors voted to make the change.

When the A's departed for Kansas City after the 1954 season, the Phillies bought the stadium for an estimated $2 million.

The Phillies played their final game at 21st and Lehigh on October 1, 1970, and the storied structure that had been the pride of baseball at its dedication 61 years earlier passed into history.

The Phillies defeated Montreal, 2-1, in the 10-inning finale, but there were moments when it appeared the game might not be played to a conclusion.

Two hundred police patrolled the premises to help maintain order, but they could not prevent a fan from running onto the field and grabbing Phillies left fielder Ron Stone just as the batter hit a ball in his direction. Stone was unable to make the catch and the Montreal runner subsequently scored the tying run.

The umpires announced that further incidents would result in a forfeit. After Oscar Gamble singled home Tim McCarver with the winning run, vandalism erupted in its ugliest form.

Club management had tried to forestall vandalism by presenting a souvenir seat slat to each fan as he entered the park. The slats turned to clubs in the hands of exuberant marauders. Ripping, slashing, crushing, the fans made a shambles of the old park. One muscular miscreant succeeded in detaching a toilet bowl and toted it triumphantly from the park.

On August 20, 1971, a fire started by two youngsters in the press box area heavily damaged the vacated stadium. Firemen battled for two hours before bringing the blaze under control. By that time the grandstand roof had collapsed on the upper deck.

A real estate company, which had purchased the property for approximately $1 million, tore down the once elegant park to make room for a housing development.

Shibe Park, also known as Connie Mack Stadium in honor of the man who managed the Philadelphia A's for 50 years, was baseball's first steel and concrete park. The exterior view (above left) shows the front entrance at 21st and Lehigh with the stadium's two names above the center gate. The overview (above right) and the panorama of the playing field (right) show the 50-foot right-field wall and the shape of the stadium, both from the outside and inside.

VETERANS STADIUM

Philadelphia

When the Phillies sold Connie Mack Stadium to a New York realty firm in 1961, they signed a three-year lease on the old park, fully expecting to be playing in a new, municipally-owned ball park by 1964.

But 1964 came and went. New leases were signed. At one point, Phils Owner R.R.M. Carpenter Jr. hinted that he might consider building his own stadium in New Jersey.

Haggling over a stadium site brought on more delays. In November of 1964 voters approved by a narrow margin a $25 million bond issue. In 1966 two sets of plans were under consideration. Meanwhile, the cost of construction had climbed to $30 million.

Eventually, a South Philadelphia site, near the 100,000-seat John F. Kennedy Stadium, was agreed upon and, because costs continued to escalate, another bond issue was passed before ground was broken October 2, 1967.

Because of delays and interruptions, the park was 3½ years in building. When it was dedicated on April 4, 1971, Veterans Stadium—or simply "The Vet"—had cost $49.5 million.

The Vet, located about six miles from Connie

Mack Stadium in North Philadelphia, occupies 14 acres and seats 65,454 for baseball. There are no stairways, but has instead two miles of ramps, eight sets of escalators and four elevators.

Sixty concessions stands, more per 1,000 seats than in any other stadium, and 62 rest rooms are spaced throughout the stadium.

Distances to the fences are 330 feet on the foul lines and 408 feet to center field.

Opening night, on April 10, 1971, attracted 55,352, the largest baseball gathering in Pennsyl-

vania history. In addition to civic dignitaries on hand, the throng included Commissioner Bowie Kuhn, National League President Chub Feeney and his predecessor, Warren Giles.

The ceremonial first baseball was dropped from a helicopter hovering over the field. Phils catcher Mike Ryan bobbled the ball, then made a clean grab of it. The catch was regarded as a good omen by those who were looking for encouragement.

After a Marine corporal tossed out the first ball from his box seat, Jim Bunning defeated the Montreal Expos, 4-1. The veteran righthander recorded the first assist in the stadium when he fielded Boots Day's grounder and tossed to Deron Johnson.

Don Money of the Phillies socked the first homer, in the sixth inning, but the park's exploding scoreboard had not yet been completely installed, so Money's feat received no electronic acknowledgement.

Unique methods for delivering the season's first baseball have become traditional at the Vet. Three times Kiteman did the honors. Once he crashed into the center-field stands, but he pulled

Veterans Stadium, 3½ years under construction, got its major league sendoff when Phillies opening-day starter Jim Bunning delivered the first pitch to Montreal's Boots Day (above).

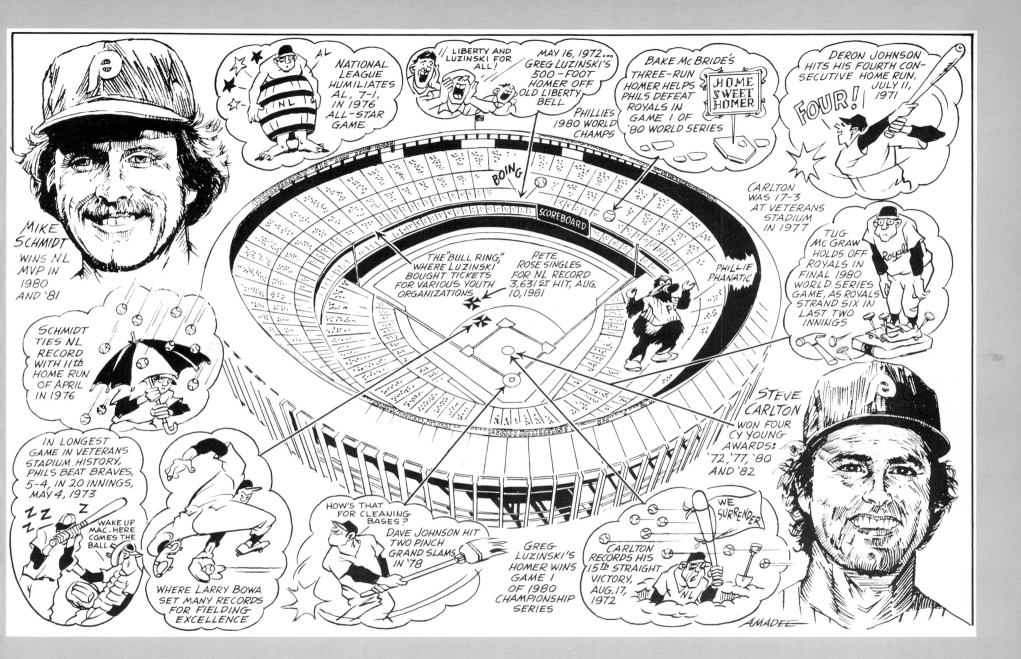

215

setting 3,631st hit.

The Phillies captured National League East Division titles in 1976, '77 and '78, but won no home games in the League Championship Series and were eliminated by the Reds the first year and the Dodgers the next two.

After deposing of the Houston Astros in the five-game Championship Series in 1980, the Phils opened the World Series at the Vet and thrilled crowds of more than 65,000 with 7-6 and 6-4 triumphs over Kansas City.

The Royals built up a 4-0 lead in the first game, but a five-run third inning, featuring a three-run homer by Bake McBride, put the Phillies ahead to stay. Carlton gained credit for the second-game victory when the Phils scored four runs in the eighth inning.

Leading three games to two after the next three contests at Kansas City, the Phils clinched their first world championship at the Vet, winning 4-1 behind the seven-hit pitching of Carlton and Tug McGraw.

The Royals loaded the bases twice against McGraw, but the veteran reliever escaped unscathed. There was only one out in the ninth frame when a walk and two singles loaded the sacks.

McGraw induced Frank White to lift a foul fly near the first base dugout. In one of the most dramatic defensive plays of the Series, catcher Bob Boone let the ball pop out of his mitt, but first baseman Pete Rose, standing nearby, alertly caught the carom for the second out.

With mounted patrolmen standing by with the canine corps to prevent postgame rowdyism, McGraw sent most of the 65,000 spectators into ecstasy by fanning Willie Wilson, who had already whiffed 11 times in the Series.

himself together and, limping away from the crash site, delivered the ball as promised.

In another season, Hugo Zacchini delivered the ball after being shot from a cannon. Monique Gutzman filled the role from a high wire. Other deliveries were made by a parachutist, Dave Merrifield dangling from a trapeze bar under a helicopter, and the U.S. Army Parachute Team.

In 1976, the United States' bicentennial year, a Paul Revere-type colonial carried the baseball from Boston on horseback. Inside the park, he presented the baseball to Rocketman, who jetted around the stadium.

Also in 1976, as the sports highlight of the Bicentennial, the All-Star Game was played at the Vet before 63,794 that included President Gerald Ford. With George Foster and Cesar Cedeno socking home runs, the National Leaguers won, 7-1. Fred Lynn homered for the lone A.L. run.

Deron Johnson crashed the record book in the Vet's first season, clouting home runs in four consecutive at-bats, three on July 11.

Other memorable achievements in the Vet's first decade were recorded by:

● Greg Luzinski, whose mammoth home run on May 16, 1972, struck the Liberty Bell, which used to be mounted on the fourth level in center field.

● Steve Carlton, who won 15 games in a row before bowing to Phil Niekro of the Braves, 2-1, in 11 innings on August 21, 1972.

● Pitcher Ken Brett, who homered in three consecutive starts in 1973, sparking victories over the Padres, Dodgers and Mets. In his next start, in Montreal, Brett extended his home run string to four games.

● Mike Schmidt, who had homered in his last at-bat the previous day, hit homers in his first three plate appearances July 7, 1979, to equal a major league mark.

● Pete Rose, who singled against St. Louis on August 10, 1981 for his National League record-

The "Bull Ring," a section in the left-field stands named in honor of former Phillies star Greg (The Bull) Luzinski, is pictured (above) in 1978.

Philadelphia's tri-complex (above) consists of Veterans Stadium (foreground), home of the Phillies and NFL Eagles, The Spectrum (center), home of the NHL Flyers and NBA 76ers, and JFK Stadium.

FORBES FIELD

Pittsburgh

Little did General John Forbes realize, when he bivouacked his Revolutionary War forces in what was to become the Oakland section of Pittsburgh, that he was giving his name to an athletic arena of the 20th century.

It remained for Barney Dreyfuss, who fled Germany at age 17 to escape compulsory military training, to honor the old general in 1909 when he christened his steel-and-concrete ball park Forbes Field. This playing field, which was home to the Pirates for 62 years, was the third enclosed park of the city's professional clubs.

The first Pittsburgh team, known as the Alleghenies, was a member of the International Association and played its home games at Union Park in 1876.

The league expired at an early date and in 1888, the Alleghenies tried again in the International League. The team succumbed on June 8, winner of only three of 26 games, the majority of which were played on the road.

Four years later, in 1892, the Alleghenies felt sufficiently bold for a third try and joined the American Association, a major league rival of the National League.

To mark their entry into the majors, the Alleghenies built Exposition Park, much larger than 2,500-seat Union Park, at the confluence of the Allegheny and Monongahela rivers and in the same general area as today's Three Rivers Stadium.

Old Expo, as the park came to be known, was

bordered on one side by the Allegheny River and the Baltimore and Ohio Railroad tracks, and on other sides by thoroughfares with current names of Galveston, Shore and Scotland streets. The park derived its name from the Exposition Grounds, a popular site for circuses and other tent shows of the 19th century.

Dimensions of Exposition Park are fogged in history, but it is generally agreed they were excessive. No drive, it is said, ever cleared the left or center-field fences, and only 11 sailed off the premises in the right-field sector.

After playing in Exposition Park for two years, the Alleghenies moved to Recreation Park, a latter-day name for refurbished Union Park.

Recreation Park was located on the North Side of the city and was bound by the Fort Wayne Railroad tracks, Allegheny, Pennsylvania and Grant avenues, and North Avenue West. It was here that the club played its first National League game on April 30, 1887, beating Chicago, 6-2.

In 1890, the Pittsburgh club of the Players League renovated Old Expo, enlarging its capacity

When Pittsburgh Owner Barney Dreyfuss decided to build a modern park in 1908, he found a location in the Oakland-Schenley Park section of the city and the result was Forbes Field (above).

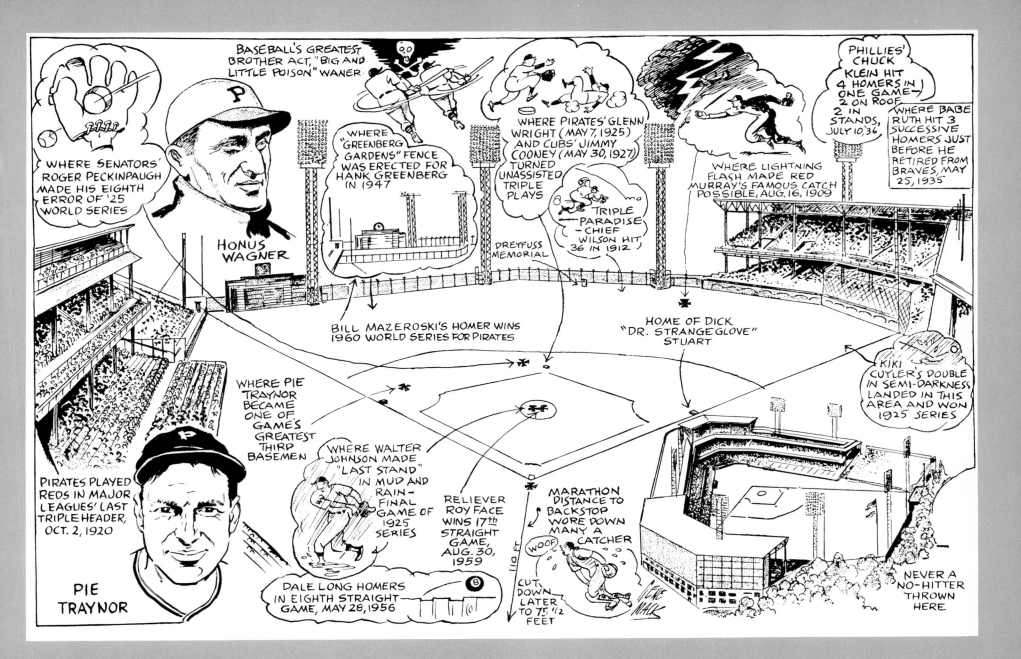

219

in the process. When the P.L. folded after one season, the Alleghenies returned to their old playground and remained there for nearly 20 years.

In the meantime, Recreation Park, which had served as a football field for the University of Western Pennsylvania (now the University of Pittsburgh), was converted into a wooden saucer for motor-paced bicycle riding. It was rechristened The Colosseum and was managed by Tim Hurst, later a well-known major league umpire.

Exposition Park was an adequate facility, except when the Allegheny River was at flood tide. At such times, it leaked badly. The most notable river encroachment occurred on the Fourth of July in 1902.

When the 10,000 fans arrived for the morning game of the holiday doubleheader, they discovered water a foot deep in the outfield. Undeterred by adverse conditions, management decided to proceed with the game. The visiting Brooklyn Superbas agreed to play after it was

decided that any ball hit into the water was an automatic single. The Pirates won the game, 3-0.

By afternoon game time, conditions had worsened. The water was now within 20 feet of second base, but again there was no thought of a postponement.

As young boys dried off the baseballs after almost every pitch, Jack Chesbro won for the Pirates, 4-0. It was one of Happy Jack's 28 victories that season.

The Pittsburgh club had scuttled its old name of Alleghenies in the aftermath of the Players League war and adopted the popular moniker of Pirates. The name traced to an innocent remark delivered during an arbitration hearing after the armistice.

One stipulation of the truce specified that the P.L. players who had jumped contracts should return to their original clubs in the National League and American Association. Through an oversight, the Philadelphia club of the A.A. neg-

lected to list second baseman Louis Bierbauer and outfielder Harry Stovey on its reserve list. Bierbauer was quickly signed by Pittsburgh, Stovey by Boston.

The Philadelphians protested vehemently, but agreed to submit the case to a board of arbitration. During the hearing, a spokesman for the Philadelphia club asserted that the action by Pittsburgh "was nothing but piratical."

Somebody on the N.L. club liked the alliterative ring to "Pittsburgh Pirates," and thus they were to remain.

One of the most fortuitous events in the history of Western Pennsylvania baseball occurred in the winter of 1899-1900, when the National League voted to reduce its membership from 12 to eight clubs. One of the disenfranchised cities was Louisville, where Barney Dreyfuss owned the baseball club.

Eager to continue in the game, Barney acquired financial backers and, accompanied by two

In 1947, a fence sliced 30 feet off the left-field home run distance. The area was christened Greenberg Gardens in honor of slugger Hank Greenberg and later dubbed Kiner Korner for Ralph Kiner.

of his star players, shortstop Honus Wagner and outfielder Fred Clarke, he moved on to Pittsburgh, where he bought a half interest in the Pirates and took over as club president.

With Wagner and Clarke added to a mediocre club, the Pirates finished second in 1900, then won three consecutive N.L. pennants. In 1902 they finished 27½ games in front.

Near the close of the 1903 race, when it appeared certain that the Pirates would win the N.L. flag and the Boston Pilgrims would do the same in the newly established American League, Dreyfuss and his Boston counterpart devised plans for a best-of-nine postseason series to determine the champion of the baseball world.

In this first tournament of the modern World Series, the Pirates won two of three games in Boston, lost three of four at Old Expo, and then dropped the finale in Boston. In their home park, the Pirates attracted throngs of 7,600, 12,322, 11,556 and 17,038.

Although they were defeated, the Pirates fared better than their adversaries because their generous boss threw the club's share of the receipts into the players pool.

The Buccos won no flags the next five years, but were constant contenders. In the winter of 1908-09, Barney decided that the club deserved a more handsome ball park, similar to the steel-and-concrete structure that Ben Shibe and Connie Mack were building in Philadelphia.

His search for a suitable location ended in the Oakland-Schenley Park section of Pittsburgh. With his friend, steel magnate Andrew Carnegie, helping to negotiate the deal, Barney bought acreage from Schenley Farms.

The choice of a site away from the city's business district subjected Dreyfuss to gentle chiding from friends and fans alike. In later years he recalled:

"There was nothing there but a livery stable and a hot house, with a few cows grazing over the countryside. A ravine ran through the property and I knew that the first thing necessary to make it suitable for baseball was to level off the entire field."

Ground for the new park was broken on March 1, 1909. Four months later, the $2 million show-place was ready for occupancy.

On opening day, June 30, a crowd of 30,338 overflowed the 25,000-seat facility into a roped-off area in the outfield. The first pitch of the game was smacked for a single by Johnny Evers of the Cubs, who beat the Buccos, 3-2.

But it was a magnificent day for the 44-year-old owner. Weeks later, he chortled: "One friend bet me a $150 suit we would never fill the park, but we filled it five times the first two weeks."

The 1910 Reach Baseball Guide reported on the new park as follows:

"The formal opening of Forbes Field . . . was an historic event, the full significance of which could be better felt than described.

For those fans who arrived early for a game at Forbes Field, Schenley Park, located beyond the left-field fence (above), provided an attractive diversion.

Rookie pitcher Babe Adams accounted for two of the Buccos' three victories at home and clinched the championship with a third win at Detroit.

The second Series contest, a 7-2 Tiger triumph, featured an umpire appealing to spectators for help on making a decision.

In the first inning, Dots Miller of the Bucs smashed a low liner to right field. As the ball neared the bleachers, fans sitting on the field in front of the barrier stood up, obscuring the vision of plate umpire Billy Evans and his partner, Bill Klem.

The arbiters had no choice but to stroll to right field and ask the fans where the ball had landed.

"It was a home run, the ball landed right there," chorused some spectators, pointing to a spot on the turf.

"If it landed there before bouncing into the stands," replied Evans, "it's a ground rule double."

Explaining his predicament later to the National Commission, the governing body of baseball, Evans suggested that, instead of permitting two backup umpires to occupy a box seat, they be assigned to positions on the foul lines to eliminate similar embarrassments in the future.

Starting with the third game of the Series, there were four umpires on the field.

The last National League tripleheader was played at Forbes Field on October 2, 1920. Because the first three teams figured in the World Series pool, N.L. President John Heydler approved the Cincinnati Reds and Pirates playing three games in one day to determine the third-place club in the senior circuit.

Although the Reds won the first two contests, 13-4 and 7-3, the third game went on as adver-

"Words also must fail to picture in the mind's eye adequately the splendors of the magnificent pile President Dreyfuss erected as a tribute to the national game, a beneficence to Pittsburgh and an enduring monument to himself.

"For architectural beauty, imposing size, solid construction and public comfort and convenience, it has not its superior in the world."

In the 1920s, Forbes Field was described as "the Hialeah of ball parks," bringing a smile from Commissioner K. M. Landis, an arch enemy of the equine fraternity.

The Pirates brought Barney's annus mirabilis to a rousing climax by winning the pennant and the seven-game World Series that pitted the majors' batting champions, Wagner and Ty Cobb of Detroit, against each other.

Due to Forbes Field's superior capacity, the Series attracted 145,000 spectators. The three Pittsburgh games alone drew over 80,000, more than saw the entire 1907 or 1908 World Series between the Tigers and Chicago Cubs.

The Cathedral of Learning, located on the campus of the University of Pittsburgh, towered over the left-field bleachers at Forbes Field.

tised, with the Pirates winning, 6-0, in a six-inning game halted by darkness.

National League pitchers never succeeded in hurling a no-hit game at Forbes Field but there were hitting accomplishments to warm the hearts of the most flinty fans.

It was here on October 15, 1925, that Kiki Cuyler smashed a bases-loaded double in the eighth inning to give the Pirates a 9-7 victory over Walter Johnson and the Washington Senators in the seventh game of the World Series.

The winning blow caused 42,856 witnesses to forget that the game had started in a drizzle and ended in a steady shower.

Forbes Field also was the scene of a remarkable batting feat on August 26, 1926, when Paul

Waner, using a different bat on each trip to the plate, collected six hits in as many tries.

Babe Ruth fired his last home run salvo here on May 25, 1935. The Bambino, recently installed as a vice president and part-time outfielder of the Boston Braves, clouted three home runs in a Boston victory. The final drive, off Guy Bush, was the first ever to clear the right-field stands and was the 714th of his career.

Five days later Ruth played in his final major league game. The legendary career, that commenced as a pitcher, was over.

Chuck Klein of Philadelphia blasted four home runs in a 10-inning game on July 10, 1936. Dale Long of the Pirates rapped his eighth homer in as many consecutive games on May 28, 1956 and

Dick Stuart, Bucco first baseman, gained distinction on June 5, 1959, when he became the first batter to hit a ball over the 457-foot mark in center field.

One of the most memorable hits in Forbes Field was struck on October 13, 1960. With the Yankees and Pirates tied, 9-9, in the ninth inning of the seventh World Series game, Bucco second baseman Bill Mazeroski rapped the second pitch from Ralph Terry over the left-field wall. The Pirates were world champions for the first time since 1925 and for the third time in history.

Defensive gems were not uncommon in Barney Dreyfuss' showplace. Two unassisted triple plays were engineered here, both by shortstops.

On May 7, 1925, Glenn Wright of the Pirates

The 1960 World Series between the Yankees and Pirates started at Forbes Field (above left) and ended there (above right) in jubilation with the arrival of Bill Mazeroski at home plate.

snared a line drive off the bat of Jim Bottomley of the Cardinals, stepped on second base to double up Jimmy Cooney and then tagged Rogers Hornsby, trying to scramble back to first.

Cooney, having been traded to the Cubs, repeated the feat on May 30, 1927. Grabbing a hard-hit smash by Paul Waner, Cooney tagged second base to retire Lloyd Waner, then tagged Clyde Barnhart, who had been running with the pitch.

One of baseball's most dramatic catches was made at Forbes Field on August 16, 1909. With the score tied, 2-2, and two Pittsburgh runners on base with two outs in the eighth inning, thunderheads rolled in thickly and menacingly. The extreme darkness forced New York pitcher Christy Mathewson to walk to within a few feet of home plate to see his catcher's signs.

Darkness obscured the outfielders and when Dots Miller lined sharply toward right-center field, all indications pointed to a game-winning hit. Suddenly, however, a flash of lightning illuminated the field long enough for everyone to see right fielder Red Murray, racing full tilt, thrust out his right arm to make a barehand catch. Moments later, a torrential downpour washed out further action.

Originally, the dimensions of the Forbes Field playing area measured 376 feet to right field, 462 feet to center and 360 feet to left.

The first change in the park occurred in 1925 when double-deck stands were erected in right field, reducing the measurement in that sector to 300 feet. A 28-foot high screen protected fans in that area.

In 1938, confident that the Pirates' early pace presaged a World Series, club officials, headed by Bill Benswanger, son-in-law of the deceased Drey-

fuss, ordered a new press box constructed on the roof of the grandstand.

When October arrived, however, the coop was empty. Gabby Hartnett's "homer in the gloamin'" at Chicago in the final week of the season had dislodged the Buccos from first place.

In 1947, the bullpens of home and visiting clubs were shifted from foul territory to left field, slicing 30 feet off the home run distance. The change was designed to provide an inviting home run target for Hank Greenberg, recently acquired from Detroit.

In his honor, the enclosure was named Greenberg Gardens. When Hank retired after the 1947 season, the bullpen area was renamed Kiner Korner for the Bucs' new young slugger, Ralph Kiner, who, aided by the handy target, poled 51 home runs in 1947 and 54 in '49. When Kiner was traded to the Chicago Cubs in 1953, the bullpens were relocated in foul territory.

For the remainder of its day, Forbes Field showed measurements of 300 feet to right field, 365 to left and 457 to center.

Like a bombshell, Pirates fans learned on November 28, 1958, that Forbes Field had been sold to the University of Pittsburgh for $2 million. The Pirates, it was added, would be allowed to use the historic facility until the completion of a proposed all-purpose municipal sports complex.

The requiem for Barney Dreyfuss' pride and joy was pronounced on June 28, 1970, when 40,918, the Pirates' largest crowd since 1956, attended a doubleheader with the Cubs. Unlike the 1909 inaugural, when the Cubs beat the Pirates, 3-2, the Buccos beat the visitors twice in their farewell appearance, giving the fans cause to smile through their tears.

The Old Lady of Schenley Park was demolished in the early 1970s to make way for the Forbes Quadrangle, comprising graduate schools of the University of Pittsburgh.

Radio announcers at Forbes Field got a real bird's-eye view of game action from their perch (above) behind home plate.

Exuberant fans attack the scoreboard (above) in search of souvenirs
after the Pirates' final game at Forbes Field on June 28, 1970.

THREE RIVERS STADIUM

Pittsburgh

Shortly before noon on April 25, 1968, Mayor Joseph Barr of Pittsburgh presided at groundbreaking ceremonies for the long-awaited municipal sports complex that would house the city's professional sports teams.

The stadium had been in the talking and planning stage for a decade and now the wheels of progress were starting to turn, if ever so slowly.

Unlike Forbes Field, which was built in four months, Three Rivers Stadium would require more than two years. Also unlike Forbes Field, the cost would be many times higher, like $55 million as compared to $2 million. The electronic scoreboard alone would set the city back $1.5 million.

The three-tier jewel overlooking the formation of the Ohio River was ready for occupancy on July 16, 1970. It received its baptism by night and 48,846 attended the rites. They discovered a symmetrical arena, a synthetic turf and baselines measuring 340 feet to the foul poles, 385 feet in the power alleys and 410 feet to center field.

They also saw the Pirates drop a 3-2 decision to the Cincinnati Reds. Shades of the Forbes Field inaugural 61 years earlier.

The first World Series night game was played at Three Rivers on October 13, 1971. The innovation, explained Commissioner Bowie Kuhn, was to enable the nation's working people to enjoy the fall classic on television.

The Pirates, beaten in the first two games at Baltimore, won Game 3 on their home lot and then tied the Series at two victories with a come-from-behind, 4-3 triumph under the lights. A crowd of 51,378, plus untold millions on TV, watched a 21-year-old pinch-hitter, Milt May, single home the decisive run in the seventh inning.

The Pirates also captured the fifth game at home, dropped the sixth contest at Baltimore, then won the seventh game behind the pitching of Steve Blass and the hitting of Roberto Clemente, who batted .414 in the seven games.

The All-Star Game, which had been played in Forbes Field in 1944 and 1959, returned to Pittsburgh in 1974. Paced by Los Angeles first baseman Steve Garvey, who belted a single and double, drove in one run and scored another, the N.L. prevailed, 7-2.

The Pirates won six East Division titles during the '70s, but only twice—in 1971 and 1979—did they make it to the World Series.

After the final game at Forbes Field in 1970, a section of the outfield wall was dismantled (above) and taken to Three Rivers Stadium for decoration in the park's Allegheny Club.

227

Matched again against the Orioles in 1979, as they were eight years before, the Pirates lost three of the first four games. They discovered their hitting formula in the fifth game, however, and scored seven runs in their last three at-bats to defeat the A.L. champions, 7-1.

After that, the pieces continued to fall into place. Spurred by the resounding chorus of "We Are Fam-a-lee," the Pirates swept the Orioles in the last two games to register their fifth world championship.

The no-hit whammy that haunted pitchers through three score of years at Forbes Field was routed early at Three Rivers. The stadium was barely one year old when Bob Gibson of the Cardinals humbled the Buccos, 11-0, on August 14, 1971.

John (Candy Man) Candelaria was the first Pirate to spin a no-hit game at Three Rivers, blanking the Dodgers, 2-0, on August 9, 1976.

Candelaria's teammate, Jim Bibby, did almost as well on May 19, 1981. After yielding a leadoff single to Terry Harper, the righthander retired the next 27 batters in a row to defeat Atlanta, 5-0.

Pirates infielder Phil Garner enjoyed a brief moment in the spotlight, September 14-15, 1978, when he smacked grand-slam homers in two consecutive games, but the decade of the '70s belonged chiefly to Willie Stargell and Clemente.

Stargell was especially devastating in 1971 when he established a major league record by hitting 11 home runs in April, including three at home on April 21. In '71 and '79 he led the Pirates to World Series titles.

Clemente, in addition to his remarkable performance in the '71 World Series, rapped his 3,000th major league hit, a double to left-center field, in the final week of the 1972 season. Three months later he was dead, at 38, the victim of a plane crash while flying supplies from Puerto Rico to hurricane victims in Nicaragua.

He was elected to the Hall of Fame in 1973.

Circular Three Rivers Stadium, viewed (above) from across the Ohio River on the scheduled opening date of May 29, 1970, didn't open until July 16 because of labor disputes.

228

The inside of Three Rivers Stadium (above) was symmetrical in design and provided a stark contrast to Forbes Field, the Pirates' home from 1909 to 1970.

SPORTSMAN'S PARK

St. Louis

In the 90-year history of Sportsman's Park, no single event captivated the public like a base on balls to a rookie pinch-hitter on August 19, 1951.

Not just any rookie pinch-hitter, but a 65-pound, three-foot, seven-inch bundle of energy who earned everlasting fame as "The Midget," Bill Veeck's super crowd-pleaser in a lifetime devoted to promotional wizardry that accelerated turnstiles, amused spectators and frequently sent pompous colleagues into blind rage.

For one brief moment of glory, Eddie Gaedel gave to Sportsman's Park a distinction that overshadowed the batting feats of Rogers Hornsby, George Sisler and Stan Musial. It was a happening that titillated 18,000 spectators, millions of fans nationwide, and drove American League President Will Harridge into a fit of rage.

In the American League's golden anniversary season, Veeck had promised more than cake and ice cream at the gate. He leaked just enough hints to convince the populace he was about to drop a blockbuster stunt between games of a Sunday doubleheader.

As though there wasn't entertainment enough with a juggler on first base, trampoline artists at second, acrobats at third, Satchel Paige beating

the drums and aerial bombs thundering overhead, a large papier mache cake was wheeled to home plate. There, on signal, a small male figure attired in a scale-model St. Louis Browns uniform leaped from the cake in a dramatic Happy Birthday salute.

The show having run its course, the spectators settled back, satisfied that Sportshirt Bill had, indeed, thrown a memorable party.

The Detroit Tigers were retired in the top half of the first inning of the second game, whereupon:

"Batting for Frank Saucier," intoned the field announcer, "No. ⅛, Eddie Gaedel."

Struck dumb for a moment, the crowd erupted. Veeck was about to serve the piece de resistance.

Plate umpire Ed Hurley summoned Browns Manager Zack Taylor to the plate, demanding an explanation for the nonsense that Veeck was about to perpetrate on the Grand Old Game.

Calmly, Taylor displayed a legal American League contract, properly signed, and a letter from the A.L. office approving the signing of player Gaedel.

From the Detroit bench, Manager Red Rolfe filed a complaint, but retreated when Hurley assured him everything was in order.

Gaedel, swinging a toy-size bat, walked into the batter's box and struck a professional pose. While Tigers catcher Bob Swift knelt in front of Hurley, Gaedel, acting on Veeck's orders, watched four pitches from Bob Cain sail by. On ball four, he trotted to first base, where he was replaced by pinch-runner Jim Delsing.

In American League headquarters, reaction to "The Midget" was swift. Harridge demanded that Gaedel be released immediately and announced that his "batting record" would not appear in official averages.

In reply, Veeck inquired sweetly, "Please advise the minimum height of players in the American League."

The controversy over "The Midget" was hardly

As a preliminary to his major league debut, Eddie Gaedel, Bill Veeck's greatest promotional triumph, popped out of a giant cake (above) between games of a Sportsman's Park doubleheader in 1951.

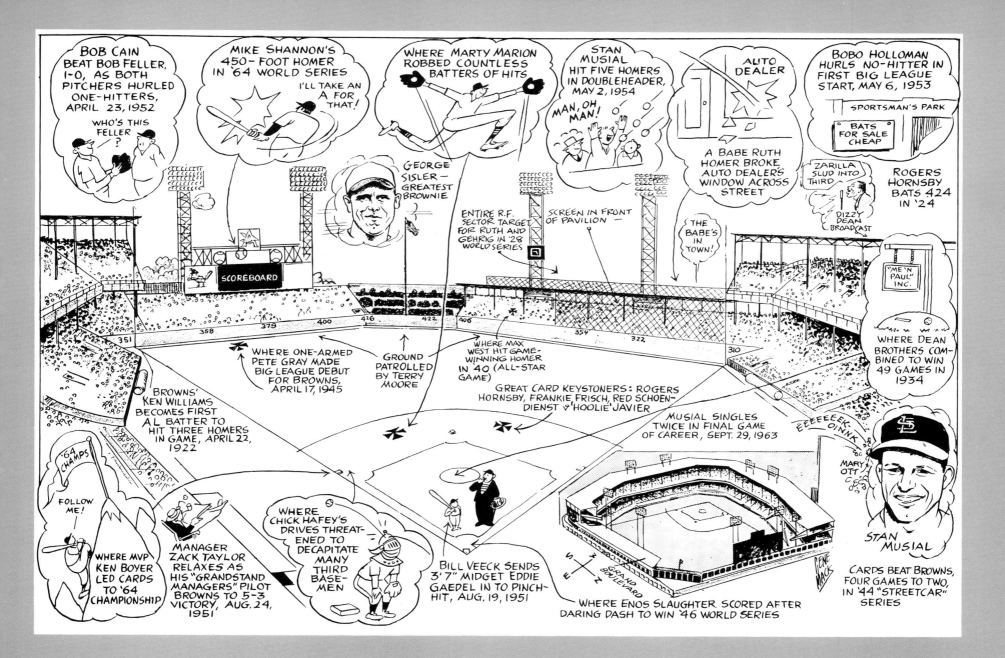

the equal of the dispute that gave birth to the Grand Avenue site as a baseball grounds prior to the advent of professional baseball in St. Louis.

The bizarre origins of the nine acres as a baseball grounds were described by Bob Burnes, sports editor of the St. Louis Globe-Democrat, in 1950:

"Many years ago a gentleman in St. Louis named Dunn owned some property on Green Street, which later became fashionable Lucas Avenue. His first name is unrecorded and the entire name of his next-door neighbor also has been lost in the dim and distant past.

"Mr. Dunn one day decided to build on his property. He had the foundation set up when his neighbor, hereinafter to be known as Mr. Fall Guy, wandered over to watch what was going on. It wasn't altogether curiosity because Mr. Fall Guy informed Mr. Dunn that he had overstepped the boundary line by nine inches.

"The builder had two choices. He could either tear down what already had been built and start over or he could make some sort of deal with neighbor Fall Guy. It seems that Dunn was not the type of chap to make deals. He tore down his foundation, moved back over the line and began anew.

"But Mr. Dunn, either to make sure he was right or because he had an ulterior motive or just was put out about the whole thing, didn't move back a mere nine inches. He moved 18.

"From what happened next it is suspected that he had something in mind. A bit later neighbor Fall Guy decided to do some building himself— and he started constructing his wall flush with Mr. Dunn's. The latter waited until the building was well advanced, then he wandered over and said, 'Ha, ha, now I've got you where you had me.

You're nine inches on my property.'

"That left Fall Guy in a predicament. His construction had progressed so far that it would have been foolish to tear it down and start anew. Besides, there was extreme danger of damaging Mr. Dunn's building.

"He offered to buy the nine inches. Mr. Dunn was adamant. The whole thing became one of the stock jokes of the time. Finally, with court action threatening, it ceased to be funny. In desperation, Mr. Fall Guy paid through the nose.

"In return for those pilfered nine inches, he turned over to Dunn nine acres he owned on the outskirts of St. Louis."

That plot eventually became Sportsman's Park, where other controversy was frequent in the years when the Browns were landlords and the Cardinals were tenants.

When the National League was founded in 1876, the St. Louis entry performed in the enclosed park with the wooden stands at Grand and Dodier. After two seasons, the Browns expired and for years the park was used for topflight exhibition games promoted by Al Spink, later the founder of The Sporting News.

By 1882 St. Louis was ripe for another major league franchise and Chris Von der Ahe, a beer garden proprietor from a block away on Grand Avenue, was willing and eager to foot the bill.

On May 21, the revived Browns made their debut in the American Association, then a major league, in refurbished Sportsman's Park, with its roofed grandstand. By 1884, the Browns had attracted legions of supporters, and competition in the form of Henry V. Lucas' club, the Maroons, of the new Union Association.

When the U.A. folded at the end of one season, however, and Lucas was awarded a franchise in

the National League, he did not hesitate to move from the Palace Park of America to a new site at Natural Bridge and Vandeventer. The Park was known as Union Park or Union Grounds.

For two years the Browns and Maroons competed for the St. Louis sports dollar. At the end of that time, Lucas tossed in the towel. His Maroons were no match for the Browns, now in the midst of prosperity that produced four consecutive pennants (1885-88).

Sportsman's Park, a name that dated from 1874, was the scene of a riotous celebration in October of 1886, when the Browns defeated Cap Anson's powerful Chicago White Stockings of the National League in the "winner take all" World Series. The deciding run was scored in the 10th inning of the final game by Chris Welsh. Newspaper accounts of the day reported that Welsh scored on a wild pitch. History has recorded the play as a steal of home. In any event, Welsh slid across the plate in what was hailed as "a $15,000 slide."

At the conclusion of their four-year reign, the Browns fell on melancholy days. The A.A. folded after the 1891 season, in which the Browns finished second, and Von der Ahe obtained a franchise in the National League for 1892.

His championship manager of the 1880s, Charley Comiskey, had defected for a managerial position at Cincinnati, and Von der Ahe, seeking to recapture lost glories, converted Sportsman's Park into "The Coney Island of the West." In addition to baseball, pleasure-seeking patrons could enjoy the chute-the-chutes, boating, wild west shows, boxing matches, horse racing and an all-girl silver cornet band.

Frequent fires—six in 10 years—forced Von der Ahe into an almost continuous rebuilding pro-

There was more than baseball on the minds of the 1918 St. Louis Browns (above) as they paraded around Sportsman's Park in a symbolic salute to the United States' efforts during World War I. By World War II, the park was the home of both the Browns and Cardinals, completely enclosed and prepared for night baseball (right).

gram at Sportsman's Park. To remain solvent, he was required to sell his better players. The combination was too big a hurdle for Von der Ahe, who disposed of his holdings after the 1898 season.

In 1899, brothers Stanley and Frank Robison, traction magnates from Fort Wayne, transferred the best players from their Cleveland club to St. Louis while stocking the Ohio club with lesser players from St. Louis. It was a fortunate move for St. Louis, disastrous for Cleveland.

The enriched St. Louis club, still known as the Browns, moved into the Natural Bridge and Vandeventer park, which quickly became Robison Field. In time, bright red caps and socks led sportswriter Willie McHale to rename the team Cardinals. The team performed at Robison Field until 1920, when it moved into Sportsman's Park, where the American League Browns had been playing since 1902 when the Milwaukee franchise was transferred to St. Louis.

The first significant change in the park's architecture was made by Robert Lee Hedges in 1909. A second deck was constructed from first base to third base, with pavilions adjoining the grandstands and bleachers in the outfield, raising the seating capacity to slightly more than 18,000.

In 1925, Phil Ball, then the Browns owner, authorized another expansion, double-decking the grandstands beyond first and third base and building a roof on the right-field pavilion, all at a cost of $500,000. The capacity swelled to 30,000.

Arc lights were installed in 1940, with the Browns marking the occasion by bowing to Cleveland, 3-2, before 25,562 on May 24. The game also was noteworthy in that winning pitcher Bob Feller backed up his own cause with his first major league home run.

The Cardinals made their home debut under the lights on June 4, 1940, bowing to Brooklyn, 10-1.

Ten years later, the Cardinals astounded other N.L. clubs by requesting permission to open the 1950 season at night. Despite protests of the Pittsburgh Pirates, scheduled opening day opponents, Owner Fred Saigh gained approval. The Redbirds won the historic inaugural, 4-2, before 20,871 with Stan Musial and Red Schoendienst hitting home runs.

The final chapter in Sportsman's Park ownership was written on April 9, 1953, when financially pinched Bill Veeck sold the structure to August A. Busch, Jr., president of the Anheuser-Busch Brewery. Busch then changed the name of the venerable park to Busch Stadium.

Busch paid $800,000 for the park and within the year had instituted a $1,500,000 rehabilitation program that included new box seats and renovated clubhouses and dugouts.

For years a distinctive feature of the park had been a screen in front of the right-field pavilion, extending from the foul pole 156 feet toward center field. In 1927, when Babe Ruth hit his record 60 home runs, the netting did not exist. The Babe lifted four round-trippers into the open area.

Three years later, Browns officials decided that home runs were too cheap in right field and erected the screen. Consequently, in 1932, when Jimmie Foxx of Philadelphia hit 58 homers, he also belted 12 drives that were stopped by the screen.

The operating arrangement between the Browns and Cardinals is evidenced (above) by the close proximity of their main offices at Sportsman's Park.

Two years later, again in the fourth game, Babe repeated the three-homer feat. Just prior to the Bambino's second round-tripper, Cardinals lefthander Willie Sherdel thought he had slipped a called third strike past Ruth. But National League umpire Cy Pfirman, working the plate, ruled that Sherdel had quick-pitched. Given another chance, The Babe rocketed the next pitch out of the park.

In the fifth game of the 1930 Series, Jimmie Foxx broke a scoreless deadlock by clouting a ninth-inning homer into the left-field bleachers off Burleigh Grimes for a 2-0 Philadelphia victory. The A's won the world championship later at Shibe Park.

A "hit" of a different sort was the feature of the 1934 Series action at the park. In the fourth game, a 10-4 Detroit victory, Dizzy Dean was inserted as a pinch-runner. Trying to break up a double play, the 30-game winner stuck his head in the path of the relay throw to first base and was knocked unconscious.

Ol' Diz returned to the mound in the fifth game —a defeat—and was on the mound in Game 7 when the Gashouse Gang humbled the Tigers, 11-0, at Detroit.

Three seven-game World Series were climaxed at Sportsman's Park. In 1931, the Cardinals put away the A's with a 4-2 victory and in 1946, Enos Slaughter ran through a coach's stop sign to score the deciding run in a cliff-hanger against the Red Sox.

In 1964, concluding a season in which they won the pennant on the final day, the Cardinals defeated the Yankees, 7-5, as Bob Gibson out-pitched five Yankee hurlers.

On two occasions tragedy cost the Yankees the services of centerfielders at Sportsman's Park.

Because of a predominantly lefthanded lineup, General Manager Dick Meyer, with the approval of Manager Eddie Stanky, removed the screen in 1955. Cardinal players had bounced 35 drives off the screen in 1954, it was emphasized, visitors only 18. Without the screen, Stan Musial would have hit 10 more homers, Red Schoendienst and Solly Hemus five more apiece.

One year later, however, Frank Lane, the new general manager, ordered the screen restored. "Keeping the ball in play is a condition, I believe, desired by the fans," said Frantic Frankie, who reasoned that banjo hitters, not sluggers, benefited most when only an 11-foot, six-inch wall stood between them and a home run.

With or without a screen, however, major league hitters registered memorable achievements within the confines of Sportsman's Park.

In 1922, Browns star George Sisler batted .420. Two years later, Rogers Hornsby, the Cardinals superstar, established a modern major league mark by hitting .424.

Babe Ruth found Sportsman's Park tailored to his slugging tastes, especially in the World Series. In the fourth game of the 1926 Series, The Babe belted three home runs.

Particularly memorable was his third-inning smash off Flint Rhem. The drive cleared the pavilion in deep right-center field, landed on Grand Avenue and smashed the show window of the Wells Chevrolet Company.

The next day, October 7, The Babe visited the auto agency and, surrounded by admirers, posed for photographers in the doorway.

After the 1946 Cardinals had defeated the Dodgers in a two-game playoff to decide the N.L. pennant, fans lined up (above) on the Grand Avenue side of Sportsman's Park to buy World Series tickets.

Another misfortune, although minor in comparison, befell Lefty Grove on August 23, 1931, while the great Philadelphia southpaw was building up to a 31-4 season. Having won 16 consecutive games, Grove opposed the Browns in what he hoped would be the victory that would surpass the A.L. record shared by Joe Wood and Walter Johnson since 1912.

Grove drew as his opponent Dick Coffman, a righthander of modest talents who, on this afternoon, shut out the powerful A's. Grove was equally as effective until left fielder Jimmy Moore, substituting for Al Simmons, misjudged a routine fly ball and permitted Fred Schulte to score the only run of the game.

The streak snapped, Grove exploded in a king-sized rage in the visitors' clubhouse, smashing furniture and demolishing lockers one by one while teammates stood by silently and helplessly.

The target of Lefty's fury was not Moore, but Simmons, who had selected this day to consult a doctor in Milwaukee, and Grove's teammates, who had failed to support Grove with even one run.

Death came to the Grand Dame of Grand Avenue at 3:15 p.m. on May 8, 1966. A 10-5 defeat by the San Francisco Giants, climaxed by Alex Johnson hitting into a double play, rang down the curtain.

As a band played Auld Lang Syne, 17,803 watched groundkeeper Bill Stocksick pry up home plate and place it aboard a helicopter for transport to Busch Memorial Stadium, the handsome new facility in downtown St. Louis.

Within a year, the grandstands were demolished and members of a boys club gamboled on sod made hallow by the spikes of Sisler, Hornsby and Musial.

Late in the 1922 season, while the Yankees and Browns were engaged in a crucial series, Whitey Witt was struck on the head by a pop bottle while tracking a fly ball in deep center field.

A more crushing tragedy occurred July 24, 1934, when Earle Combs, wilted by the blistering heat, crashed into the concrete left-field wall. Carried from the field with a fractured skull, shoulder and knee, the Kentucky Colonel hovered between life and death for four days. Amazingly, he recovered, but the mishap virtually ended his career. He retired a year later at age 36.

Although few spectators were aware of it, a near-tragedy occurred the night of May 19, 1965, while the Cardinals were playing the Phillies. During a ticket window holdup, a trigger-happy gunman fired a shot that ricocheted off a girder and grazed the neck of a 13-year-old girl sitting 400 feet away near third base.

This view (above) of a 1960 game at Sportsman's Park (by then known as Busch Stadium) shows the shape of the grandstand area with press box inhabitants getting a bird's-eye view of the action.

236

The panoramic view (above) of the playing field at Sportsman's Park
was photographed during a Browns' batting practice prior to their
April 25, 1938, game against Detroit.

BUSCH MEMORIAL STADIUM
St. Louis

For years there had been dialogue about a large midtown St. Louis sports stadium that would help revitalize the area's sagging economy.

But talk became reality when Anheuser-Busch pledged $5 million to the private equity capital. The balance of the $20 million needed to convert conversation into construction followed, as did a city referendum to clear a 30-acre tract of land just a stone's throw from the Mississippi River.

On May 24, 1964 ground was broken for a multi-purpose structure that, the chairman of the Civic Center Redevelopment Corporation said, "will kindle the fires of progress through the entire St. Louis area."

Two years later, on May 12, 1966, the two-tier masterpiece was ready for the Cardinals' first game—well, almost. Supervisory personnel would have welcomed a few more days for final preparation, but the date had been set and there was no time for change.

The message board did not function, elevator service was sporadic, the clubhouse had no heat and the installations for gas to grill hot dogs were not completed.

But there were compensations for the 46,048 first-nighters. The largest sports throng in St. Louis history swilled hot coffee on a chilly night and marveled at the two-section $1.5 million scoreboard with the electronic redbird that fluttered erratically, with accompanying chirps, during the seventh-inning stretch and whenever a player clouted a home run. The board, it was reported, contained 35,000 lights and its electri-

cal consumption was equivalent to that of a town of 2,000 inhabitants.

The discomfort and inconvenience was quickly forgotten when the Cardinals engaged the Atlanta Braves. Entering the last of the ninth, the Redbirds trailed, 3-2, but Jerry Buchek's single drove home the tying run, and Lou Brock's 12th-inning single produced a 4-3 victory.

The win was credited to reliever Don Dennis while Phil Niekro was charged with the loss.

Gary Geiger, an ex-Cardinal farmhand, rapped the first hit in the new park and teammate Felipe Alou smashed the first home run. Alou, in fact, smacked a pair, the first off starter Ray Washburn, the second off Tracy Stallard.

Mike Shannon was credited with the first St. Louis safety, a single in the opening frame, and the first RBI, with a third-inning triple.

Some of the opening night shivers would have been appreciated two months later when 49,936 sweltered through 105-degree heat at the All-Star Game.

First-aid attendants treated 135 heat victims during the 10-inning game that was decided when Maury Wills singled to drive in Tim McCarver, who had singled and advanced on a sacrifice.

One of the survivors of the cauldron-like temperature who retained his sense of humor was Casey Stengel, honorary coach of the National League team. Asked for his opinion of the new stadium, Ol' Case quipped, "Well, I must say, it sure holds the heat well."

Initially, grass covered the playing field, but

Fireworks light up the sky and fans pour onto the Busch Memorial Stadium playing field (above) after the Cardinals had wrapped up their 1982 World Series title with a victory over Milwaukee.

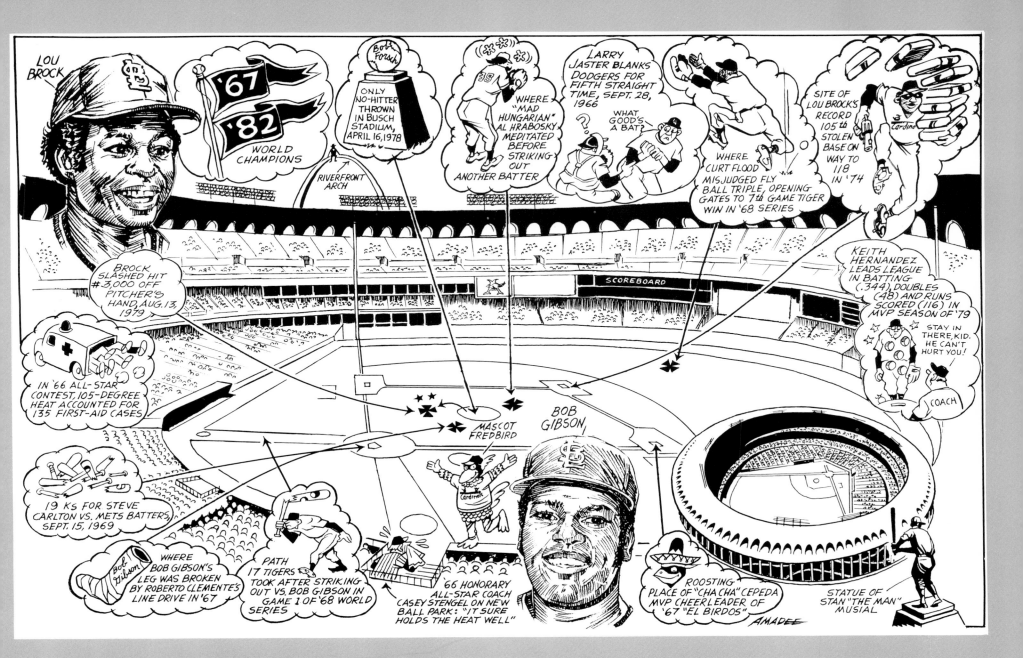

that gave way to synthetic turf in a few years. The foul lines have remained constant at 330 feet, but power-alley and center-field distances have been shortened. In 1973 an eight-foot high inner fence reduced the power alleys from 386 feet to 376 and center field from 414 feet to 404. The Cardinals' home run production failed to climb appreciably, however, and a few years later the inner fence was removed.

No St. Louis players dominated action as masterfully during the park's first decade as Bob Gibson and Lou Brock, the Hall of Fame pitcher with strikeout proclivities and the fleet-footed outfielder with the larcenous soul.

Gibby was almost unhittable in the late 1960s. In '67, after suffering a broken leg as the result of being hit by a line drive on July 15, the fireballing righthander recuperated in time to win 13 games. He followed with three victories over the Red Sox in the seven-game World Series—including a shutout at home.

A year later, in the World Series opener against Detroit, Gibby was superb. A Series-record total of 17 strikeouts was achieved by Gibson as Tiger batters gazed helplessly or swung weakly in a 4-0 Cardinal shutout.

Gibby's strikeout performance was not a record for Busch Memorial Stadium. That was set by Steve Carlton, a St. Louis southpaw, who fanned 19 New York Mets while losing, 4-3, on September 15, 1969.

When Brock shattered the record for most stolen bases in a season on September 10, 1974, he did it before the home folks. His 105th theft thrilled 27,000 admirers who had little else to applaud as Dick Ruthven and the Phillies beat the Birds, 8-2.

Brock pilfered 16 bases against the Phils that season, more than he got against any other club during a record season that netted 118 steals.

The most severe case of public embarrassment in the stadium's first 15 years was suffered by Curt Flood, normally a flawless outfielder.

Flood's miscue occurred in the seventh inning of the seventh game of the 1968 World Series with more than 54,000 pair of eyes trained on him.

The Cardinals, who had permitted the Tigers to deadlock the Series at three games apiece the previous day, were locked in a scoreless tie when Norm Cash and Willie Horton hit back-to-back singles off Gibson.

When Jim Northrup stroked a drive to center field, Flood, momentarily losing sight of the ball against the crowd background, broke in, then tried to reverse direction. He was too late. The ball sailed over his head for a two-run triple. Northrup scored later and the Tigers were well en route to a title-clinching, 4-1 victory.

As it turned out, that would be the last time the Cardinals would appear in a World Series for 14 years. In 1982, a club built through clever deals by General Manager-Manager Whitey Herzog captured the world championship, defeating the Milwaukee Brewers, four games to three, in an exciting World Series.

Trailing three games to two after losing two of the three Series games in Milwaukee, the Cardinals battled back to win Games 6 and 7 at Busch Memorial Stadium. The Series ended with Bruce Sutter, the Cardinals relief ace, striking out Brewers slugger Gorman Thomas in a 6-3 St. Louis triumph. It was the Cardinals' ninth world title in 13 Series appearances, an N.L. record.

The view (above), taken during Game 3 of the 1967 World Series against Boston, shows the symmetrical design of Busch Memorial Stadium, pre-AstroTurf.

The Gateway Arch and Mississippi River form the backdrop for circular
Busch Memorial Stadium in this 1967 aerial view (above).

SAN DIEGO STADIUM

San Diego

When the National League was organized in 1876, San Diego was a sleepy seacoast village of 2,500 people only a shade larger than when it was founded by Father Juniperro Serra as a Franciscan mission in the 18th century.

In 1936, six decades after the birth of the N.L., professional baseball arrived in Southern California chiefly because of hard times. H. W. (Hardrock Bill) Lane, a one-time miner, experienced rough sledding in Hollywood and moved his Pacific Coast League club to San Diego.

Awaiting Lane was a partially constructed stadium built by the Works Progress Administration, a federally funded program to provide employment during the Great Depression.

Disregarding warnings that the shift would rob him of his last $11,000, Lane moved into the park at the foot of Broadway.

The team, named the Padres because of the nearby mission, made its home debut on March 31, 1936. With 8,178 in the 9,100-seat stadium, Herman Pillette defeated Seattle, 6-2.

In the Padres lineup were future major leaguers Bobby Doerr, George Myatt and Vince DiMaggio. During the season Doerr collected six hits in one game, the last against Lefty O'Doul, the San Francisco manager.

Also during that first season, Lane signed a gangling youngster who had attracted attention with his slugging feats at Herbert Hoover High School.

The youngster batted .271 as a Padre rookie and amused the spectators by losing his cap

while running the bases and smacking long foul balls into the Pacific Ocean, 100 yards from home plate.

Ted Williams hit no home runs in 42 games his first season, but he rapped two triples and eight doubles while driving in 11 runs. The next year he

batted .291 with 23 homers and 98 RBIs.

Because there was no roof on Lane Field at the start, there also was no foul screen. Foul balls regularly zipped into the crowd, inflicting broken noses and bruised jaws.

A chummy right-field barrier, 325 feet from the plate, made the field a favorite batting range for lefthanded batters. In 1949 Max West clouted 48 homers and Luke Easter poled another 25 as a two-man demolition crew. "They drove 20 dozen baseballs out of the park during batting practice in one week," a former teammate remembered.

Jack Graham socked 48 home runs in 1948 and appeared a cinch to break Tony Lazzeri's PCL record of 60 until he was beaned in mid-season by Red Adams of Los Angeles.

Easter was credited with hitting the longest home run in Lane Field, a 500-foot drive against the center-field scoreboard.

Because of Big Luke's slugging prowess, crowds jammed Lane Field for batting practice. In 1949 they whirled the turnstiles 493,780 times, the highest total in the park's 22 years.

The two most dramatic home runs in Lane Field were smashed by Bob Elliott in a one-game playoff to decide the 1954 championship. The one-time National League MVP clouted two homers and drove in five runs as the Padres defeated Hollywood, 7-2. The old Mission team of San Francisco had been moved to Hollywood following the departure of Bill Lane's club.

The most notable batting accomplishment at Lane Field was registered by Hollywood outfielder

Ted Giannoulas, alias the San Diego Chicken (shown above doctoring umpire Rich Garcia), started out modestly as a San Diego attraction, but has expanded his horizons to parks throughout the country.

243

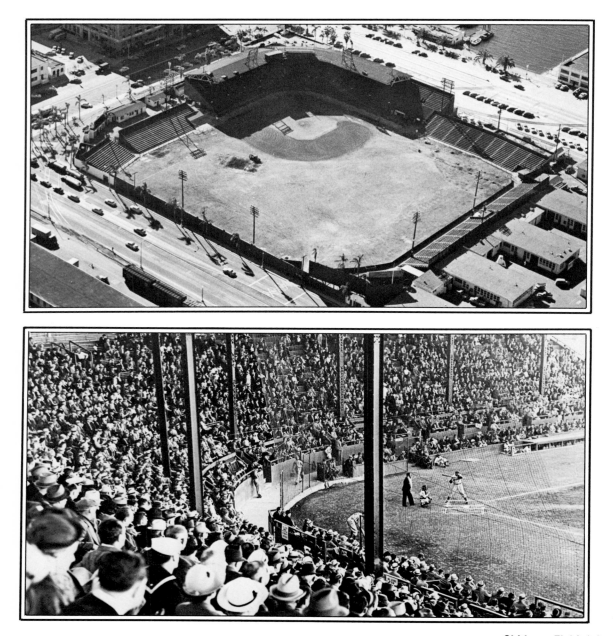

Ted Beard on April 4, 1953. The former Pittsburgh Pirate set a PCL record by clouting four home runs in five at-bats as the Stars defeated the Padres, 6-5.

All of Beard's homers cleared the right-center field fence and traveled about 375 feet. In his only non-homer appearance, Beard struck out.

One day after Beard's achievement, San Diego outfielder Herb Gorman, who had doubled in his first two at-bats, collapsed in the field and died of a heart attack while en route to the hospital.

But there were more memorable moments than those supplied by hitters at Lane Field.

One spectacular pitching duel took place in 1938 when Frank Shellenback, manager of the Padres, beat an 18-year-old righthander for Seattle, 2-1, in a seven-inning second game of a Sunday doubleheader. The youngster, who was making his professional debut, was Fred Hutchinson, later a mainstay of the Detroit Tigers and manager of the Tigers, Cardinals and Reds.

On August 30 of the same year, Dick Ward of the Padres pitched 12⅔ hitless innings against Ray Prim of Los Angeles before winning, 1-0, on a two-hitter.

It was the last game Bill Lane ever saw. The owner suffered a heart attack after the game and died later that year.

Dick Stigman hurled 10⅔ hitless frames against Salt Lake City on May 20, 1939. He departed the mound in the 12th inning and did not figure in the 12-inning victory.

In the latter years of Lane Field, a curious groundkeeper discovered that the distance from home plate to first base was only 87 feet, instead of the standard 90, and that the right-field foul line was 325 feet long, not 335 as was painted on the fence.

Old Lane Field (above), located at the foot of Broadway on San Diego Bay, was the home of the original Padres. The park (below in 1938) eventually was eaten away by termites and torn down.

Following the death of Lane, his estate operated the franchise until 1945, when it was acquired by Bill Starr and his associates. Starr, a catcher for the Padres from 1937 to '39, enjoyed the distinction of being the only player to pinch-hit for Ted Williams in Ted's two years at San Diego. Starr was sent to the plate to bunt.

In 1951, after vendors had increased their commission demands, Starr replaced them with machines, which catered to customer appetites until the following year, when vendors agreed to accept smaller commissions.

After the 1957 season the Starr group sold the Padres to C. Arnholt Smith for nearly $350,000.

The beginning of the Smith tenure signaled the end of Lane Field. The termite-ridden structure gave way to a parking lot while the Padres moved to Westgate Park, an 8,200-seat facility in Mission Valley.

Westgate Park was built with Smith money on Smith property. The park, with 5,732 box seats and 2,516 grandstand seats, was completely roofed over. Foul lines measured 320 feet and the center-field barrier, a 6-foot high wire fence, was 410 feet away.

The Padres dedicated the new field with a day-night doubleheader against Phoenix on April 29, 1958, drawing crowds of 4,619 and 7,129.

The park, named for Smith's Westgate-California Tuna Packing Corp., had a parking lot capable of handling 3,000 cars. More than $20,000 worth of trees, shrubs, flowers and tropical plants were imported to beautify the grounds.

For years San Diego city fathers had dreamed of a major league franchise. That dream took a turn toward reality in May 1965 when the City Council approved the plans of a 50,000-seat, $27.75 million stadium. They directed the city

Westgate Park (above and below), an 8,200-seat facility in Mission Valley, replaced Lane Field in 1958 and featured a grandstand area that was completely roofed over.

The final step toward a major league baseball franchise was taken in 1967 when San Diego Stadium (above) was dedicated with a football game between the Chargers and Detroit Lions.

246

manager to acquire the necessary acreage in Mission Valley for the four-tier structure.

When the proposition was presented to the voters, it passed by an overwhelming 72 percent majority.

Before construction could begin, however, it was necessary to divert the San Diego River, which flowed through the proposed stadium site. The next step was the removal of 2.5 million cubic yards of dirt so that the stadium could be built on a mound 40 feet above the playing surface.

The stadium extends 12 blocks in one direction and six in another. It consists of 1,715 massive pieces of pre-cast concrete in 234 different shapes, some weighing 39 tons. Other items include 1,500 steel pilings, each 40 to 60 feet long, 40,000 cubic yards of concrete, an $815,000 plumbing complex, over 60 public rest rooms, a $300,000 heating-ventilating system, and 2,000 directional signs.

San Diego Stadium was formally dedicated on August 29, 1967 with a football game between the San Diego Chargers and Detroit Lions. Baseball fans obtained their first glimpse of the city's newest pride and joy in a two-day open house, February 17-18, 1968. A total of 15,000 toured the premises, taking in the 330-foot foul lines, the 370-foot power alleys, the center-field fence 410 feet away and the 17-foot high fence surrounding the outfield.

In their first season in the new park, the Pacific Coast League Padres, a second-place club, attracted 203,000 fans. In the meantime, Westgate Park, five miles away, was demolished to make way for Fashion Valley, a shopping center.

Major league baseball arrived in San Diego in the form of a National League expansion fran-

ald's hamburger chain.

Kroc's career as a baseball magnate got off to an inauspicious start in the Padres' home opener in 1974. Kroc grabbed the public address microphone and told 39,000 fans, "This is the most stupid ball playing I've ever seen."

The next day, censured by Commissioner Bowie Kuhn and Marvin Miller, executive director of the Major League Baseball Players Association, Kroc offered a public apology.

Willie Mays, en route to 660 lifetime home runs, got his 600th at San Diego Stadium as a San Francisco pinch-hitter on September 22, 1969. Lou Brock of St. Louis gained fresh laurels on August 29, 1977 when he stole the 893rd base of his career, surpassing the record set by Ty Cobb.

The 49th major league All-Star Game was played to the cheers of 51,000 spectators on July 11, 1978 and resulted in a 7-3 N.L. victory.

Steve Garvey, with a triple and a two-run single, was named the game's most valuable player.

Of all the personalities who have performed in the Mission Valley arena, none has attracted as many laughs as a non-athlete standing 5'4" tall and weighing 125 pounds.

He is Ted Giannoulas, a former San Diego State journalism student who, colorfully attired in a henhouse costume, has amused millions of spectators and mimicked hundreds of players as the San Diego Chicken.

The Chicken's native habitat, known initially as San Diego Stadium, was rechristened Jack Murphy Stadium in 1981, within a year after the death of the San Diego Union sports editor who for years had campaigned vigorously for a modern stadium and major league franchises in baseball and football.

chise on April 8, 1969 and the Padres rewarded 23,370 customers with a 2-1 victory over Houston. Dick Selma allowed the Astros only five hits while striking out 12. The Padres reached Don Wilson and Jack Billingham for only four safeties, one of which was a fifth-inning home run by Ed Spiezio, the first by a major league Padre.

Ollie Brown's sixth-inning double scored Roberto Pena with the deciding run.

Dock Ellis of Pittsburgh hurled the only no-hitter in the stadium's first 14 major league seasons, blanking the Padres, 2-0, on June 12, 1970.

But there nearly was another.

On July 21, 1970, Clay Kirby held the New York Mets hitless for eight innings, but trailed 1-0 when he was lifted for a pinch-hitter by Manager Preston Gomez. Two walks, a double steal and an infield out produced a first-inning run for the Mets, who collected three hits in the ninth off Jack Baldschun and won the game, 3-0.

After five consecutive last-place finishes, the Padres were ardently wooed by would-be buyers in Washington, D.C. However, the club was saved for San Diego by Ray Kroc, founder of the McDon-

After opening-day ceremonies (above) in 1969, the major league Padres rewarded 23,370 fans with a 2-1 victory over the Houston Astros.

248

By 1960, the Cardinals were operating under the ownership of August A. Busch and Sportsman's Park (above) was operating under the alias of Busch Stadium.

Busch Memorial Stadium (above left, during the 1982 World Series) is located near the St. Louis riverfront in the shadow of the Gateway Arch (below left).

San Francisco's Candlestick Park lies in the shadow of the ever-present Candlestick Point (above, beyond the fence), overlooking San Francisco Bay. A panoramic look at Philadelphia's Veterans Stadium is seen on pages 252-253.

The baseball scoreboard at Exhibition Stadium in Toronto is located well back of the right-field fence at the open end of the facility.

The Cascade Mountains form a scenic backdrop (above) for the
Kingdome, home of the Seattle Mariners.

CANDLESTICK PARK

San Francisco

According to reliable research, the first baseball game in San Francisco was played on February 22, 1860. There is no mention of the diamond site or the time consumed between the first pitch and the last putout. All that is known is that the game lasted nine innings and wound up in a 33-33 tie between the Eagles and the Red Rovers. The contest was halted after regulation time because the Rovers protested "unfair" practices by the Eagles pitchers.

The city was represented in the "outlaw" California League in the late 1800s and entered Organized Baseball as a member of the Pacific Coast League in 1903.

Early teams performed on a diamond at Eighth and Harrison streets near downtown San Francisco. The great earthquake of 1906 destroyed the park and the club finished the season as a tenant of the Oakland team.

In the rebuilt city of 1907, a new park, named Recreation Park, was constructed at 15th and Valencia. This 15,000-seat park in the Mission District served as home for the PCL Seals until 1931, with the exception of 1914. In that season, the team switched to Ewing Field, which was abandoned after one year because of game delays and interruptions due to fog.

One of the most remarkable Pacific Coast League games was played in San Francisco on June 8, 1909 when the Seals and Oakland battled 24 innings before the Seals squeezed out a 1-0 victory. Clarence (Cack) Henley of the winners and Jimmy Wiggs each went the distance in the three-hour and 35-minute struggle. The game was decided when Nick Williams, later manager of the Seals, smacked a two-out single to right field.

According to the San Francisco Chronicle, "The crowd at the start was not of immense proportions, but increased as the game progressed. Before the end there was a mob of howling fans who yelled on every play and went home to cold suppers satisfied that they had had their money's worth."

In 1931, the San Francisco club moved into its new park, Seals Stadium, at 16th and Bryant streets. The 18,600-seat facility incorporated the best features of other minor league parks as determined in a year's research by owners Charles Graham, Dr. Charles Strub and George Putnam.

The concrete and steel structure contained three clubhouses and, surprisingly for that era, individual player lockers. The lighting system, reputed to be the finest in the minor leagues, consisted of six towers with banks of lights at a height of 122 feet.

For a couple of reasons, Seals Stadium was built without a roof. First, the fans preferred to sit in the sun, and the heat never became excessive. Second, the city receives very little rainfall during the baseball season. In one five-year period, the Seals lost only three games because of rain.

Dimensions of the playing area were 340 feet to left field, 385 to right and 400 to center. A 30-foot high fence enclosed the field.

Seals Stadium, erected in the depth of the Great Depression, cost only $600,000. Dr. Strub once explained that unemployed laborers would leap on the running board of his car early in the morning and beg for the opportunity to work on the project at $3 a day.

The stadium was dedicated on April 7, 1931 when a packed house watched the Seals shut out Portland, 8-0. Playing third base for the Seals was Babe Pinelli, later a National League umpire. The shortstop was Frank Crosetti, who was to join the New York Yankees the following year.

When Joe DiMaggio, not yet 19, established a

With the exception of one season, Recreation Park (above) was the home of San Francisco's Pacific Coast League franchise from 1907 through 1930.

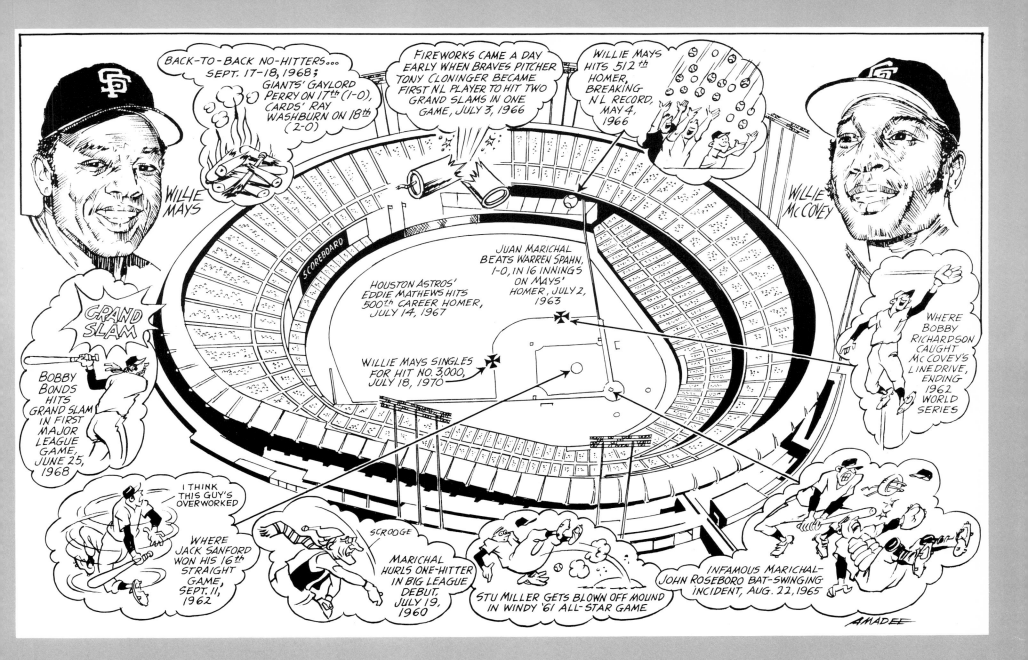

The Giants spent their first two seasons in San Francisco, 1958 and 1959, at Seals Stadium (above), longtime home of the city's minor league club.

PCL record in 1933 by hitting safely in 61 consecutive games, he started the streak at Portland on May 25 and was stopped at home on July 26. Oakland pitcher Ed Walsh Jr., son of the Chicago White Sox immortal, blanked DiMag in five trips to the plate. Twenty-one of the games during the streak were played at Seals Stadium.

The Seals and Portland Beavers battled for 21 innings, the fourth longest game in PCL history, on August 5, 1953 before the visitors pulled out a 4-2 triumph. The four-hour and 20-minute marathon, witnessed by 1,394, was decided when, with two outs, Teddy Shandor yielded a single, a walk and RBI singles by Fletcher Robbe and Bob Marquis.

Seals Stadium expired as a Pacific Coast League park on September 13, 1957 when the Seals, having clinched the pennant, clowned their way to a 14-7 loss to Sacramento before 15,484.

Seals Manager Joe Gordon, then 42, pitched and played shortstop as well as his old second base position. Outfielder Albie Pearson played five positions, including pitcher, and was charged with the loss after yielding two hits in one inning of work.

The height of farce was attained when Sacramento Manager Tommy Heath inserted himself in the opposition's lineup as a pinch-runner for Gordon, who collected two hits.

Major league baseball arrived in San Francisco in 1958 as a result of Horace Stoneham transferring the New York Giants to greener pastures. The Giants settled in at Seals Stadium until the city could fulfill its promise to construct a new stadium.

Seals Stadium, with a capacity less than half that of the abandoned Polo Grounds in New York, was not the profit inhibitor that might have been

Photos showing Candlestick Park as it appeared in 1966 (above right), six years after the stadium opened, and how it looks at the present (below right) offer a startling contrast.

259

expected. The 1958 Giants attracted 1.27 million customers, almost double their gate of the previous season.

Opening day in 1958 attracted a crowd of over 23,000. They reserved their most thunderous ovation for Mrs. John McGraw, widow of the legendary Giants manager.

The Giants marked their California debut by thumping the Los Angeles Dodgers, 8-0, as Ruben Gomez beat Don Drysdale. Home runs by Daryl Spencer and Orlando Cepeda fueled the winners' 11-hit attack.

"Imagine," chortled winning Manager Bill Rigney, "winning with three men on the field who had never appeared in a big-league game acting as if they had been around for years!"

The reference was to first baseman Cepeda, right fielder Willie Kirkland and third baseman Jim Davenport.

In their two seasons at Seals Stadium, the Giants played to nearly 2.7 million customers, and then transferred to their new stadium.

To determine a name for the new facility, a contest was conducted by the City Recreation and Parks Commission. More than 20,000 entries and 2,000 names were submitted. The judges, who were sports editors of the city's four daily newspapers, selected Candlestick Park as the winning name because the stadium is situated on Candlestick Point, overlooking San Francisco Bay.

Initially, the capacity of the park was 42,553, but the installation of additional general admission seats soon raised the capacity to 43,765.

The first major league park to be constructed exclusively of reinforced concrete, Candlestick Park also was, in 1960, "the only heated open-air stadium in the world." Because many of the Giants games were scheduled at night, when temperatures in the 40s are not uncommon, a radiant heating system was installed in the 20,000-seat reserved seating section. Three-quarter inch wrought iron pipe, placed below pre-cast concrete seats, circulated water heated by a boiler independent of the remainder of the stadium's heating plant.

The new stadium traced its origins to November 1954, when voters approved a $5 million bond issue for a new park when and if the city acquired a major league franchise.

From that point the project passed through numerous stages, such as:

May 1957—Mayor George Christopher asks for surveys of possible sites for the park.

June 1957—Contractor Charles Harney offers ground at Candlestick Point.

July 1957—Mayor accepts the Harney offer, calls it "fabulous."

August 1957—Harney says park can be built in eight months.

November 1957—Harney awarded $30 per square foot to remove 300,000 feet of hill to clear way for park.

January 1958—Stadium Inc., a non-profit organization, was designated to handle details of construction.

February 1958—Horace Stoneham approves blueprints.

March 1958—Bay View property owners protest the widening of streets for access roads.

July 1958—Supervisors approve stadium plans; Mayor turns over $5 million to Stadium Inc.

August 1958—Work starts on stadium.

September 1958—Grand jury orders probe of financing, particularly of payment for Harney's land.

Situated on Candlestick Point overlooking San Francisco Bay, the
Giants' Candlestick Park (above) was the first major league stadium
to be constructed entirely of reinforced concrete.

42,269, including Vice President Richard Nixon, Governor Pat Brown, Commissioner Ford Frick and Mrs. John McGraw.

The customers, many of whom arrived by helicopter, cabin cruisers and yachts, were told by Brown: "San Francisco always has been a city of giants. Now we have a home for them."

The Giants brought the occasion to a rousing climax by defeating the St. Louis Cardinals, 3-1, as Sam Jones outpitched Larry Jackson. Willie Mays drove in all the winners' runs with a first-inning triple and a third-inning single. Leon Wagner's fifth-inning homer accounted for the Cards' only run.

The contest was only three innings old when Giants Manager Bill Rigney huddled with umpires Augie Donatelli, Ken Burkhart, Ed Vargo and Jocko Conlan to the puzzlement of the fans.

Eventually, it was revealed that a question had arisen over the placement of the foul poles on the playing field—rather than off the playing area.

"If you don't like where they are, get a shovel, dig a hole, and put 'em where you want 'em," Rigney told the umpires.

It was decided that any ball that caromed off the poles and into the seats would be a ground-rule double.

National television viewers gained a clear understanding of the diabolic winds that plague the stadium while watching the first 1961 All-Star Game. In the ninth inning, Stu Miller, a 165-pound San Francisco reliever, was blown off the pitching mound by a near gale. The costly balk figured in the American League's two-run rally that tied the score. The A.L. scored again in the 10th inning but the N.L. won the contest, 5-4, when Hank Aaron singled, Willie Mays doubled and Roberto Clemente singled.

December 1958—Harney threatens to stop work unless some items are removed from the contract.

July 1959—Stadium Inc. announces Candlestick cannot possibly be ready for the final weeks of the season as promised.

August 1959—Grand jury probes the awarding of parking contract.

September 1959—Teamster strike holds up seat installation.

November 1959—Harney bars Giants from park because Stadium Inc. won't accept his work.

Stoneham refuses to accept "unplayable infield." Harney agrees to put in a new one.

January 1960—City Fire Prevention Bureau calls Candlestick a "fire trap."

February 1960—Dove of peace flies over park as Harney finally lets Giants move in, using player clubhouse for temporary offices.

Foul lines at Candlestick Park measure 335 feet, while the center-field fence is 400 feet from home plate. A 7,000-car parking lot adjoins the stadium.

Opening day on April 12, 1960 attracted

While Candlestick Park has been noted for its swirling winds, the stadium has had other weather problems. Fog swept the field (above) during a 1960 game, forcing a 30-minute delay.

Candlestick's acclaimed radiant heating system brought on a lawsuit before the park was a year old. A disgruntled fan charged the Giants with breach of warranty by selling him a box seat in an area where the system did not function properly. The fan testified that on several occasions he was forced to leave his seat in the midst of exciting rallies because his feet were "freezing."

Horace Stoneham agreed that the system did not work, but maintained that the Giants did not install it—and therefore were not responsible. The irate fan's feelings were soothed by a jury award of $1,597.

Candlestick Park fell into quick disfavor because of the chilling winds that frustrated right-handed hitters and supplied jet stream force behind balls hit by lefthanded batters. Wind velocity developed into such a potent issue that a study was ordered to determine what, if anything, could be done to correct the situation.

The report offered no relief. "Changing the shape of the stadium would only change the direction of the winds," it noted. "If the winds had been checked before construction, the stadium might have been shifted a few hundred yards to a more comfortable site."

Eventually, Mayor Joseph Alioto proposed that Candlestick Park be scrapped and a $50 million multi-purpose stadium be built in midtown San Francisco. When his suggestion failed to draw public support, the mayor instructed the Board of Supervisors and the Recreation and Parks Commission to proceed with expansion and improvements on Candlestick Park.

As a result of the discussions and high-level decisions, a $16.1 million renovation was completed before the 1971 season. Synthetic turf

replaced natural grass; movable seats were installed in right field to be used during the football season; an escalator was built to transport fans from the parking lot into the stadium; the park was converted into a bowl and the seating capacity increased to 58,000. The artificial turf was replaced by a natural surface in 1979.

While the rebuilding project was under way, architect John Bolles assured everyone that there would no longer be a wind problem.

Bolles was partially correct. Wind velocity was lessened, but was not eliminated entirely.

One of baseball's most bizarre episodes occurred at Candlestick on August 22, 1965 when Giants pitcher Juan Marichal, batting for the home club, bludgeoned Los Angeles catcher John Roseboro on the head with his bat. Marichal was angry because he thought Roseboro intentionally threw too close to his head when returning a ball to Dodger pitcher Sandy Koufax. Roseboro suffered a gash on his head and a bump on his hand. Marichal was handed an eight-game suspension and a $1,750 fine by National League President Warren Giles.

With pro football's San Francisco 49ers joining the Giants as Candlestick Park tenants in 1971, the stadium took on a different appearance (above).

KINGDOME

Seattle

When a Seattle baseball fan in the late 19th century wished to attend a weekday game, he found his way by private or public conveyance to 12th and Jefferson streets, where he could watch the local nine perform in the YMCA Park.

If he wished to attend a Sunday contest, he would journey to the Madison Park picnic grounds, site of all the Sabbath contests.

According to a clipping from the Seattle Times, "In 1903 the team moved to a ball park at Fifth Avenue and Republican Street. Next, in 1907, came the first Dugdale Field, also known as Band Box Park, at 13th and Yesler."

Dugdale Field was named for Dan Dugdale, a Peoria, Ill., native who had caught briefly in the major leagues for Kansas City and Washington before migrating to Seattle where, in 1898, he managed the Northwest League club.

In the early years of this century, Seattle teams, known as the Indians, moved from the Northwest League to the Pacific Coast League to the Pacific Northwest League to the Northwestern League to the Pacific International League and back to the PCL in 1919.

While the city had a franchise in the Northwestern League in 1913, Dugdale built a wooden park seating 15,000 at Rainier and McClellan streets. Dugdale Field remained the home of the Indians until July 4, 1932 when it was destroyed by fire, supposedly the result of holiday fireworks set off in the vicinity.

When the Indians returned from a trip and found their old home in ashes, they moved into Civic Field. Built originally for high school sports, Civic Field consisted of a dirt playing surface and seating accommodations for about 15,000.

When the PCL club moved into modern quarters in June 1938, a correspondent of The Sporting News reported:

"The fine grass field at the new stadium is like soothing salve to the much-punished underpinning of the players. For six long years the outfielders pounded the turf of Civic Field and received more than their share of sore legs and Charley horses. Infielders have taken many a bump from ricocheting balls and the fans endured the inconvenience of view-obstructing wooden light poles and the chill winds from the nearby Puget Sound waters. Use of the Civic grounds was an emergency measure occasioned by the burning of old Dugdale Field. The Civic Field was never meant for pro ball."

The new home of the PCL club was Emil George Sick's Seattle Stadium, a $350,000 structure that seated 15,000 in a concrete grandstand and wooden bleachers. The park was located at Rainier and McClellan, site of old Dugdale Field.

The franchise had been purchased late the previous year by Sick, reputed to be the most successful brewer in the Far West.

Within six months Sick had discarded the traditional team name of Indians and rechristened it the Rainiers. He also erected a park with 325-foot foul lines and a center-field fence 400 feet from home plate. Instantly, baseball enthusiasm in the Northwest skyrocketed.

A crowd of 12,000 greeted the Rainiers in their new home on June 15, 1938. The following evening, despite inclement weather and a one-hour rain delay, 7,000 turned out for the first night game in the new park.

With Jack Lelivelt as manager, the Rainiers challenged for the pennant in Sick's first year of ownership, then captured two successive championships. When Lelivelt died suddenly following the 1940 season, Sick hired Bill Skiff, who produced the third consecutive flag and won for Sick The Sporting News designation as Minor League Executive of the Year for 1941.

Acknowledging his citation, Sick noted: "Really, I took a sporting chance when I went into a business about which I knew nothing. I thought the town deserved a better break than it was getting in baseball.

"The way the baseball-starved community reacted to my decision was wonderful. In fact, the citizens and the newspapers were so enthusiastic after I announced I was going to build a new park and a new team that one of my daughters, on reading the latest edition, said: 'Daddy, did you just buy a baseball team or save the country from disaster?' "

For years Seattle factions had clamored for a major league franchise. The city, it was emphasized, was the 28th largest in the United States with a population of 1.3 million. It was a gold

A wide-angle shot of Seattle's Kingdome (above) gives the indoor
stadium a cavernous look. The Mariners played their first game under
the roof on April 6, 1977.

mine waiting to be tapped.

The eagerly awaited moment arrived in October 1967 when American League club owners, meeting in Chicago, awarded Seattle an expansion franchise for 1969. Franchise owners were William Daley, former majority stockholder of the Cleveland Indians, and the Soriano brothers, Dewey, president of the Pacific Coast League, and Max, an attorney. The franchise cost $6 million and another $2.5 million was spent in preparing the team, known as the Pilots, for its A.L. debut.

The first season, it was said, the team would play in Sick's Stadium, enlarged to a 25,000 seating capacity with the addition of seats beyond the first and third base areas. This facility, now city-owned, would be used temporarily, until the city could construct a multi-purpose domed stadium, which voters had approved in a $40 million bonds issue several years earlier.

Almost from the start there was friction between the Pilots and city officials, who had promised to bring the stadium up to major league standards.

Expansion work on the park did not begin until January 1969, three months before the start of the season. Instead of the promised 25,000 seats by opening day, only 18,000 were ready. Ticket manager Harry McCarthy was forced to ask 700 fans to wait an hour on April 11 until carpenters could put the finishing touches on their seats.

Throughout the season the complaints mounted. The rest rooms, maintained Dewey Soriano, were "disgraceful." Other improvements, it was alleged, were done at the club's expense.

Lack of water pressure created another headache. If attendance climbed above 14,000, the pressure almost disappeared. After an August series, New York players were required to return to their hotel to shower. One nettled baseball writer griped that there was insufficient pressure to supply water to the press box.

But water pressure was of scant importance on opening day when 17,150 watched the Pilots defeat the Chicago White Sox, 7-0, as Gary Bell scattered 10 hits. The next night Diego Segui and Jack Aker scattered four hits and the Pilots won again, 5-1.

As late as mid-August, Joe Schultz's club occupied third in the American League West Division, but the loss of 18 of 20 games punctured the Pilots' hopes for a respectable season. They wound up last.

To break even on their maiden venture, the Pilots needed an attendance of 850,000. They attracted only 677,944. Their top draw was 23,657 for a game with the Yankees in August. At season's end club ledgers showed a deficit of $800,000.

Under their five-year lease agreement, the Pilots were to pay an annual rent of $165,000, which was to be used for park improvements. In October 1969 city officials demanded that the club post a $660,000 letter of credit, representing the four remaining years of rent, plus a $150,000 bond to insure the return of the stadium to the city in good condition, or face eviction.

Maintaining that the city had failed to live up to its terms of the lease, the Pilots refused to pay up, a position which was supported by the American League.

Climaxing the Pilots' problems, the Pacific Coast League demanded $1 million in damages for the loss of one of its strongest franchises. The Pilots offered to settle for $80,000. The matter was submitted to arbitration and the indemnity was set at $300,000.

Efforts were launched to find more oppulent owners and the American League voted a $650,000 loan in a bid to keep the Pilots afloat. Until late March 1970, Seattle continued as a viable franchise in the American League.

On March 30-31, however, the Pilots expired without a gurgle. On March 30 A.L. club owners, in a telephone poll, approved the club's move to Milwaukee. On the second date a bankruptcy court referee in Seattle ruled that a $10.8 million offer from Milwaukee Brewers Inc. was in order.

Seattle remained out of Organized Baseball for two years, then returned as a member of the Northwest League. After five seasons in the Class A circuit, Seattle received a second opportunity to demonstrate its qualifications as a major league city.

The return was not so easily achieved, however. First there was the domed stadium, a prerequisite for a second chance. The site was a problem in itself. Should it be in the downtown area or in the suburbs? For every proposed location there was an equal and vociferous reaction. The World's Fair site of the 1960s was struck down in a referendum because it lacked parking areas. Eventually, in the fall of 1972, the Stadium Commission settled on a plot on the southern perimeter of downtown Seattle. Construction of the domed arena seating 59,438 for baseball and almost 65,000 for football, commenced on the day that a King County executive pressed a symbolic gold home plate into the turf and announced, "This is the place."

By 1977 the Queen City of the Northwest was ready to try its hand at major league baseball once more. The Kingdome, costing $67 million, was completed and the American League had

granted the city another expansion franchise. Prominent among the new owners was movie star Danny Kaye.

Unlike its first major league venture, the city was fully prepared in 1977. The new club, christened the Mariners, played its first game under the roof on April 6, 1977, losing to the California Angels, 7-0. Diego Segui, the only Seattle player to perform for the old Pilots, drew the opening pitching assignment and, at 38, was immediately dubbed "The Ancient Mariner."

Joe Rudi took hitting honors for the winners, rapping three hits, including a home run, and driving in four runs in support of Frank Tanana.

The game attracted 57,762, including Commissioner Bowie Kuhn, A.L. President Lee MacPhail and U.S. Senator Henry Jackson, who threw out the first ball.

The players were unanimous in their praise of the Kingdome's beauty. Those who were in a position to judge declared the baseball carried better in the Kingdome than in baseball's first covered ball park, the Houston Astrodome.

First-year attendance in the Kingdome totaled 1.3 million, but it wasn't until the Mariners' sixth American League season, 1982, that the club again cracked the one-million mark (with a figure of 1,070,404).

During the same period the M's floundered in the depths of the A.L. West. Their best effort was a fourth-place finish in the 1982 season.

The Kingdome's brightest day in the spotlight occurred on July 17, 1979 when Lee Mazzilli and Dave Parker sparked the National League to a 7-6 victory in the 50th All-Star Game. Mazzilli clouted an eighth-inning pinch homer and drew a bases-loaded walk in the ninth inning to force in the deciding run.

Parker collected one hit and an RBI and threw out two runners, including Brian Downing at the plate in the eighth inning when the score was tied, 6-6, to win MVP honors. The game was witnessed by more than 58,000.

Ironically, although the Kingdome is a hitter's haven, a pitching feat which had occurred only 14 other times in the history of baseball took place there on May 6, 1982.

Gaylord Perry, a 43-year-old pitcher and undisputed master of the spitball, defeated the New York Yankees that night, 7-3, for his 300th career victory. A pitcher no other major league club wanted in spring training, Perry won 10 games for the Mariners in 1982 and finished the season with 307 for his career.

Pilot fans had little to cheer about at Sick's Stadium (above left) in 1969, but eight years later a new team (the Mariners) and a new park (the Kingdome, above right) brightened Seattle's outlook.

EXHIBITION STADIUM

Toronto

At the close of the 1967 baseball season, the city of Toronto held the distinction of having the longest uninterrupted membership in the International League—72 years.

The Toronto Maple Leafs also lost $400,000 over four seasons and had drawn only 67,000 fans in 1967. So there was little, if any, surprise in early October when the franchise was sold for $65,000 and moved to Louisville.

Before three months had elapsed, the auctioneer's gavel sounded at Maple Leaf Stadium on West Lakeshore Boulevard and souvenir enthusiasts walked off with, among other treasures: two mud-encrusted home plates at $5 apiece; seven trunks at $5 each; 134 bats at $1.15 each; a box of batting practice baseballs worth 40 cents apiece; a whirlpool bath for $85; a ticket-counting machine at $160 and a trunk of uniforms for $84.

Prior to the auction the Toronto Harbor Commission, landlord of the stadium, bought the public address system, turnstiles, ticket boxes and the lighting system which had been installed four years earlier.

Physically, the 19,224-seat park was showing

the ravages of its 42 years. The roof had sprung leaks and a portion of the outfield fence had yielded to vandals. Within a few years the stadium was razed and replaced by a public park and picnic grounds.

Toronto made its debut in Organized Baseball as a member of the Canadian League in 1885. Games were played at the Jarvis Street Lacrosse Grounds at Jarvis and Wellesley, which rented for $100 a month. For that sum the club was permitted to use the grounds three days a week.

By early 1886 construction was underway on

the city's first baseball park, a $7,000 facility on an eight-acre plot south of Queen Street and adjacent to the Don River.

The park, with covered stands, accommodated 2,000 spectators and was built in the shape of a half octagon. The main entrance was on Queen Street with exits for fans with carriages on Eastern Avenue, Kingston Road and Scadding Street.

A 550-seat reserved section occupied the center portion of the stands. General admission was 25 cents, but a fan could buy a seat for an extra dime and a reserved location for still another dime. Seats were equipped with arms, cushions and back rests.

The park, known as Sunlight Park because of its proximity to the Sunlight Soap Works, was enclosed by a fence "which will tax the acrobatic talents of the smartest to surmount," according to a local journal. A distinguishing feature of the park was sliding doors on three sides which "would be used by the players to recover baseballs when hit over the fence, which is not likely to happen very often."

Until construction was completed, the 1886

By 1974, an enlarged Exhibition Stadium (above) was ready for major league baseball. But Toronto baseball enthusiasts had to wait until 1977, when the expansion Blue Jays made their debut.

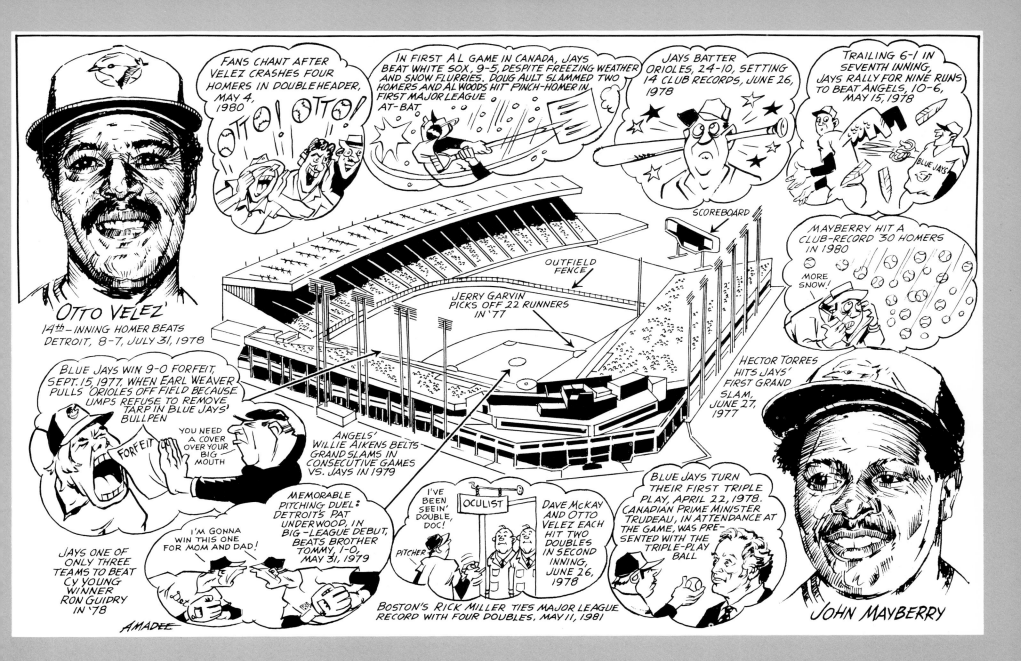

team played its early games at the Rosedale Athletic Grounds. Sunlight Park was ready for occupancy on May 22, and the home club climaxed a gala day with a 10-3 victory over Rochester before 5,000 partisans.

Toronto won its first pennant in 1887 behind the redoubtable Ned (Cannonball) Crane. The pitcher-outfielder won 33 games and batted .428.

Toronto dropped out of Organized Baseball in 1891 when the league collapsed as a result of the turmoil created by the Brotherhood War between the upstart Players League and the established National League and American Association.

In 1896 Toronto acquired the Erie franchise in the Eastern League, later the International, and began more than 70 years of continuous repre-

sentation in professional ball.

In 1897 the Maple Leafs moved into a new park on Hanlan's Point, an island on the Don River. To reach the stadium, fans first were required to dodge railroad traffic at a street crossing and then take a ferry to the island.

The Leafs remained on the island until 1901, when they moved to Diamond Park on Fraser Avenue.

The 1902 team, under the management of Ed Barrow, later the architect of the New York Yankees' dynasties, won the pennant. Barrow's salary in Toronto was $1,500 a year with a $300 bonus if the Leafs finished first or second.

Diamond Park served as the Leafs' home until 1908, when they returned to Hanlan's Point. The

stay on the island was short-lived, however, because of a fire that leveled the park in 1909 and sent the team back to Diamond Park.

One year later, the team was back at Hanlan's Point. The stadium, now known as Maple Leaf Park, was to have been dedicated on May 9, 1910, but the ceremonies were delayed for one day by the death of King Edward VII of Great Britain. The delay did not handicap the Leafs, who defeated the Baltimore Orioles, 4-3, before 13,000.

Babe Ruth socked his first home run as a professional in the Toronto park on September 5, 1914. The Providence pitcher stroked a three-run homer over the right-field fence in a one-hit, 9-0 triumph. Since this was Ruth's only minor league

season, his home run also was his only one before graduating to the major leagues.

Toronto baseball returned to the mainland in 1926 following the construction of Maple Leaf Stadium, a $750,000 park seating 20,000 at the foot of Bathurst Street. The park was built on seven acres of reclaimed land known as the Fleet Street Flats.

The park, with "Maple Leaf Stadium" painted in large white letters against a red background on the outfield fence, was dedicated on April 29, 1926 when 13,000 saw the season opener against Reading. Trailing 5-0 after eight and a half innings, the Leafs tied the score in the ninth and won in the 10th on a squeeze bunt.

The Harbor Commission took over the stadium in 1931 after the owners accumulated $60,000 in debts through non-payment of taxes and rent.

Night baseball arrived in Toronto on June 28, 1934 and it was an occasion to remember for 16,000 customers. To entertain the fans until it was totally dark, management hired Nick Altrock, a famed Washington comedian who overplayed his act a trifle—the game did not begin until 10 o'clock. A peanut vendor's brawl in the seventh inning interrupted play and the game did not end until 1 a.m. Making matters more grievous, Rochester defeated the Leafs, 8-2.

The largest opening-day crowd in Maple Leaf Stadium history, 22,216, turned out in 1953 and watched the Leafs score a pulsating victory on Ed Stevens' 10th-inning triple.

By this time Toronto was a pillar of minor league baseball. With a fourth-place club in 1952, attendance was 440,000. Over a 10-year period, the Leafs drew 3.26 million. When Dick Williams guided the team to playoff titles in 1965 and '66, however, the club ledgers showed a deficit.

One of the major reasons for the city's decline as a minor league bulwark, it was alleged, originated within the Leafs organization. Jack Kent Cooke, club owner from 1951 to '63, repeatedly extolled the area as a lucrative major league market, and on four occasions made offers for a major league franchise.

In preparation for the day when the city would join the major league family, Toronto officials talked publicly of an appropriate playing site. In

Maple Leaf Stadium (above) served as home of Toronto's International League team for 42 years.

October 1957 a special committee recommended the expansion of the Canadian National Exhibition grandstand to 64,000 at a cost of $6 million.

The proposal was defeated. Later, the city Parks Committee received a proposal for a three-stage $4.75 million expansion of CNE that would provide nearly 40,000 seats for baseball. This proposal was hailed by Cooke as "the biggest step ever taken toward bringing major league ball to Toronto."

That proposal also collapsed. In 1965 a group of businessmen talked of a domed stadium approximately 14 miles from mid-city. Included in the package were a 50,000-seat stadium and parking for 25,000 cars.

Like all other plans, this, too, floundered. On September 4, 1967 the Maple Leafs expired, losing to Syracuse, 7-2, before only 802 mourners.

By 1971 talk of a domed stadium was revived, but by now the cost had climbed considerably. Spokesmen for the group hoped to persuade the federal government to contribute 50 percent of the sum, the province of Ontario 25 percent and the city of Toronto the remaining 25 percent.

By 1974 action had replaced words in the city of 2.5 million. The Metro Council approved a $15 million expenditure that would enlarge CNE Stadium to approximately 40,000 for baseball and 55,000 for football.

The provincial government of Ontario loaned the city $7.5 million for the project, and the remainder was borrowed from private lenders.

On a visit to Toronto, Commissioner Bowie Kuhn gave his blessings to the enlarged stadium, and by the time the Los Angeles Dodgers met the Oakland A's in the World Series that year, Metro Council Chairman Paul Godfrey was ready to make his pitch. He impressed upon major league club owners the untapped resources of his city and demonstrated via brochures the attractiveness of a 40,000-seat stadium.

The west stands, Godfrey pointed out, would contain 9,958 chair-back seats. There would be a stadium club, VIP boxes and a lower deck accommodating 3,261. With 25,303 seats in the south stands, there would be a total of 38,522 new seats.

In early January 1976, Toronto residents read blaring headlines like: GIANTS AGREE TO SALE; TORONTO WARMS UP FOR BASEBALL. The National Exhibition Company, the corporate name of the San Francisco Giants, had accepted a $13.25 million offer from a company comprising the Labatt Breweries, Vulcan Assets Dominion and the Canadian Imperial Bank of Commerce. The club, it was reported, would move to Toronto and compete in the National League West Division.

All that remained to make the deal official was approval of nine of the 11 other club owners.

Unfortunately for the fans of Toronto and the province of Ontario, that approval never came. Weeks later, in the wake of a court injunction, threatened lawsuits and the emergence of Bay Area monies to purchase the club from Horace Stoneham, the N.L. magnates voted to keep the Giants in San Francisco.

By 1977, however, Canadian aspirations were realized. Toronto, along with Seattle, was granted an American League franchise. A contest to determine a name for the city's new club produced the name of the Blue Jays.

The Jays made their debut on April 7, with 44,649 huddling in near-freezing temperatures to watch Roy Hartsfield's team defeat the Chicago White Sox, 9-5.

Predictions that the park, with its 330-foot foul lines, would produce a bumper crop of home runs failed to materialize in the first season. American League batters pounded 139 homers, only about the average for league parks.

Although the fledgling Blue Jays compiled the poorest major league record—54 wins and 107 losses—fan enthusiasm never waned. At season's end the turnstile count had topped the 1.7 million mark.

Not only were the Jays popular on the field, but in the souvenir market as well. Irwin Toy Ltd. of Toronto had exclusive license to all non-food related items and did an estimated $10 million worth of business in toys, T-shirts and souvenirs.

"People all over Canada feel an addiction for the team," declared Chairman Arnold B. Irwin. Ninety percent of the sales were made in "baseball boutiques," installed in some of the nation's largest retail outlets at the suggestion of Irwin.

Sales for the year included 700,000 bats at $5 apiece and 300,000 T-shirts priced between $5 and $8.

By May 1978, with the Jays on their way to a 1.5 million gate, there was talk of expanding the stadium by 10,000 seats, to 54,000, if the club could register a two-year won-lost percentage of .500. Those discussions produced no results, however.

There also was a lot of chatter on June 26, 1978 after the Jays had engaged the Baltimore Orioles before 16,184 at Exhibition Stadium. In the two-hour and 58-minute game, the Jays rapped 24 hits, including two homers, two triples and seven doubles, and buried the Birds, 24-10. The winners scored nine runs in the second inning and led 24-6 after five innings. In the course of their explosion, the Jays broke or tied numerous club records.

Exhibition Stadium, an open-ended facility with an open expanse behind the right-field fence, seats over 40,000 and is also home of the Canadian Football League Argonauts during the winter.

GRIFFITH STADIUM

Washington

For most of its 70 years, Griffith Stadium was the home park for United States Presidents. Starting in 1910, no major league baseball season opened officially unless a Chief Executive appeared in a flag-draped front-row box on baseball's inauguration day and arched the ceremonial first pitch to a throng of waiting players.

William Howard Taft, a former ball player from Cincinnati, introduced the practice in 1910. Through the years other White House pitchers included Woodrow Wilson, Warren Harding, Calvin Coolidge, Herbert Hoover, Franklin Roosevelt, Harry Truman, Dwight Eisenhower and John Kennedy.

As seasons progressed, it was almost certain that every game would be witnessed by elite members of three branches of government.

The ancient playing grounds on Florida Avenue possessed a charm and character missing from other parks in Philadelphia, New York and Boston.

The stadium also provided the background for the illustrious achievements of a Kansas farm boy named Walter Johnson, for boy Managers Bucky Harris and Joe Cronin, for three World Series, two All-Star Games and an injury that curtailed the

career of Hall of Fame Cardinals pitcher Dizzy Dean.

Two years before the Confederates fired on Fort Sumter in 1861, the game was already a popular pastime in the nation's capital, drawing substantial crowds to games played by government clerks.

In the immediate postwar years when Andrew Johnson sought relief from his daily cares, the 17th President, it was recorded, strolled from the White House to the nearby White Lot to join as many as 6,000 others in watching games of the

National Athletic Club.

The city's first enclosed baseball park was constructed in 1870 by Mike Scanlon, at 17th and S streets NW, seating 500 spectators. This was the home of the Washington Olympics in 1871 and the Olympics and Nationals in the National Association in 1872. When both teams dropped from the league in 1873, few shed tears because neither had performed in a manner to make a city proud.

Beginning in 1884, a succession of major and minor league teams entertained the Washington fans, all failing in their attempts to swell the city's pride.

Noteworthy was the four-season ownership (1886-89) of the Hewitt brothers, Robert and Walter. They constructed 6,000-seat Capitol Park on Capitol Avenue between F and G streets, changed the name of their National League entry to Senators and brought up a young catcher named Cornelius McGillicuddy, who, as Connie Mack, broke in with a 10-game batting average of .361 in 1886 and captured the hearts of the spectators with his sparkling performance behind the plate.

One of the early fields in the nation's capital was Capitol Park (above), where a catcher named Cornelius McGillicuddy, later known as Connie Mack, made his major league debut in 1886.

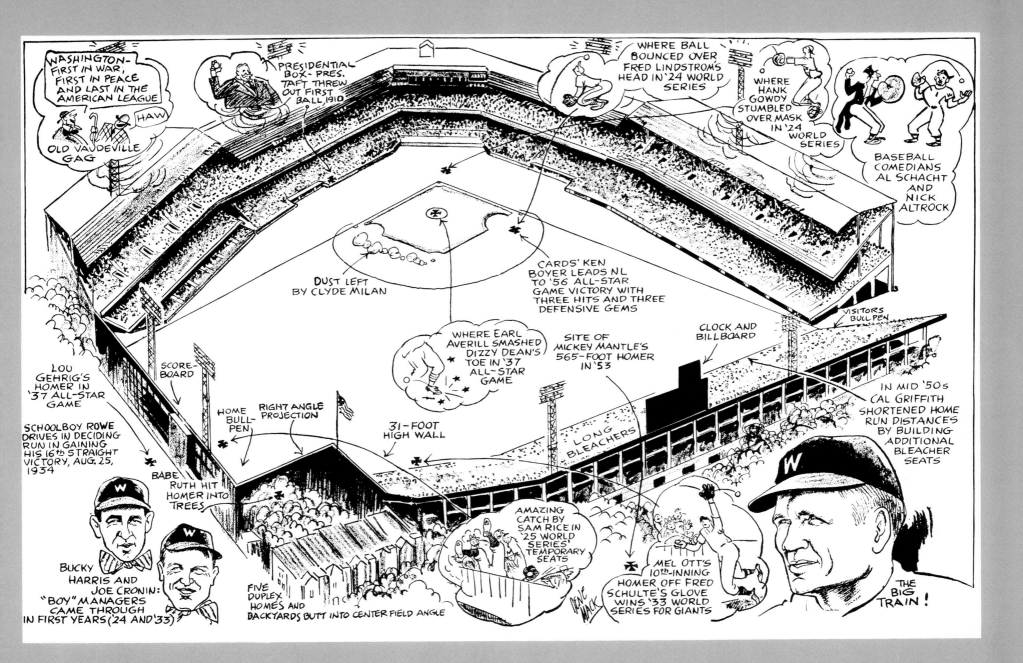

Another brother act, George and Jacob Earle Wagner of Philadelphia, acquired a major league franchise in 1892 when the National League expanded to 12 teams. The D.C. citizens greeted the Wagners enthusiastically, particularly when they built 6,500-seat National Park at The Boundary, at the intersection of 7th Street NW and Florida Avenue, the eventual site of Griffith Stadium.

Disenchantment with the Wagners, however, came early. It peaked in 1893, when the Wagners transferred a three-game series with the Phillies to Philadelphia where the teams had attracted 15,000 to a recent game. Another three-game series was transferred to Cleveland.

As disaffection grew and attendance fell, the owners traded established players for cash and youngsters. At the end of the 1899 season, the National League bought the faltering franchise and the ball park lease from the Wagners for $46,500.

The National League retrenched to eight clubs in 1900, however, leaving Washington without major league representation. The situation was remedied in 1901 when Ban Johnson, proclaiming his American League a new major circuit, transferred the Kansas City franchise to Washington.

Because the N.L. still held the lease on National Park, Owners Jimmy Manning and Frederick Postal were forced to find another site for a ball park. They selected a plot at 14th Street and Bladensburg Avenue NE. They christened the new wooden structure American League Park, which was dedicated on April 29, 1901 before a crowd of over 10,000, including Admiral Dewey, the hero of Manila Bay in the Spanish-American War.

When peace came to the major leagues after the 1902 season, the Senators switched to National Park. Before doing so, however, they intro-

Future President Franklin D. Roosevelt was Assistant Secretary of the Navy when he marched ahead of Washington players (above) in a salute to the U.S. war effort prior to the 1917 opener at Griffith Stadium.

duced a practice that soon became universal in baseball.

E. Lawrence Phillips became the original megaphone man, announcing lineups to the spectators and relieving the umpires of that chore. Before Phillips retired in 1928, his innovation had been copied throughout baseball.

In 1911, while the Senators were in spring training, fire destroyed all but a small section of bleachers in National Park. Within 18 days, however, the park was rebuilt. Although there was no roof over the single-deck stands running from first to third base, and no box seats except for the Presidential box, the Senators opened the season on schedule.

Eventually, the park was completed. In 1920, after Clark Griffith became president and gave his name to the park, the stands were double-decked beyond first and third base. Curiously, the roof of the new stands was built higher than the roof of the old stands, giving the impression that the new stands had been built by a carpenter with a faulty foot rule.

In 1950, Griffith installed 1,000 box seats in left and left-center fields, reducing the distances from 405 feet to 386 feet in left field, and from 391 feet to 372 feet in left-center.

Griffith had arrived in Washington in 1912, assuming the management of a club that boasted one bona fide star, Walter Johnson. The young righthander had signed several years earlier out of the Snake River Valley League in Idaho for a $100 bonus, a $350 monthly salary, plus transportation to Washington and, if he failed to stick with the Senators, his guaranteed return fare to Idaho.

News of the fireballing phenom had preceded Johnson eastward. Manager Joe Cantillon let pub-

lic expectancy grow before he unveiled Johnson in the first game of a doubleheader on August 2, 1907. Cantillon picked no pushover for the 19-year-old righthander, sending him against the Detroit Tigers with their power-laden lineup featuring Ty Cobb and Sam Crawford.

Ten thousand fans were in the stadium, now renamed American League Park, for the historic occasion. Johnson pitched eight innings and allowed six hits, including one by Cobb. The score was 2-1, Detroit, when Johnson departed.

Five days later, Johnson made his second start, beating Cleveland, 7-2, on four hits. It was the first of his 416 major league victories, all with Washington.

By 1908, Johnson was a full-fledged gate attraction on a mediocre team. He gained national acclaim in a late-season series in New York when he shut out the Highlanders in three consecutive games. Only an off-day on Sunday interrupted the streak.

Johnson pitched the first of his 14 home openers in 1910, a doubly historic occasion because it also marked the first appearance by a United States President for opening day ceremonies. After Taft did the honors, Johnson took over the pitching chores and shut out Philadelphia, 3-0, on one hit, the first of his seven opening day shutouts.

In 1912, Johnson reeled off 16 consecutive wins, setting a league record. The streak was snapped in St. Louis when Johnson, relieving Tom Hughes with two runners on base, yielded a two-run single that beat the Senators, 4-2. Under later scoring rules, Hughes would have been charged with the loss.

St. Louis also proved a jinx park for Johnson in 1913, when the Big Train's shutout pitching

Washington fans celebrate during a victory parade (above) for the 1924 world champions. Vice President John Garner (below left) and Clark Griffith help usher in the 1933 pennant-winning season.

streak was snapped after 55⅔ innings.

For the first 17 years of his major league career, Walter Johnson struggled manfully to pitch the Senators to a pennant. In 10 consecutive seasons he won 20 games or more and in two years he topped the 30-victory mark. His efforts were of little consequence. Only the vaudeville comics saw anything funny in the inept club with their sure-fire laugh-provoker: "Washington, first in war, first in peace and last in the American League."

When the Senators won their first American League flag, under Boy Manager Bucky Harris in 1924, Johnson was approaching his 37th birthday. The smoke was gone from the Big Train's fastball, but he still was able to contribute 23 victories, while losing only seven games.

The first game of the World Series, on October 4, was a showcase for government dignitaries. President Calvin Coolidge attended the game, accompanied by his wife, Grace, an incurable baseball fan. Cabinet members, military brass and diplomats also brightened the premises.

Johnson pitched creditably in his postseason debut but lost to southpaw Art Nehf, 4-3, in 12 innings. The outcome might have been different if management had not chosen to install temporary seats in front of the left-field bleachers. The new seats helped swell attendance to 35,760, but they also turned fly balls by George Kelly and Bill Terry, normally routine putouts, into home runs.

After the Senators knotted the Series, winning 4-3 on Roger Peckinpaugh's RBI double, the Giants won two of three games at the Polo Grounds and needed only one more victory to spoil the Nats' first appearance in the World Series.

Game 6 attracted 34,254 to Griffith Stadium,

A 37-year-old Walter Johnson (above) receives congratulations from his brother Leslie after shutting out Pittsburgh in Game 4 of the 1925 World Series at Griffith Stadium.

including the Coolidges for the third time. The throng was rewarded with a 2-1 Washington victory as Tom Zachary outdueled Art Nehf and Bucky Harris singled home both of the winners' runs. The decisive seventh game, played before 31,667 spectators, including the Coolidges once more, was a baseball classic, starting with an unusual bit of strategy by the youthful Harris.

With the acquiescence of Griffith, Harris started Curly Ogden on the hill. Harris chose the right-handed Ogden, a late-season acquisition from Philadelphia, so that New York Manager John McGraw would load his lineup with lefthanded batters. Ogden struck out Fred Lindstrom to open the game, then issued a walk to Frank Frisch and took a walk himself, to the bench.

The meaning of Ogden's sudden departure was soon evident. Secretly, Harris had instructed left-hander George Mogridge to warm up under the stands. Mogridge was now called into the game to face the predominantly lefthanded Giants lineup, including Bill Terry, who had batted .500 in the first six games. With Mogridge pitching, Harris reasoned, Terry's effectiveness would be reduced. It turned out even better than that. Terry was lifted for a pinch-hitter in the sixth inning.

By then the Senators had taken a 1-0 lead on Harris' second homer of the Series. In the sixth inning, however, Mogridge weakened and the Giants scored three runs, aided by two Washington errors. Firpo Marberry relieved Mogridge in the frame. In the eighth, the Senators were down

to their last four outs when Harris rapped a two-run single, tying the score, 3-3.

Harris now needed a pitcher to hold the Giants until the Nats could mount a rally. His choice was Johnson, already a two-time loser in the Series.

The move worked. Johnson held the Giants and Lady Luck smiled on the Senators in the bottom of the 12th when Earl McNeely's grounder hit a pebble and bounded crazily over third baseman Lindstrom's head and drove home the winning run. The Senators were champions of the world and the nation's capital plunged into world-class hysteria.

When the Senators repeated as A.L. champions in 1925, beating Philadelphia by 8½ games, Griffith Stadium was the site for the third, fourth and

The Griffith Stadium of 1956 (above left) and 1961 (above right) was double-decked beyond the first and third-base lines and had bleacher seats that extended from left to left-center field.

By 1964, the Griffith Stadium field (above) once inhabited by the likes of Walter Johnson was no longer discernible and only one year away from demolition.

fifth Series games. The Senators and Pirates split the first two games in Pittsburgh, and when the Nats captured the first two games at home, another world title seemed inevitable. But the Pirates, down three games to one, bounced back to win three in a row.

After a six-year drought, the Senators captured a third pennant in 1932. And again Griffith Stadium took on a holiday atmosphere.

Once more in the World Series the Senators were matched against the Giants, their 1924 rivals. By the time the Series got to Washington, the Senators trailed two games to none.

Those two defeats combined with threatening weather to hold the crowd for Game 3 to slightly more than 25,000. Franklin Delano Roosevelt, in his first year as President, was on hand, along with a huge Congressional contingent that shared in a pregame shower.

Earl Whitehill cooled Giants bats in Game 3, winning 4-0 on five hits before the Giants finished off the Senators in five games with extra-inning victories, 2-1 in 11 and 3-2 in 10. A drive by Mel Ott that flicked off center fielder Fred Schulte's glove for a home run accounted for the title-winning run.

Next to Walter Johnson, no Griffith Stadium pitcher enjoyed as great a popularity as Louis Norman (Bobo) Newsom. At least Bobo was popular with management, which acquired the showboating righthander five separate times.

One of Newsom's finest moments occurred on opening day in 1936 when he defeated Lefty Gomez and the Yankees, 1-0, in most trying circumstances.

In the first inning, Bobo darted off the mound as though to field a bunt toward third base. Suddenly, Bobo pulled up short, then stood idly by as Ossie Bluege fielded the ball and uncorked a throw toward first base. Fifteen feet from Bluege's hand was Newsom's head. Bluege's throw scored a direct hit. Staggering crazily, Newsom found his way to the bench where he doctored his aching head with a cold towel. Newsom returned to the mound and completed his shutout before President Roosevelt and 31,000 spectators.

Newsom's injury was mild compared to that suffered by Dizzy Dean on the same field in 1937. Dean was the starter for the National League in the fifth All-Star Game and was within one out of completing his three-inning stint when Earl Averill's scorching drive back to the mound struck him on the foot and fractured a toe. Later, Dean, trying to adjust to the handicap, altered his pitching style and developed a sore arm that shortened his brilliant career.

The A.L. won that game, 8-3, but succumbed, 7-3, in the 23rd All-Star Game in 1956 when Ken Boyer collected three hits and performed brilliantly at third base. Willie Mays and Stan Musial homered for the winners, Ted Williams and Mickey Mantle for the losers.

Mantle's homer did not rate, for distance, with his mammoth clout of April 17, 1953, in the same park. Batting righthanded against southpaw Chuck Stobbs, Mantle walloped a ball over the left-field wall and into a yard behind a three-story tenement. According to Red Patterson, the Yankees' publicity director who computed the distance, the ball traveled 565 feet.

When the Senators pulled up stakes at the close of the 1960 season to become the Minnesota Twins, Griffith Stadium obtained a new tenant, an expansion club also known as the Senators.

But the end was fast approaching. A new stadium was already under construction on the banks of the Potomac, to be known as the District of Columbia Stadium. The young American League club would move there, with its 45,000 seats, in 1962.

In the final inaugural at Griffith Stadium in 1961, President John F. Kennedy did the first-pitch honors, then watched the Chicago White Sox defeat the Nats, 4-3.

Significantly, the old Senators—now the Minnesota Twins—and the one-year-old Senators performed the last rites over Griffith Stadium on September 21, 1961. Only 1,498 attended the final services. The Nats lost the game, 6-3.

The old stadium, care-worn and decrepit, remained standing for four years, at which time the demolition crew went to work. The light towers, erected in 1941, were the first to fall, then the concrete stands that had been built hurriedly after the fire in 1911.

The Howard University Hospital now occupies the site.

For the next 10 seasons, baseball was to survive in Washington with the "New Senators" playing in their new stadium. Unfortunately, District of Columbia Stadium, later to be named Robert F. Kennedy Stadium, is remembered not so much for the baseball accomplishments within its circular confines as for the manner in which major league baseball bid it farewell on September 30, 1971.

The Senators, completing their final season in the huge oval, were leading the New York Yankees, 7-5, with two out in the ninth inning when hundreds of spectators, angered that Owner Bob Short was transferring the club to Arlington, Tex., streamed onto the field.

Park police had been reinforced in anticipation of such a demonstration, but they were powerless to cope with the undisciplined fans, who ripped up the bases, pried up home plate, destroyed the pitching mound, danced on the bullpen roofs, tore up swatches of turf and removed letters from the scoreboard. Within seconds, it was apparent that the game would never be completed and eventually umpire-in-chief Jim Honochick forfeited the game to the Yankees.

Chief victim of the forfeit was Paul Lindblad, the Washington reliever who lost credit for a victory. All other individual statistics went into the records.

The bizarre ending was in sharp contrast to the beginning, when in April of 1962, President John F. Kennedy and 44,383 others watched the Senators defeat Detroit, 4-1.

"I'm leaving you in first place," JFK quipped to General Manager Ed Doherty as he left the presidential box.

Without Kennedy's help, the Senators fared poorly. In the 10-club American League they finished last three times, ninth once and eighth twice. When the loop switched to division play in 1969, the Nats were noncontenders for their last three seasons in the Capital.

Kennedy's appearance at the 1962 inaugural carried more than ceremonial significance. The Chief Executive had followed stadium progress closely ever since Oren Harris, an Arkansas Democrat, had introduced a bill authorizing construction of the facility with public funds.

The stadium, Kennedy hoped, "will be an enduring symbol of the American belief in the importance of physical fitness and of the contributions which athletic competition can make to our way of life."

First-time visitors to the stadium invariably were impressed with its clean lines, the result of a decision by the city's Fine Arts Commission, which rules on the design of all public buildings. Because the stadium is on a direct line with the United States Capitol and the Lincoln and Jefferson Memorials, the Fine Arts people ruled out light towers for esthetic reasons. As a consequence, lights were installed on the rim of the roof.

Built on reclaimed swamp land, the stadium was subjected early to the barbs of local wits. One compared it to a wet straw hat. Another said it resembled a waffle whose center stuck to the gridiron.

Sports fans could ignore such putdowns and appreciate the unobstructed view of the field. There were no port holes in the huge oval and the temperature grew uncomfortably high in daytime, but there was always the consolation that most games were played at night.

Hitters approved the design because the ball carried well. Pitchers disliked it for the same reason. During its 10 years as a major league baseball park, no pitcher hurled a no-hitter in RFK Stadium.

The park contained no lower deck in the outfield. The nearest seats to home plate were in the mezzanine, 410 feet away. Foul lines measured 335 feet.

The first home run into the upper deck was smacked, fittingly enough, by Roger Maris on April 27, 1962, barely seven months after the

District of Columbia Stadium (above), renamed Robert F. Kennedy
Stadium in 1968, is a huge oval with some esthetic touches that set it
apart from other ball parks.

Yankee outfielder had set a season record with 61 homers.

Other features include a ground-level scoreboard in center field, measuring 375 feet by 35 feet and costing nearly $400,000; air-conditioned dugouts with overhead lights, 24 ticket booths, 45 rest rooms, 28 concessions stands, 14 sets of ramps pitched at 15 degrees and parking space for 12,500 cars.

The name of the stadium was changed shortly after the assassination of U.S. Sen. Robert F. Kennedy in 1968.

Another assassination, of Martin Luther King Jr. on April 4, 1968, touched off nights of riots and looting in the city and postponed the opening game until April 10.

Tension remained sufficiently high on opening day for the National Guard and the 82nd Airborne Division to be patrolling the streets and the stadium when Vice President Hubert Humphrey uncorked two pitches, one to outfielder Hank Allen, the other to coach Nellie Fox of the Senators.

The Senators lost the uneasy opener to the Minnesota Twins, 2-0, and played a number of ensuing games in the afternoon, at considerable cost to the club, as a means of allaying public anxiety over attending games.

President John F. Kennedy (above left) did the honors in the 1962 inaugural game at District of Columbia Stadium, which later carried the name (above right) of his brother.

Index to Cities and Parks

Continued